IYANU™

CHILD OF WONDER

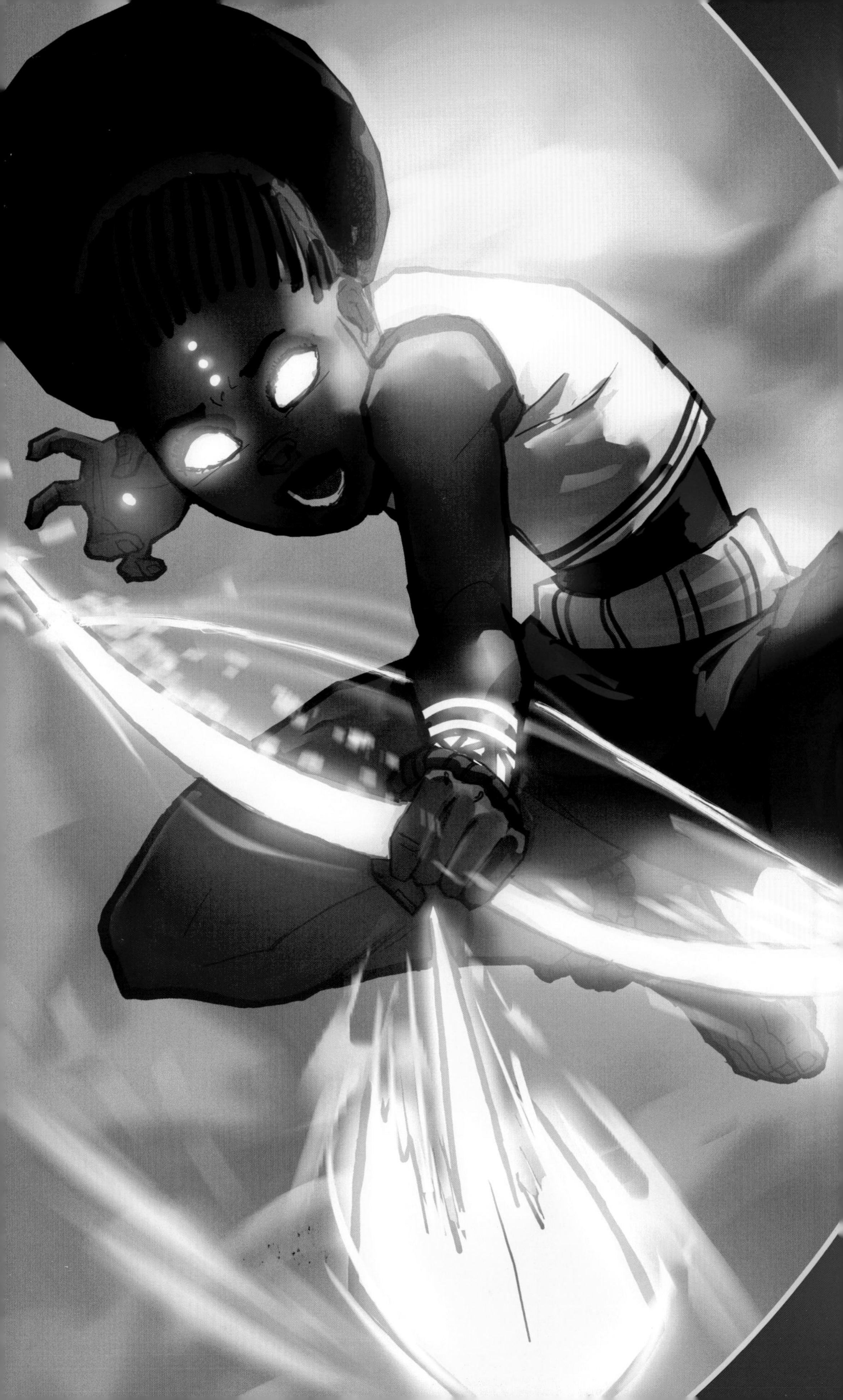

IYANU™

CHILD OF WONDER

VOLUME TWO

Creator and Writer
ROYE OKUPE

Cover and Interior Art
GODWIN AKPAN

Letters
SPOOF ANIMATION

YOUNEEK
STUDIOS

DARK HORSE BOOKS

Publisher
MIKE RICHARDSON

Associate Editor
JUDY KHUU

Designer
KATHLEEN BARNETT

Senior Editor
PHILIP R. SIMON

Assistant Editor
ROSE WEITZ

Digital Art Technician
ADAM PRUETT

IYANU: CHILD OF WONDER VOLUME 2

Published by Dark Horse Books | A division of Dark Horse Comics LLC
10956 SE Main Street, Milwaukie, OR 97222
DarkHorse.com

To find a comics shop in your area, visit comicshoplocator.com

Library of Congress Cataloging-in-Publication Data

Names: Okupe, Roye, writer. | Akpan, Godwin, artist, colourist. | Spoof Animation, letterer.
Title: Iyanu : child of wonder / writer, Roye Okupe ; artist, Godwin Akpan ; colors, Godwin Akpan ; letters, Spoof Animation.
Description: Milwaukie, OR : Dark Horse Books, 2021. | Series: Iyanu ; volume 1 | Audience: Ages 10+ | Audience: Grades 7-9 | Summary: "A teenage orphan with no recollection of her past, suddenly discovers that she has abilities that rival the ancient deities told in the folklore of her people."-- Provided by publisher.
Identifiers: LCCN 2021009242 | ISBN 9781506723044 (trade paperback)
Subjects: LCSH: Graphic novels. | CYAC: Graphic novels. | Folklore, Africa--Fiction. | Fantasy--Fiction. | Orphans--Fiction. | Ability--Fiction. | Adventure and adventurers--Fiction.
Classification: LCC PZ7.7.O424 I93 2021 | DDC 741.5/973--dc23
LC record available at https://lccn.loc.gov/2021009242

First edition: September 2022
Ebook ISBN: 978-1-50672-315-0
Trade Paperback ISBN: 978-1-50672-305-1

1 3 5 7 9 10 8 6 4 2

Printed in China

FSC
www.fsc.org

MIX
Paper from
responsible sources
FSC® C169962

CHAPTER SIX

Past and
Present

The story so far . . .

Iyanu, a teenage orphan with no recollection of her past, discovers that she has abilities that rival the ancient deities told of in folklore. This makes her "the Chosen," but with this great power comes great scrutiny from the community of Elu, the last walled city in all of Yorubaland. A land that is terrorized by the Corrupt—cursed wildlife and divine beasts determined to destroy humanity.

One day while wandering through the forest region of Elu, Iyanu spots Toye, a shy but brilliant boy being bullied. She intervenes. The next day, while walking through the forest, Iyanu spots Toye and some other kids in danger. This time though, it's not bullies. It's a corrupt serval who slipped through a crack in the walls. In an attempt to save Toye and the rest, Iyanu inadvertently activates her powers in public for the first time. This puts her under the radar of the evil Chancellor Nuro—second only to the King in Elu—who then orders the Eso Warriors, led by Toye's father, Kanfo, to capture Iyanu. It is unclear why Nuro is after Iyanu, but one thing is certain, it is not for benevolent reasons.

Iyanu quickly returns home to report to Olori, her mentor and mother figure, with the Eso in hot pursuit. When she arrives, Olori, the last of the Agoni priestesses—self-proclaimed keepers of the secrets of Yorubaland—holds off the Eso on her own as Iyanu escapes outside the walls and heads for "the Source" as Olori instructed.

Alone and outside of the walls of Elu for the first time, Iyanu encounters Ekun, the corrupt, giant, divine leopard of legends. However, with the help of her powers, which are accidentally activated yet again, Iyanu manages to escape Ekun. But just barely.

Meanwhile, back in Elu, the people of the Workers' District are threatening to revolt if their leaders on the council (the Elu Mesi) don't solve the issue of squalor. Abject poverty has spread rampantly throughout their district. Fearing civil war, Foreign Minister Uwa, younger brother of the king, urges his older brother and the council to help the people of the Workers' District. But Chancellor Nuro is only concerned with the capture of "the Chosen," AKA Iyanu. He manages to somehow convince the king and council that their number one priority should be Iyanu and not the people of the Workers' District.

Back outside the walls, Iyanu meets Biyi, a carefree and fun-loving teenage boy whose recklessness usually gets him into more trouble than he bargained for. Biyi is from one of the exiled settlements—communities containing exiles who have been banished by the king from the safety of the walls of Elu. Although they both get off to a rough start due to their glaring personality differences, Iyanu and Biyi eventually learn to work together when they are attacked by a corrupt rhino. During the encounter, Iyanu once again activates her powers by mistake, but this time, she heals the corrupt rhino, which transforms back to its original, peaceful state after Iyanu transfers her powers to it. Iyanu passes out, and Biyi is stunned that he has finally found the Chosen—a child of destiny prophesied to heal the lands of the corrupt and bring back the Age of Wonders—and we begin . . .

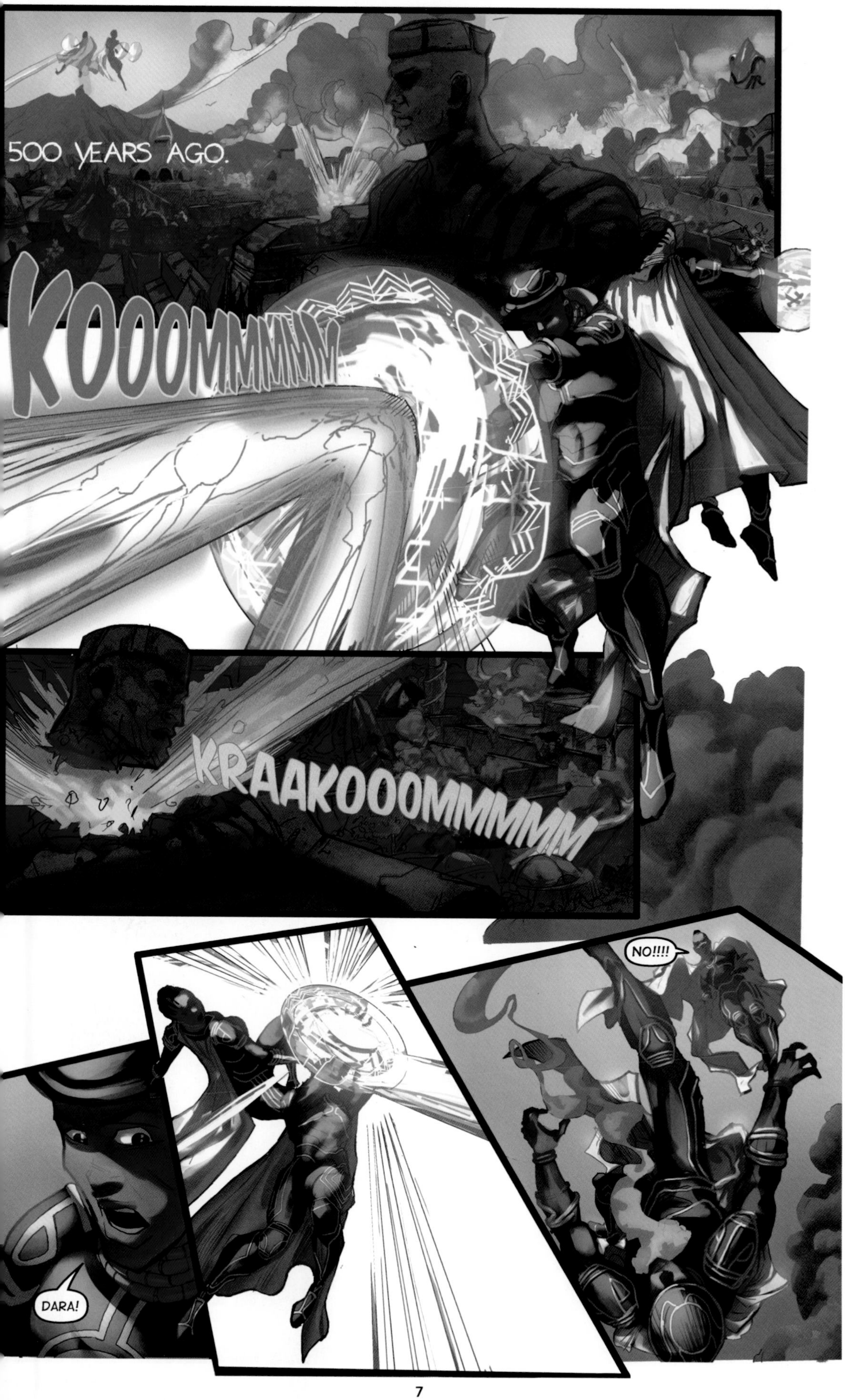
500 YEARS AGO.
KOOOMMMMM
KRAAKOOOMMMMMM
DARA!
NO!!!!

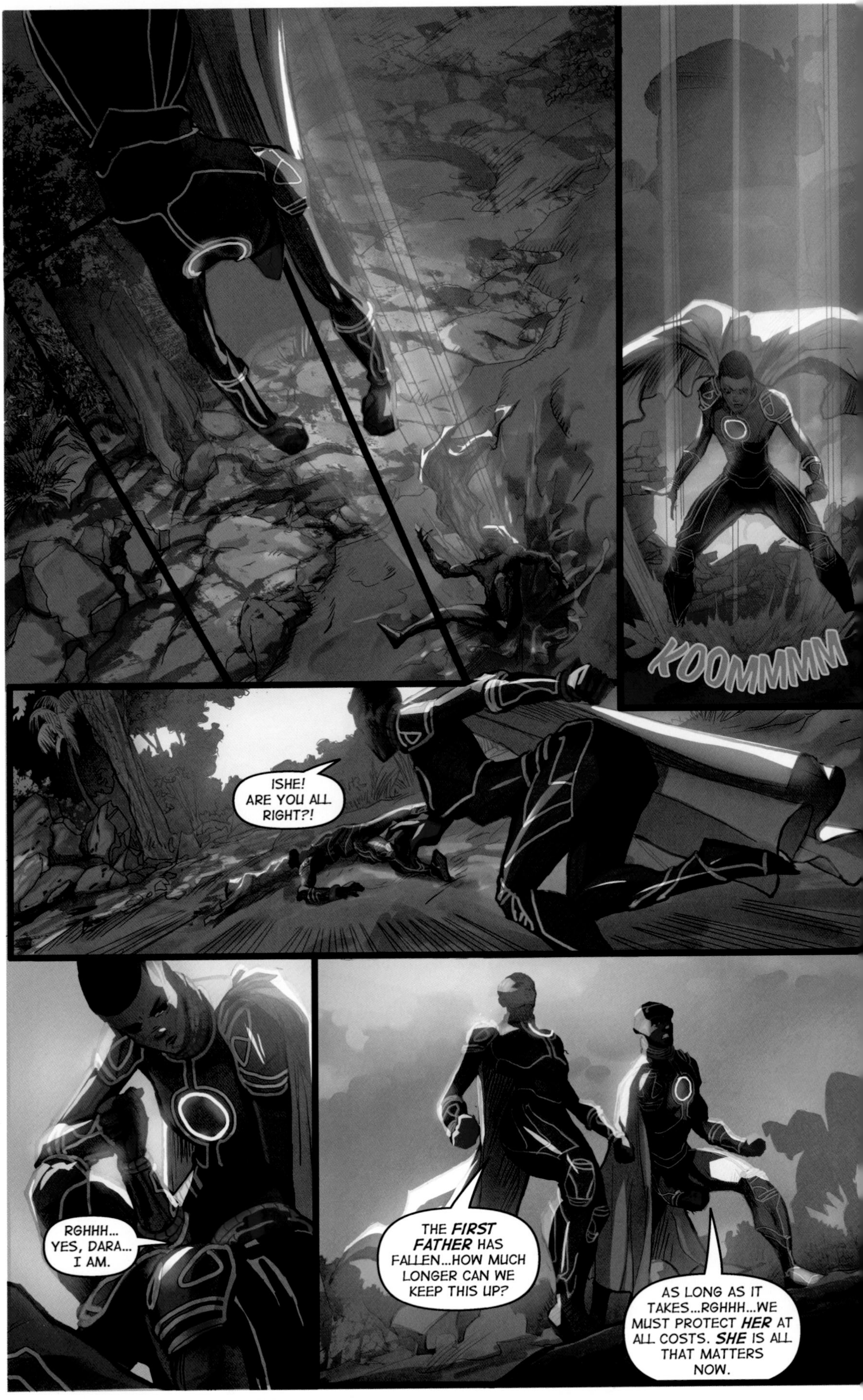
KOOMMMM
ISHE! ARE YOU ALL RIGHT?!
RGHHH... YES, DARA... I AM.
THE FIRST FATHER HAS FALLEN...HOW MUCH LONGER CAN WE KEEP THIS UP?
AS LONG AS IT TAKES...RGHHH...WE MUST PROTECT HER AT ALL COSTS. SHE IS ALL THAT MATTERS NOW.

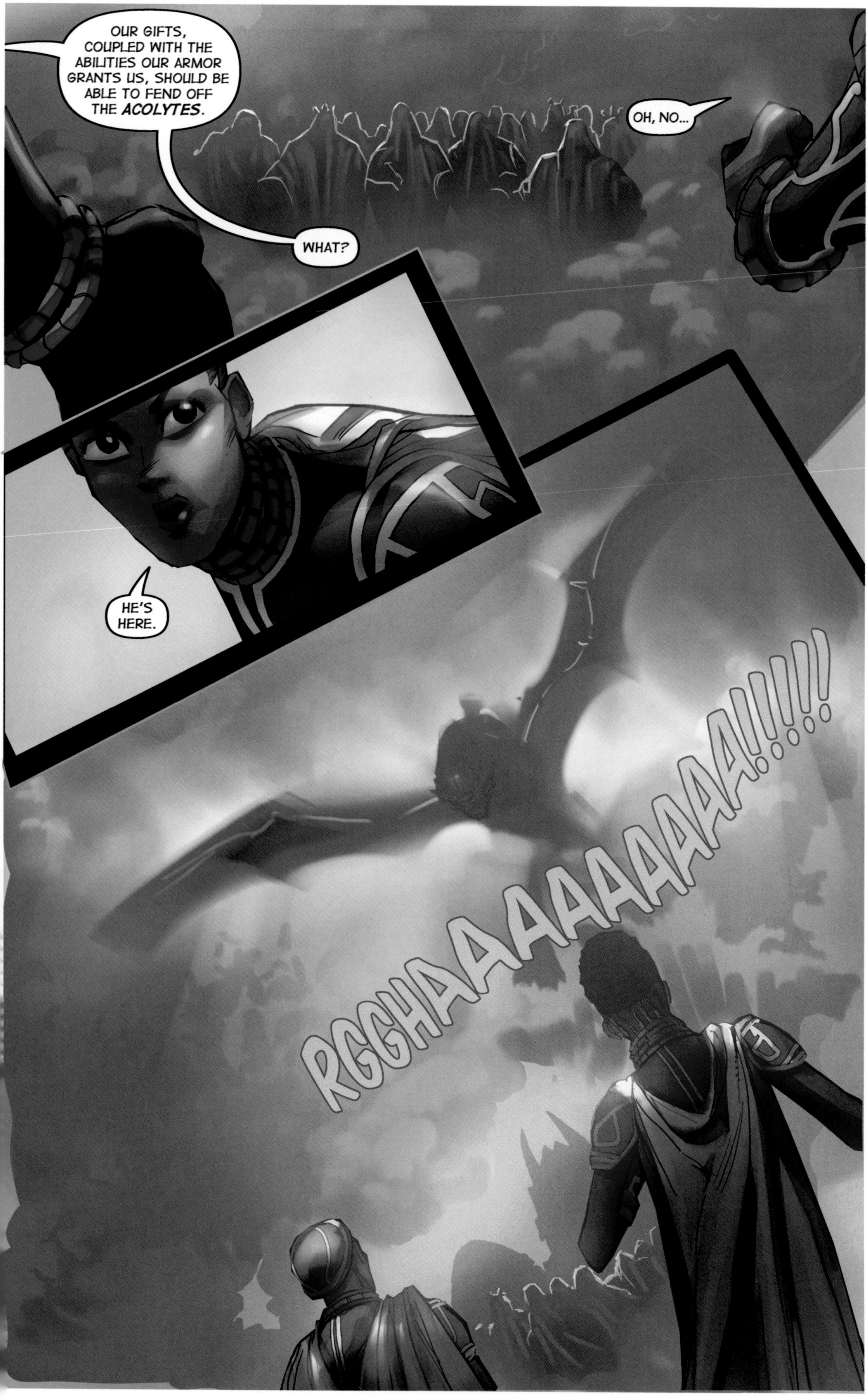
OUR GIFTS, COUPLED WITH THE ABILITIES OUR ARMOR GRANTS US, SHOULD BE ABLE TO FEND OFF THE *ACOLYTES*.
OH, NO...
WHAT?
HE'S HERE.
RGGHAAAAAAAAA!!!!!!

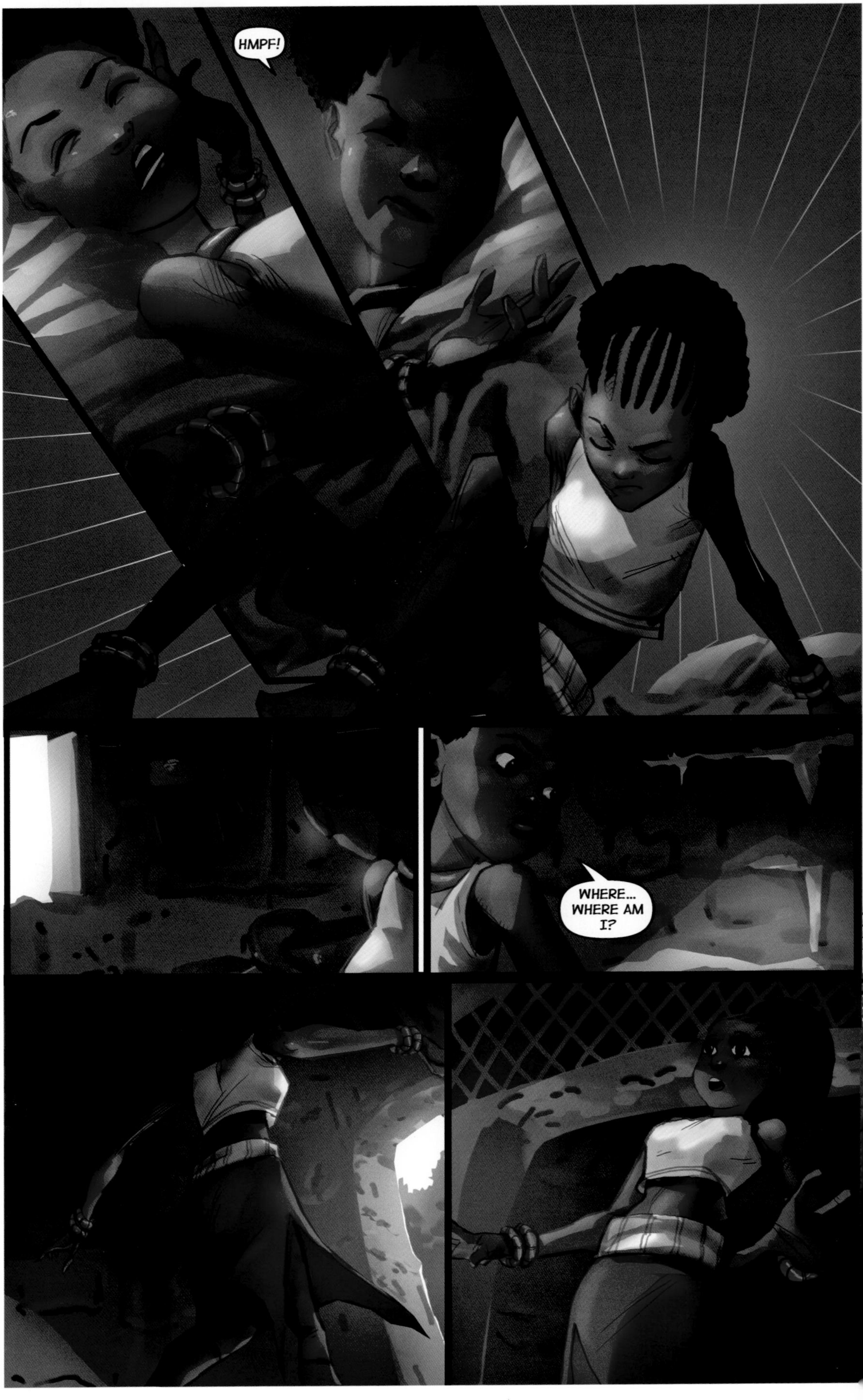
HMPF!
WHERE... WHERE AM I?

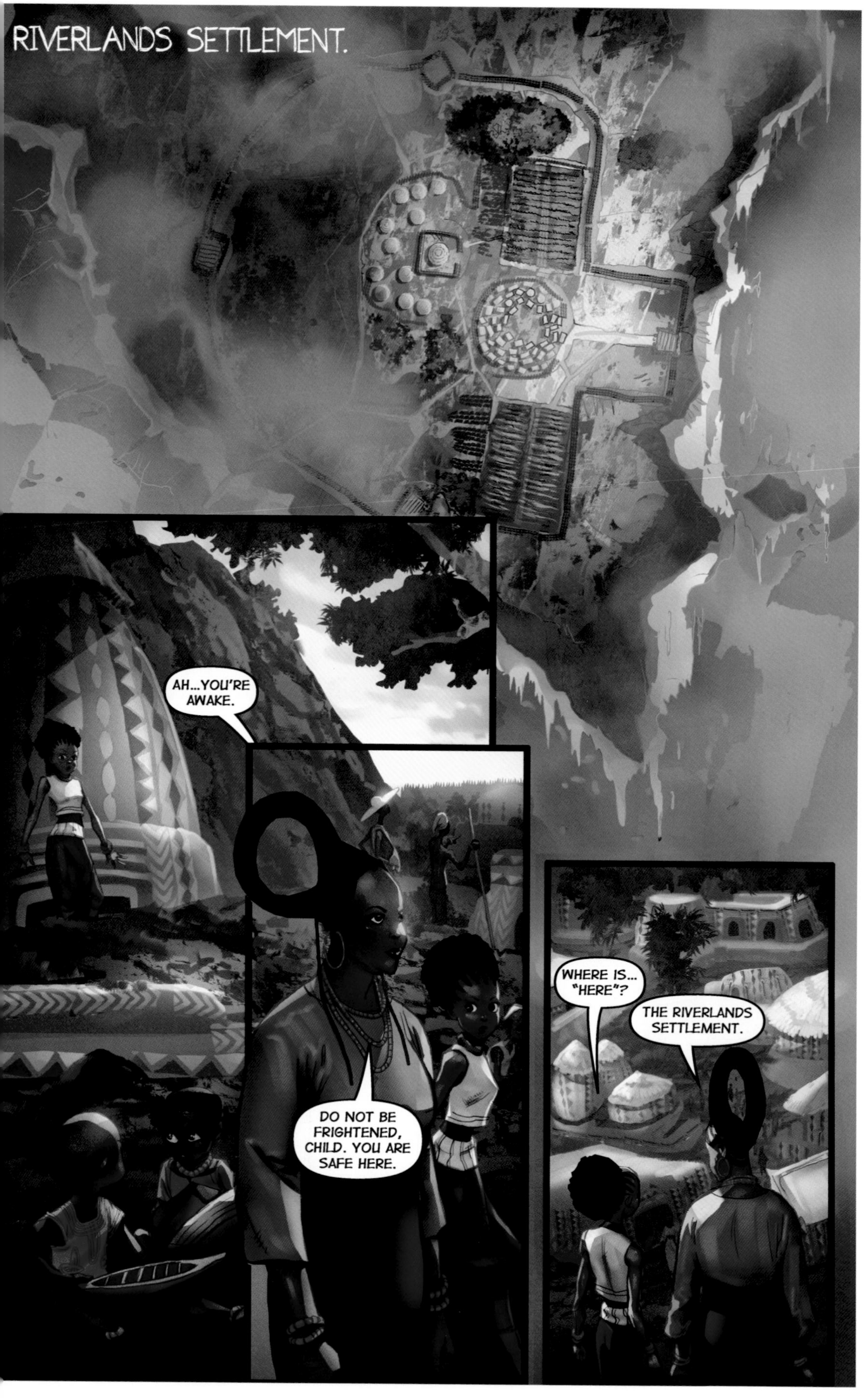

RIVERLANDS SETTLEMENT.
AH...YOU'RE AWAKE.
DO NOT BE FRIGHTENED, CHILD. YOU ARE SAFE HERE.
WHERE IS... "HERE"?
THE RIVERLANDS SETTLEMENT.

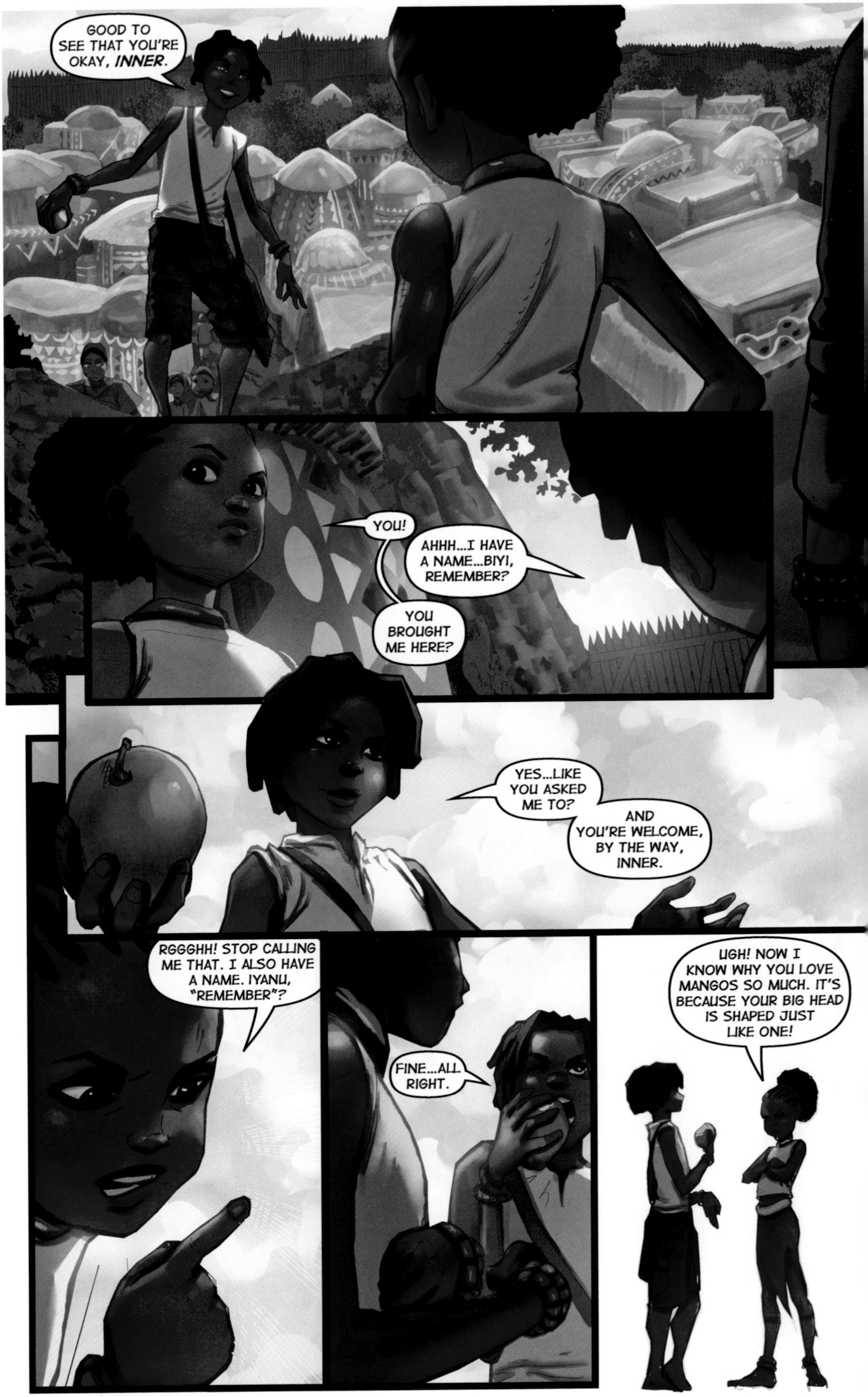
GOOD TO SEE THAT YOU'RE OKAY, INNER.
YOU!
AHHH...I HAVE A NAME...BIYI, REMEMBER?
YOU BROUGHT ME HERE?
YES...LIKE YOU ASKED ME TO?
AND YOU'RE WELCOME, BY THE WAY, INNER.
RGGGHH! STOP CALLING ME THAT. I ALSO HAVE A NAME. IYANU, "REMEMBER"?
FINE...ALL RIGHT.
UGH! NOW I KNOW WHY YOU LOVE MANGOS SO MUCH. IT'S BECAUSE YOUR BIG HEAD IS SHAPED JUST LIKE ONE!

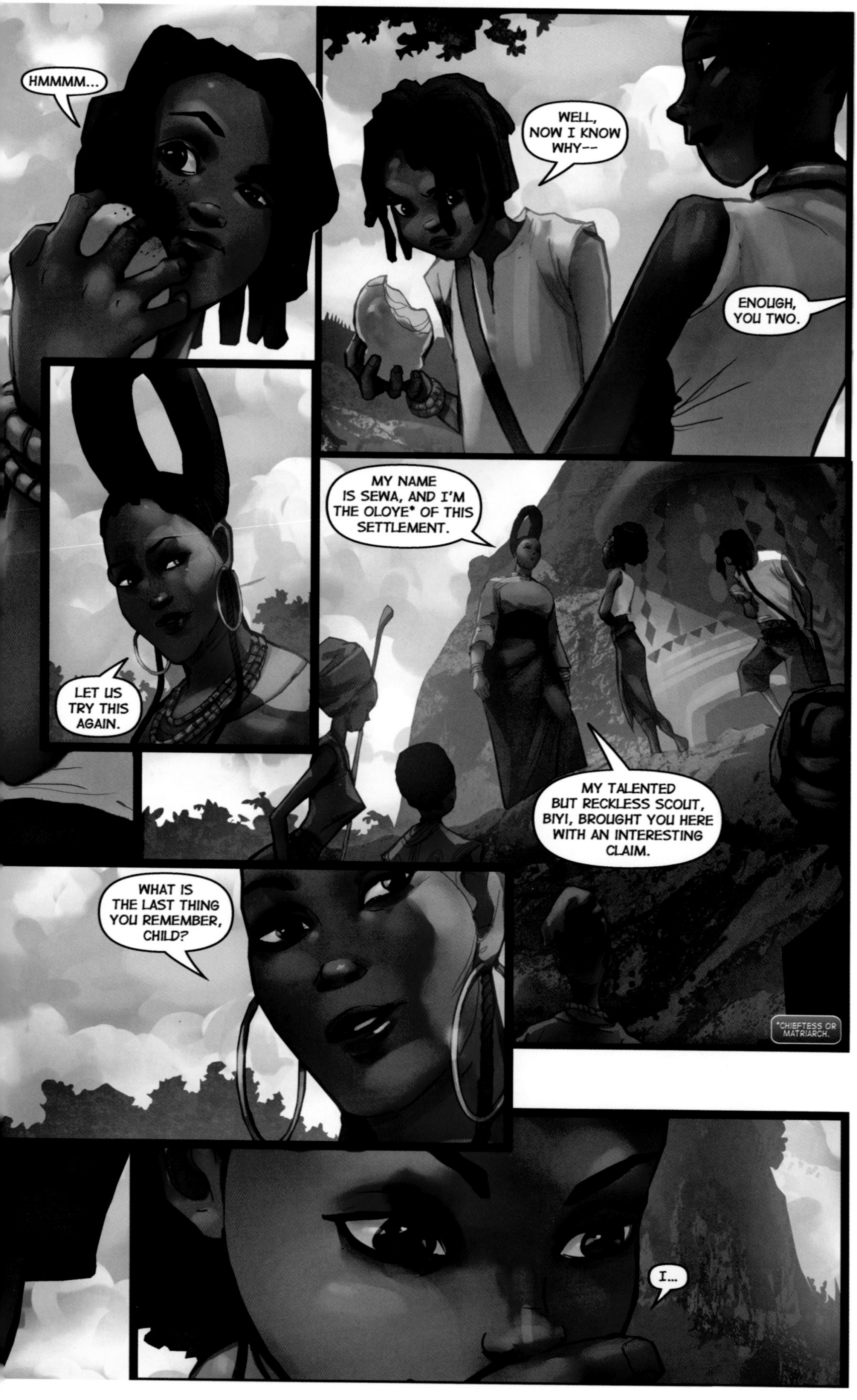

HMMMM...
WELL, NOW I KNOW WHY--
ENOUGH, YOU TWO.
LET US TRY THIS AGAIN.
MY NAME IS SEWA, AND I'M THE OLOYE* OF THIS SETTLEMENT.
MY TALENTED BUT RECKLESS SCOUT, BIYI, BROUGHT YOU HERE WITH AN INTERESTING CLAIM.
*CHIEFTESS OR MATRIARCH.
WHAT IS THE LAST THING YOU REMEMBER, CHILD?
I...

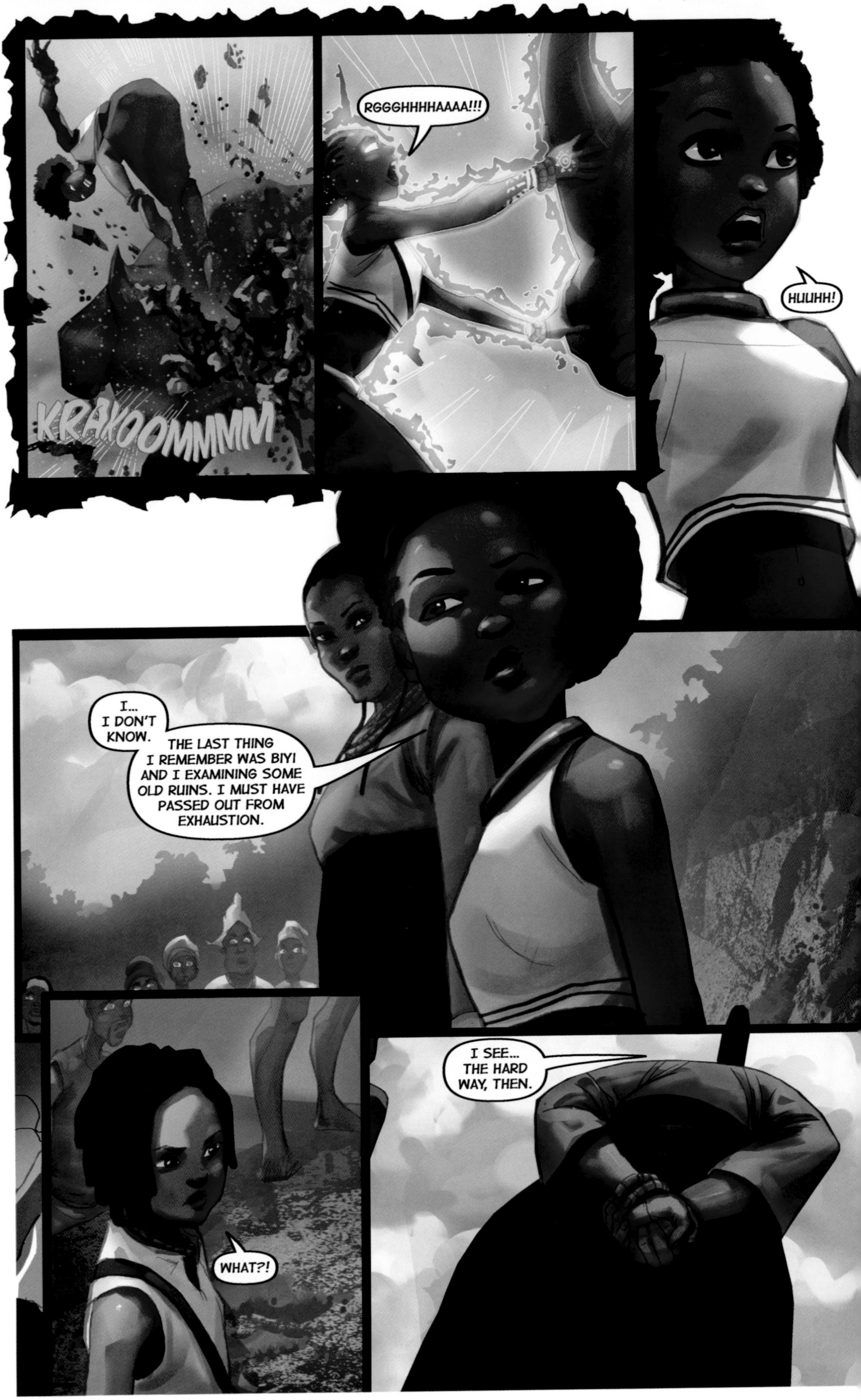
KRAKOOMMMM
RGGGHHHHAAAA!!!
HUUHH!
I... I DON'T KNOW.
THE LAST THING I REMEMBER WAS BIYI AND I EXAMINING SOME OLD RUINS. I MUST HAVE PASSED OUT FROM EXHAUSTION.
WHAT?!
I SEE... THE HARD WAY, THEN.

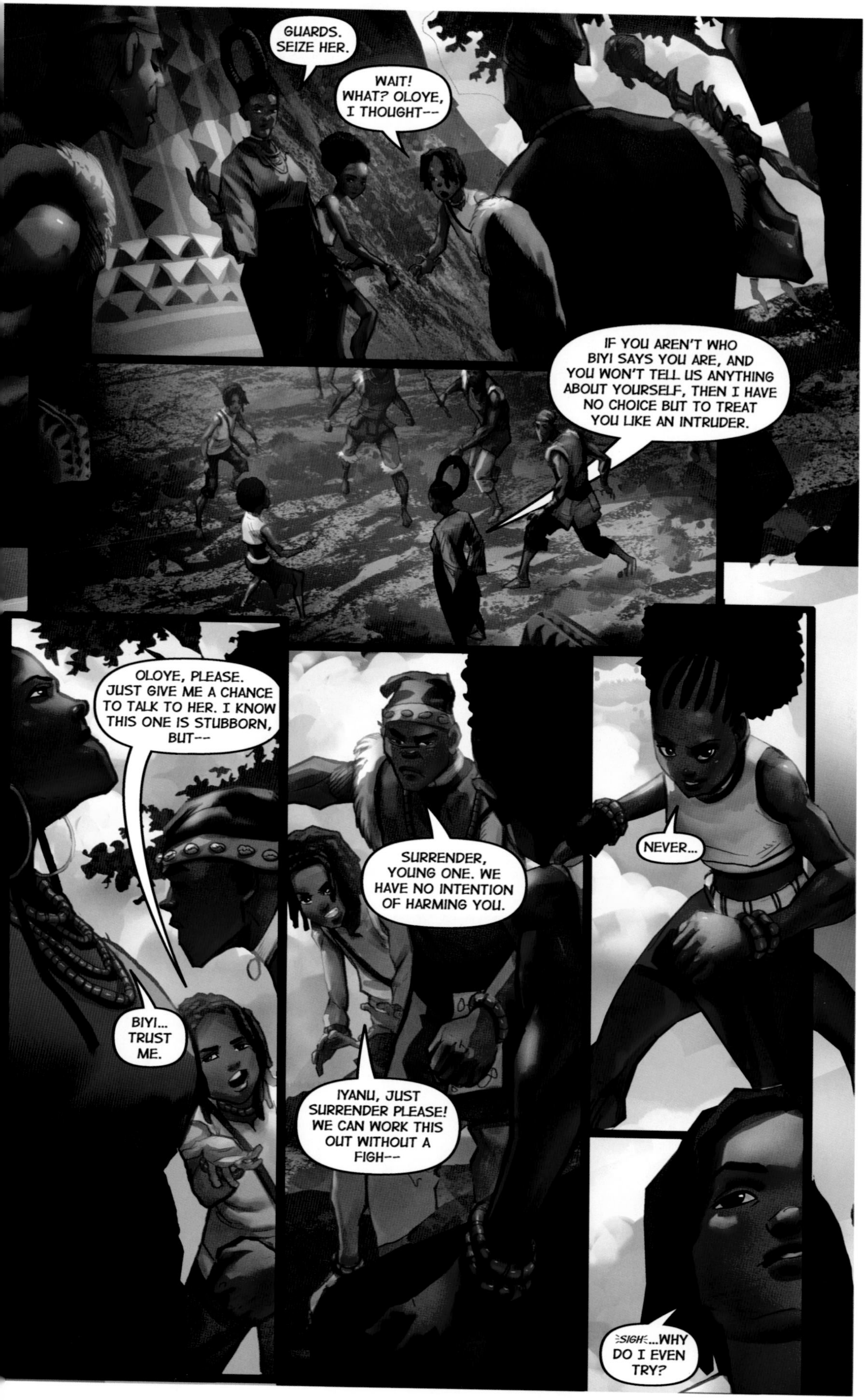
GUARDS. SEIZE HER.
WAIT! WHAT? OLOYE, I THOUGHT--
IF YOU AREN'T WHO BIYI SAYS YOU ARE, AND YOU WON'T TELL US ANYTHING ABOUT YOURSELF, THEN I HAVE NO CHOICE BUT TO TREAT YOU LIKE AN INTRUDER.
OLOYE, PLEASE. JUST GIVE ME A CHANCE TO TALK TO HER. I KNOW THIS ONE IS STUBBORN, BUT--
BIYI... TRUST ME.
SURRENDER, YOUNG ONE. WE HAVE NO INTENTION OF HARMING YOU.
IYANU, JUST SURRENDER PLEASE! WE CAN WORK THIS OUT WITHOUT A FIGH--
NEVER...
SIGH...WHY DO I EVEN TRY?

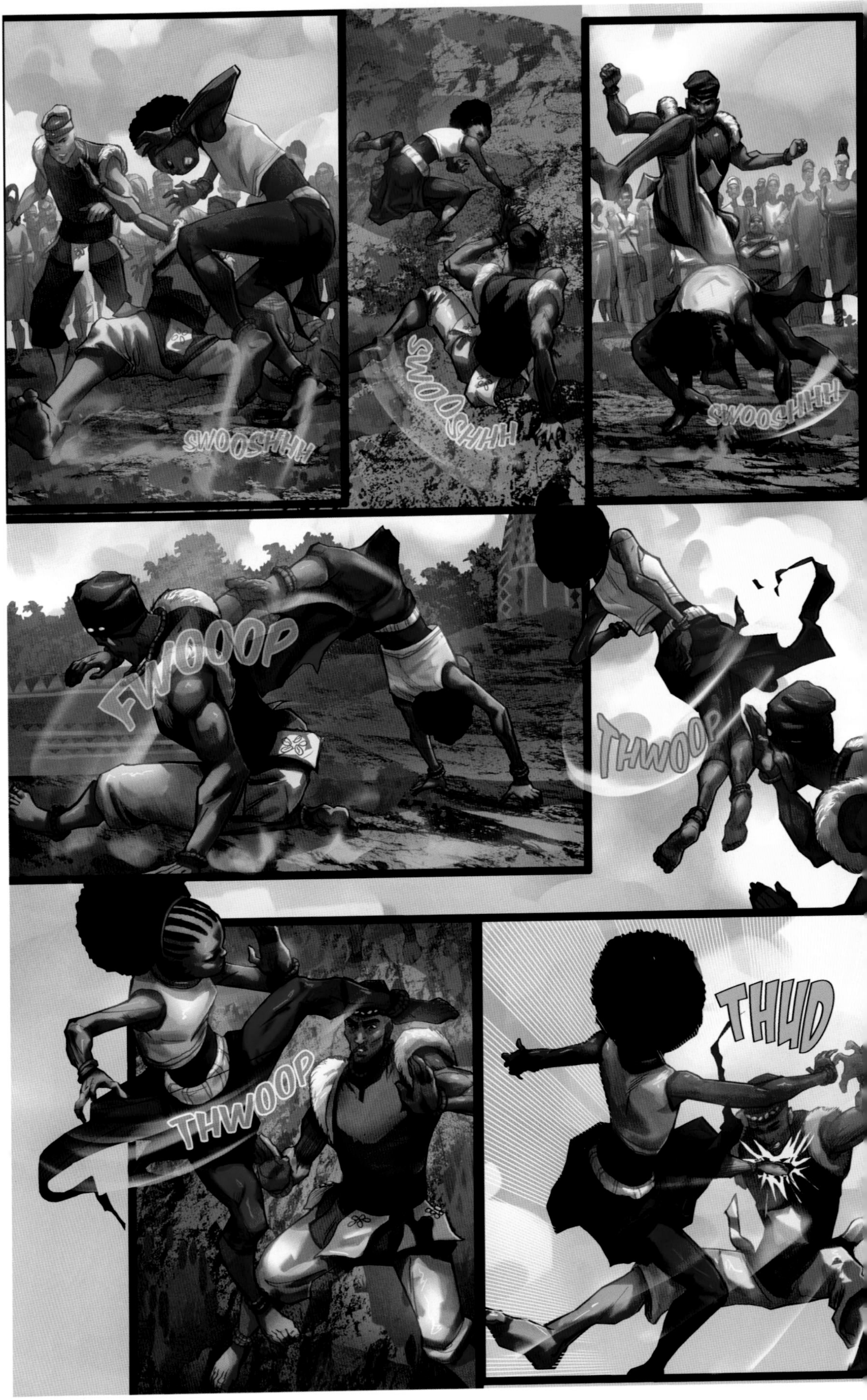
SWOOSHHH
SWOOSHHH
SWOOSHHH
FWOOOP
THWOOP
THWOOP
THUD

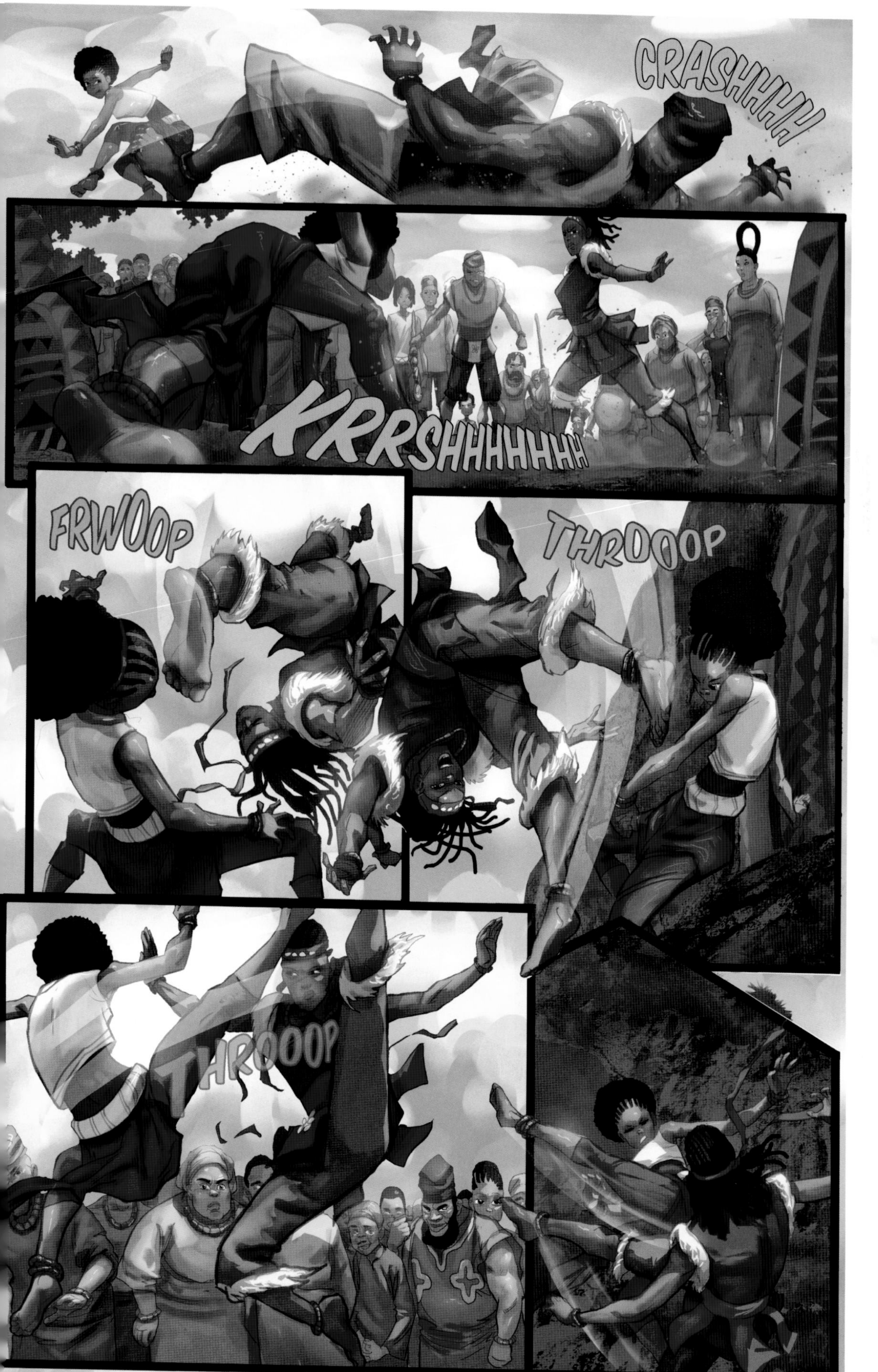
CRASHHHH
KRRSHHHHHHH
FRWOOP
THROOOP
THROOOP

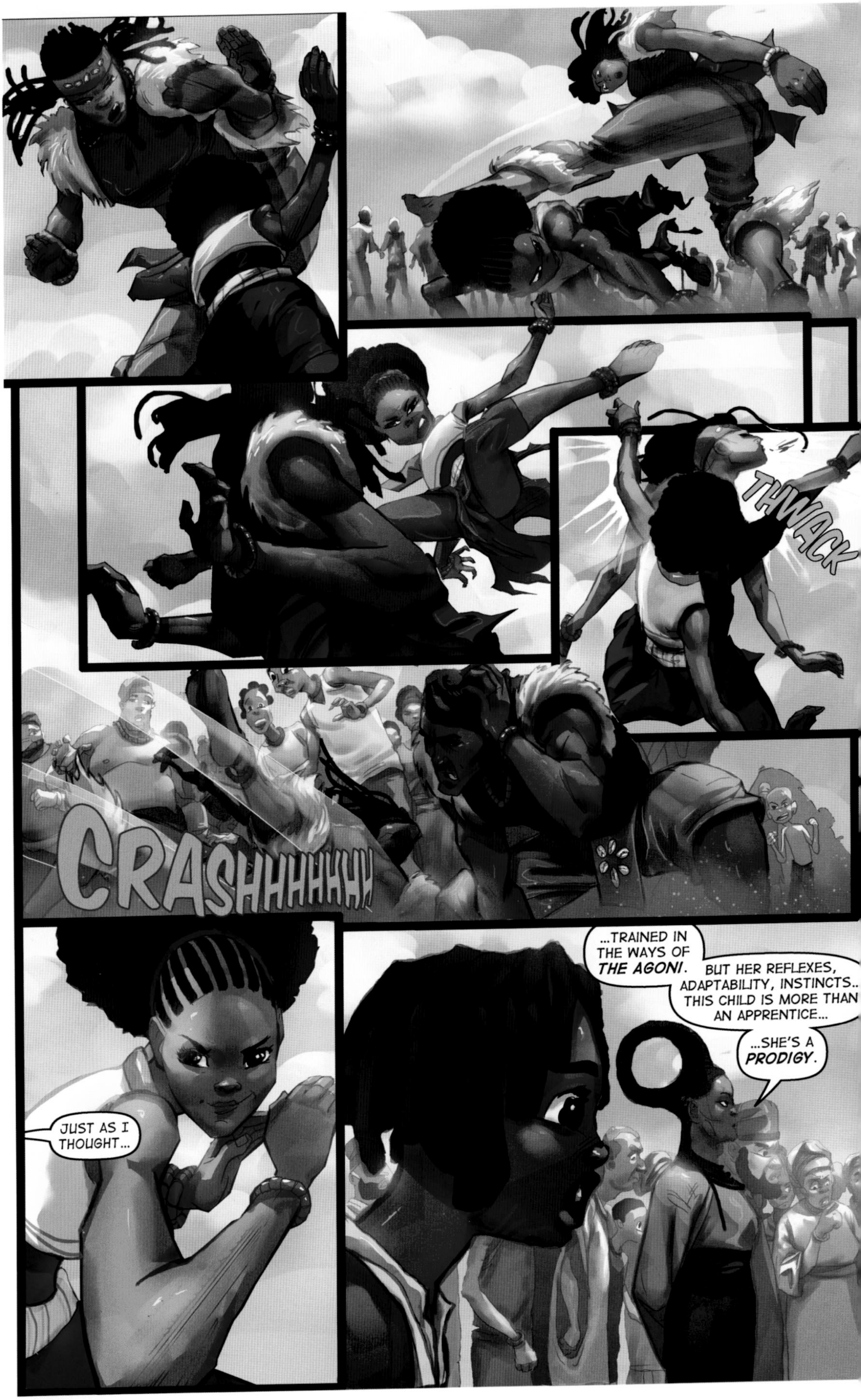
THWACK
CRASHHHHHH!
JUST AS I THOUGHT...
...TRAINED IN THE WAYS OF THE AGONI.
BUT HER REFLEXES, ADAPTABILITY, INSTINCTS.. THIS CHILD IS MORE THAN AN APPRENTICE...
...SHE'S A PRODIGY.

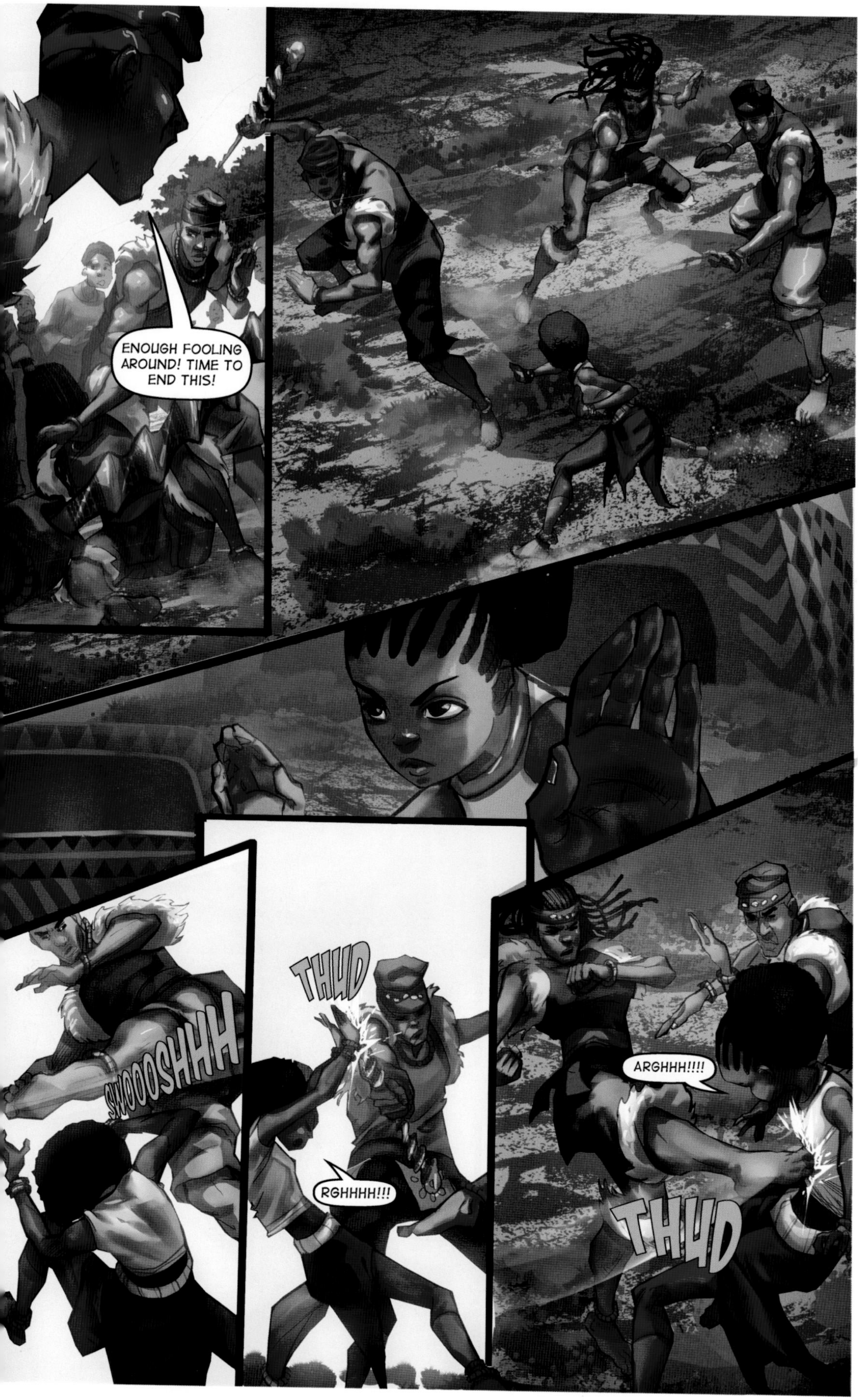
ENOUGH FOOLING AROUND! TIME TO END THIS!
SWOOOSHHH
THUD
RGHHHH!!!
ARGHHH!!!!
THUD

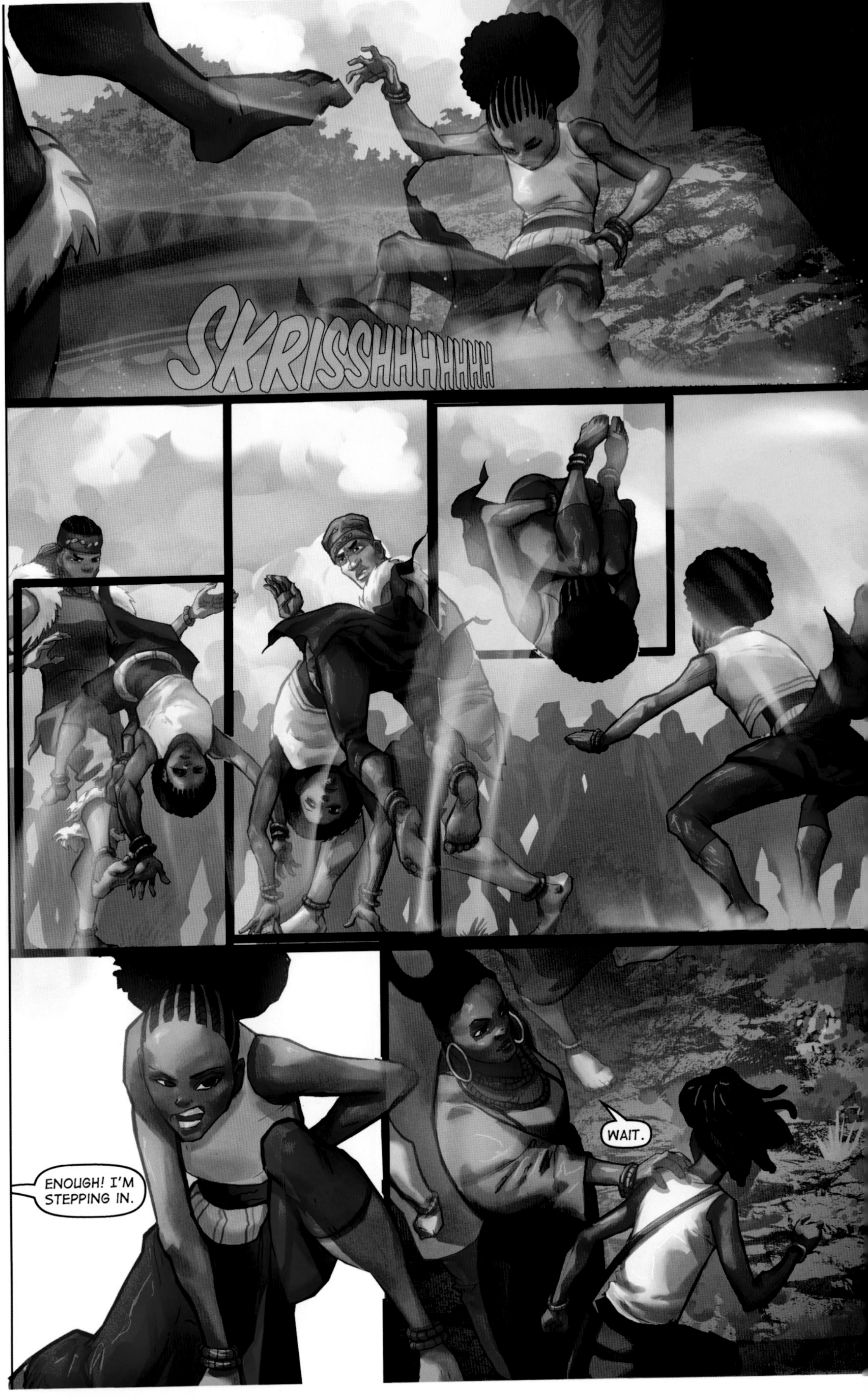
SKRISSHHHHHHH
ENOUGH! I'M STEPPING IN.
WAIT.

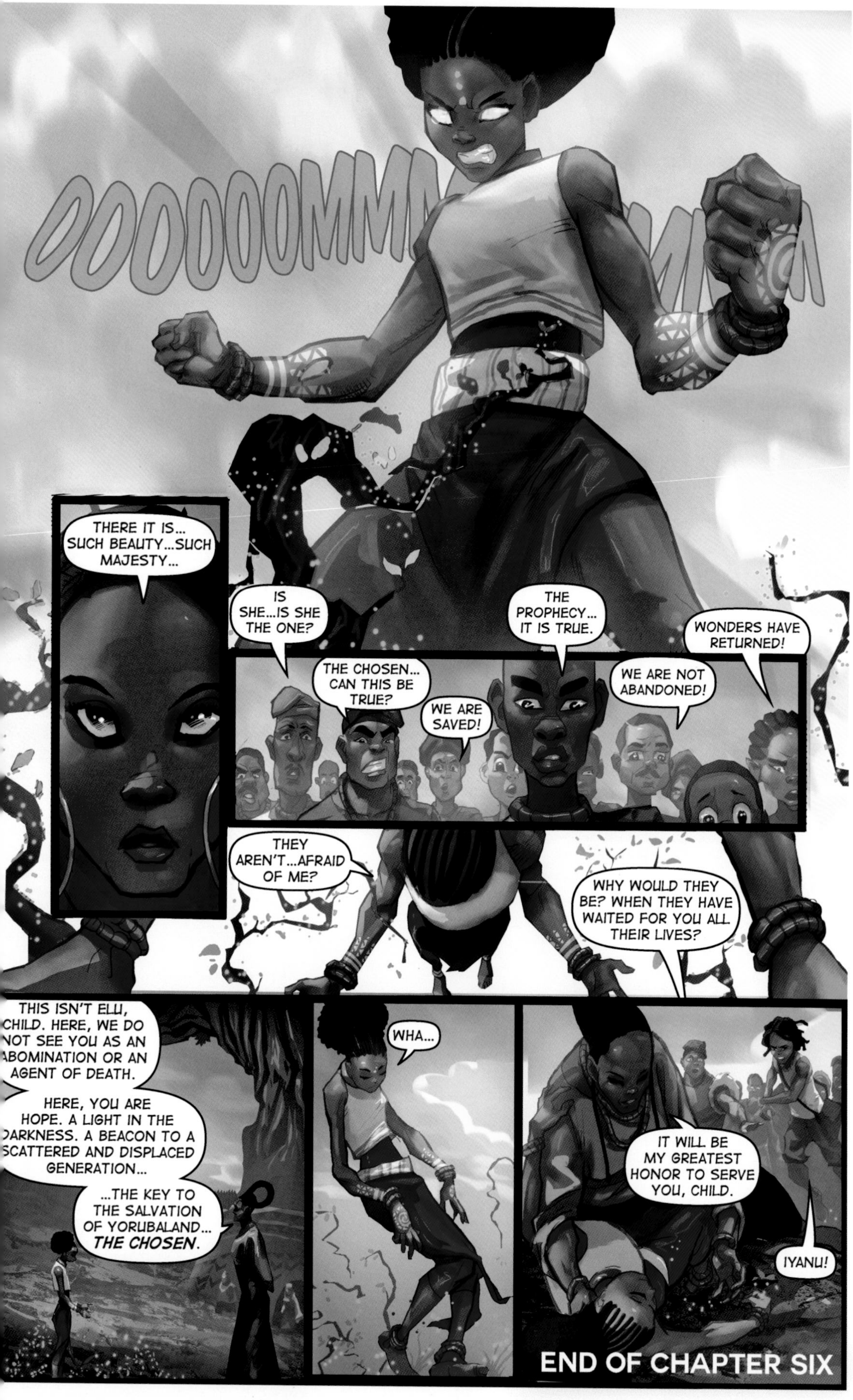
OOOOOOMMMMMMMM
THERE IT IS... SUCH BEAUTY...SUCH MAJESTY...
IS SHE...IS SHE THE ONE?
THE PROPHECY... IT IS TRUE.
WONDERS HAVE RETURNED!
THE CHOSEN... CAN THIS BE TRUE?
WE ARE SAVED!
WE ARE NOT ABANDONED!
THEY AREN'T...AFRAID OF ME?
WHY WOULD THEY BE? WHEN THEY HAVE WAITED FOR YOU ALL THEIR LIVES?
THIS ISN'T ELU, CHILD. HERE, WE DO NOT SEE YOU AS AN ABOMINATION OR AN AGENT OF DEATH.
HERE, YOU ARE HOPE. A LIGHT IN THE DARKNESS. A BEACON TO A SCATTERED AND DISPLACED GENERATION...
...THE KEY TO THE SALVATION OF YORUBALAND... THE CHOSEN.
WHA...
IT WILL BE MY GREATEST HONOR TO SERVE YOU, CHILD.
IYANU!
END OF CHAPTER SIX

CHAPTER SEVEN

The Exiled Settlements

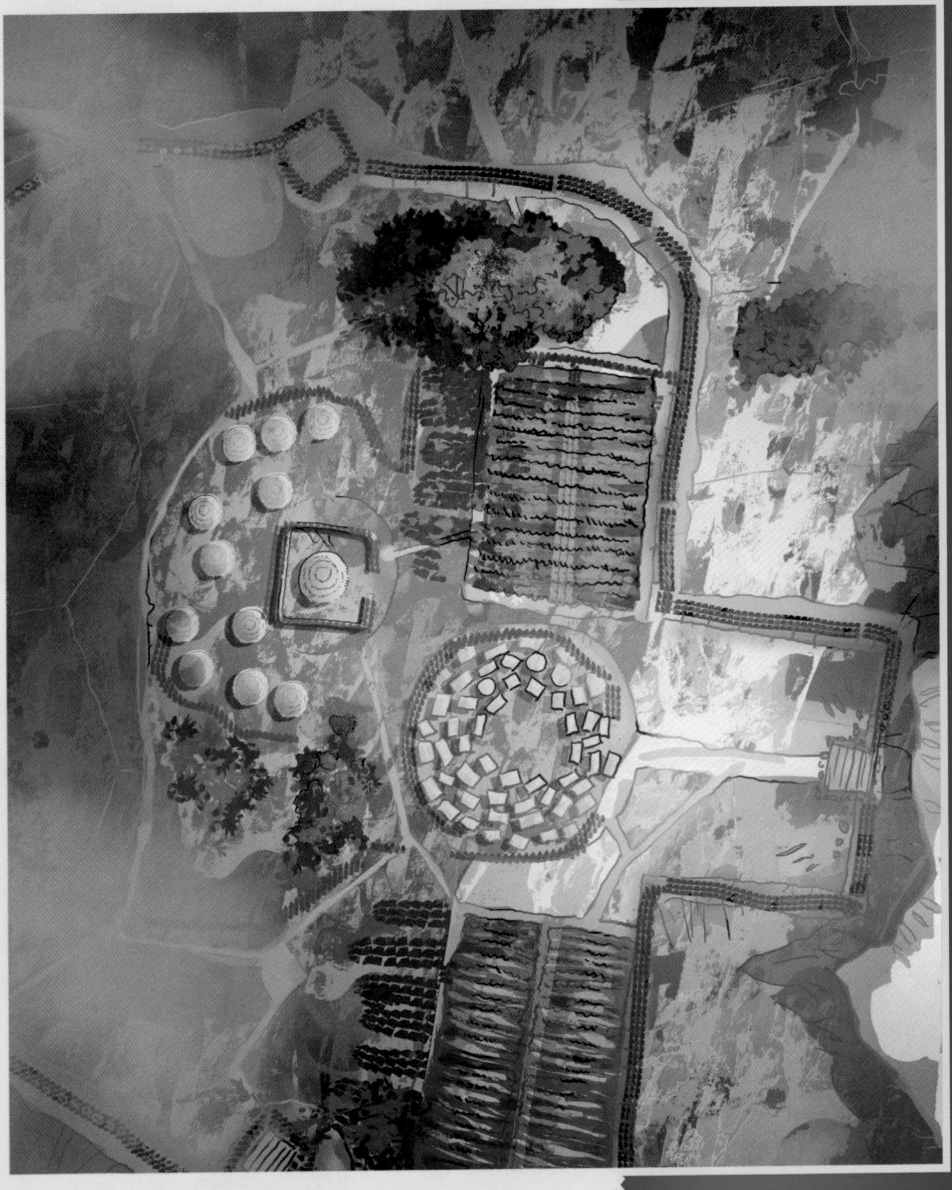

The exiled settlements are small villages that exist outside the walls of Elu. These villages are composed of two kinds of people. First, are people that have at one time or another been banished from Elu for crimes. The other is their offspring. There are currently only five known exiled settlements in Yorubaland.

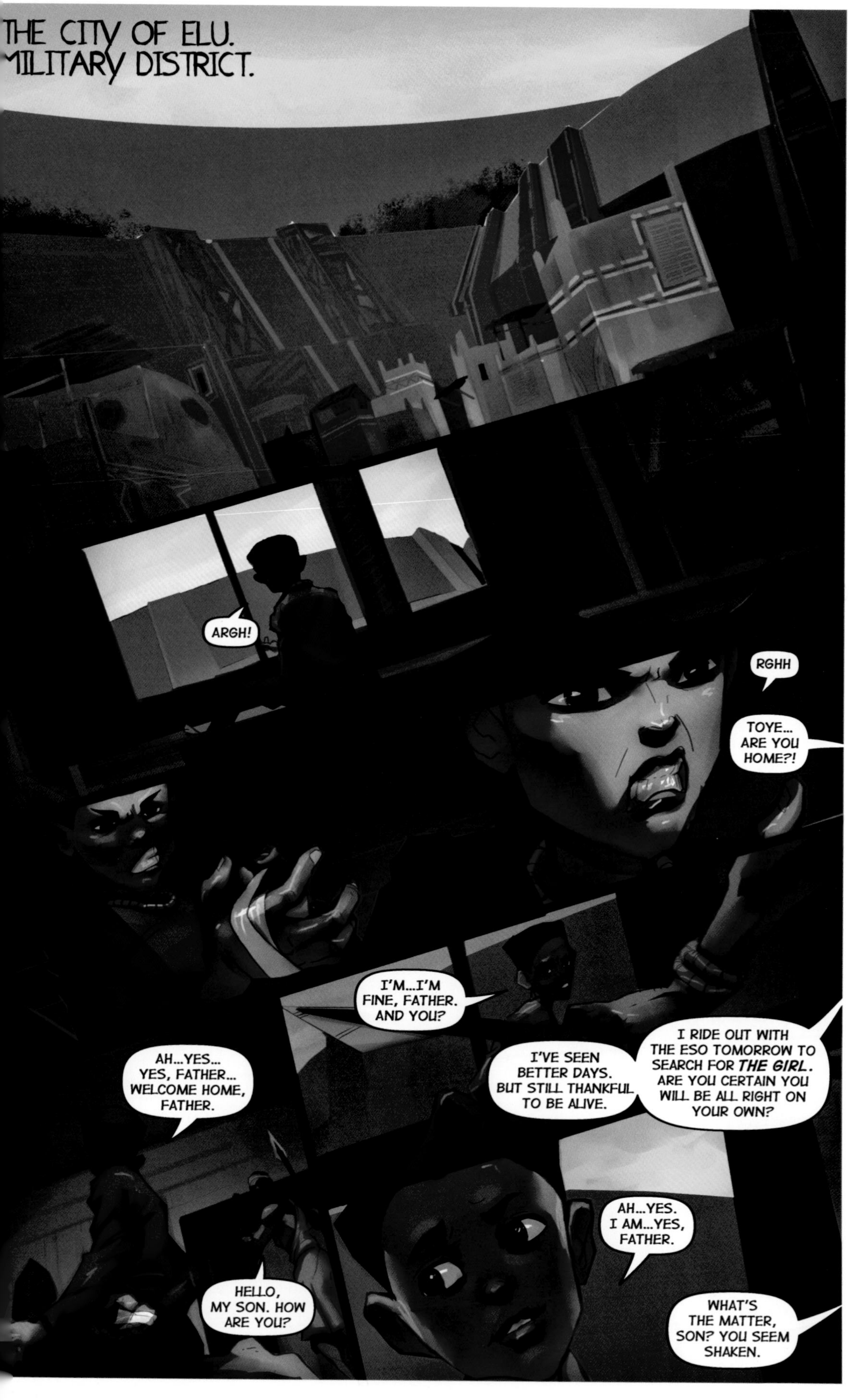
THE CITY OF ELU.
MILITARY DISTRICT.
ARGH!
RGHH
TOYE... ARE YOU HOME?!
I'M...I'M FINE, FATHER. AND YOU?
AH...YES... YES, FATHER... WELCOME HOME, FATHER.
I'VE SEEN BETTER DAYS. BUT STILL THANKFUL TO BE ALIVE.
I RIDE OUT WITH THE ESO TOMORROW TO SEARCH FOR THE GIRL. ARE YOU CERTAIN YOU WILL BE ALL RIGHT ON YOUR OWN?
HELLO, MY SON. HOW ARE YOU?
AH...YES. I AM...YES, FATHER.
WHAT'S THE MATTER, SON? YOU SEEM SHAKEN.

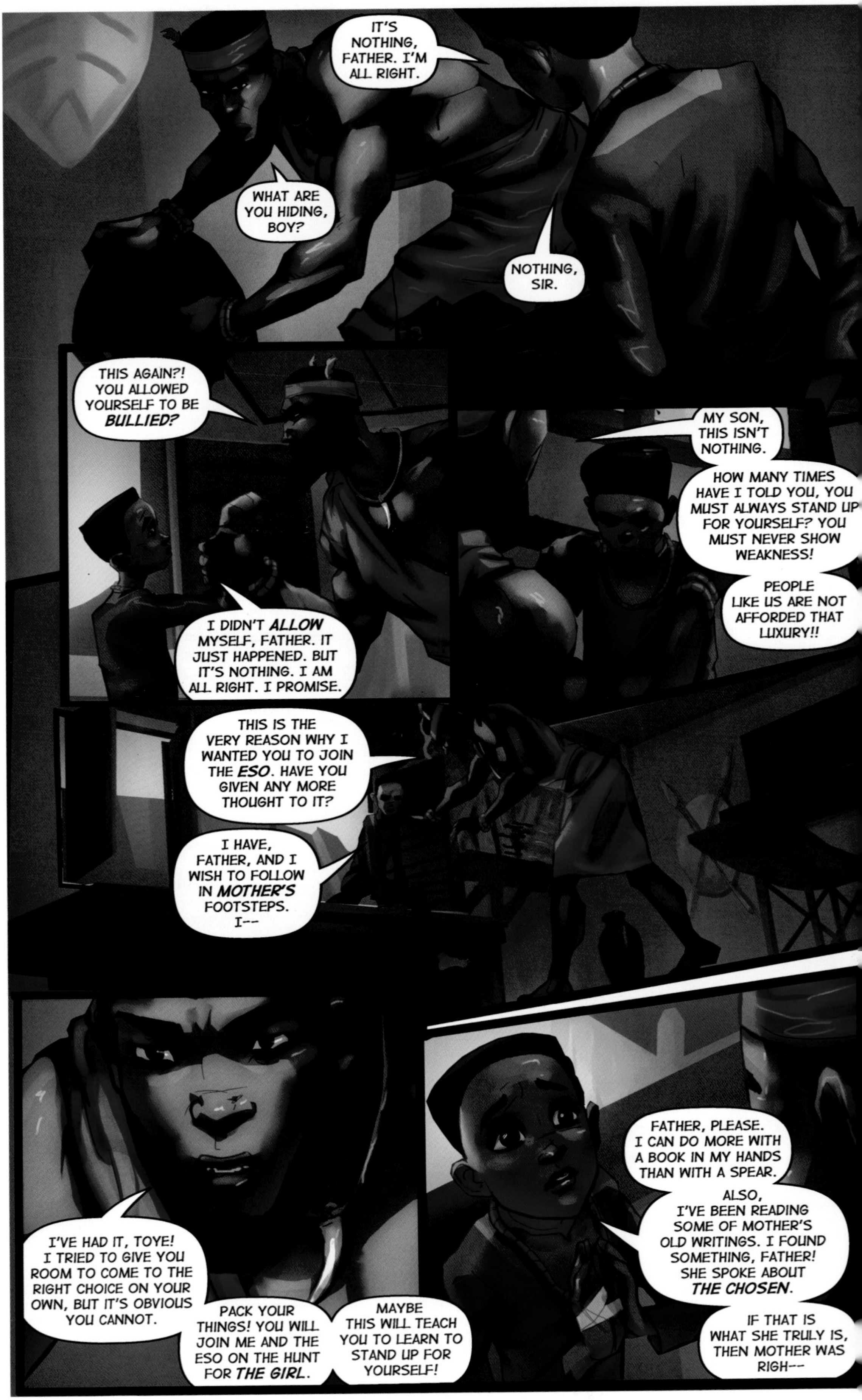
IT'S NOTHING, FATHER. I'M ALL RIGHT.
WHAT ARE YOU HIDING, BOY?
NOTHING, SIR.
THIS AGAIN?! YOU ALLOWED YOURSELF TO BE BULLIED?
I DIDN'T ALLOW MYSELF, FATHER. IT JUST HAPPENED. BUT IT'S NOTHING. I AM ALL RIGHT. I PROMISE.
MY SON, THIS ISN'T NOTHING.
HOW MANY TIMES HAVE I TOLD YOU, YOU MUST ALWAYS STAND UP FOR YOURSELF? YOU MUST NEVER SHOW WEAKNESS!
PEOPLE LIKE US ARE NOT AFFORDED THAT LUXURY!!
THIS IS THE VERY REASON WHY I WANTED YOU TO JOIN THE ESO. HAVE YOU GIVEN ANY MORE THOUGHT TO IT?
I HAVE, FATHER, AND I WISH TO FOLLOW IN MOTHER'S FOOTSTEPS. I--
I'VE HAD IT, TOYE! I TRIED TO GIVE YOU ROOM TO COME TO THE RIGHT CHOICE ON YOUR OWN, BUT IT'S OBVIOUS YOU CANNOT.
PACK YOUR THINGS! YOU WILL JOIN ME AND THE ESO ON THE HUNT FOR THE GIRL.
MAYBE THIS WILL TEACH YOU TO LEARN TO STAND UP FOR YOURSELF!
FATHER, PLEASE. I CAN DO MORE WITH A BOOK IN MY HANDS THAN WITH A SPEAR.
ALSO, I'VE BEEN READING SOME OF MOTHER'S OLD WRITINGS. I FOUND SOMETHING, FATHER! SHE SPOKE ABOUT THE CHOSEN.
IF THAT IS WHAT SHE TRULY IS, THEN MOTHER WAS RIGH--

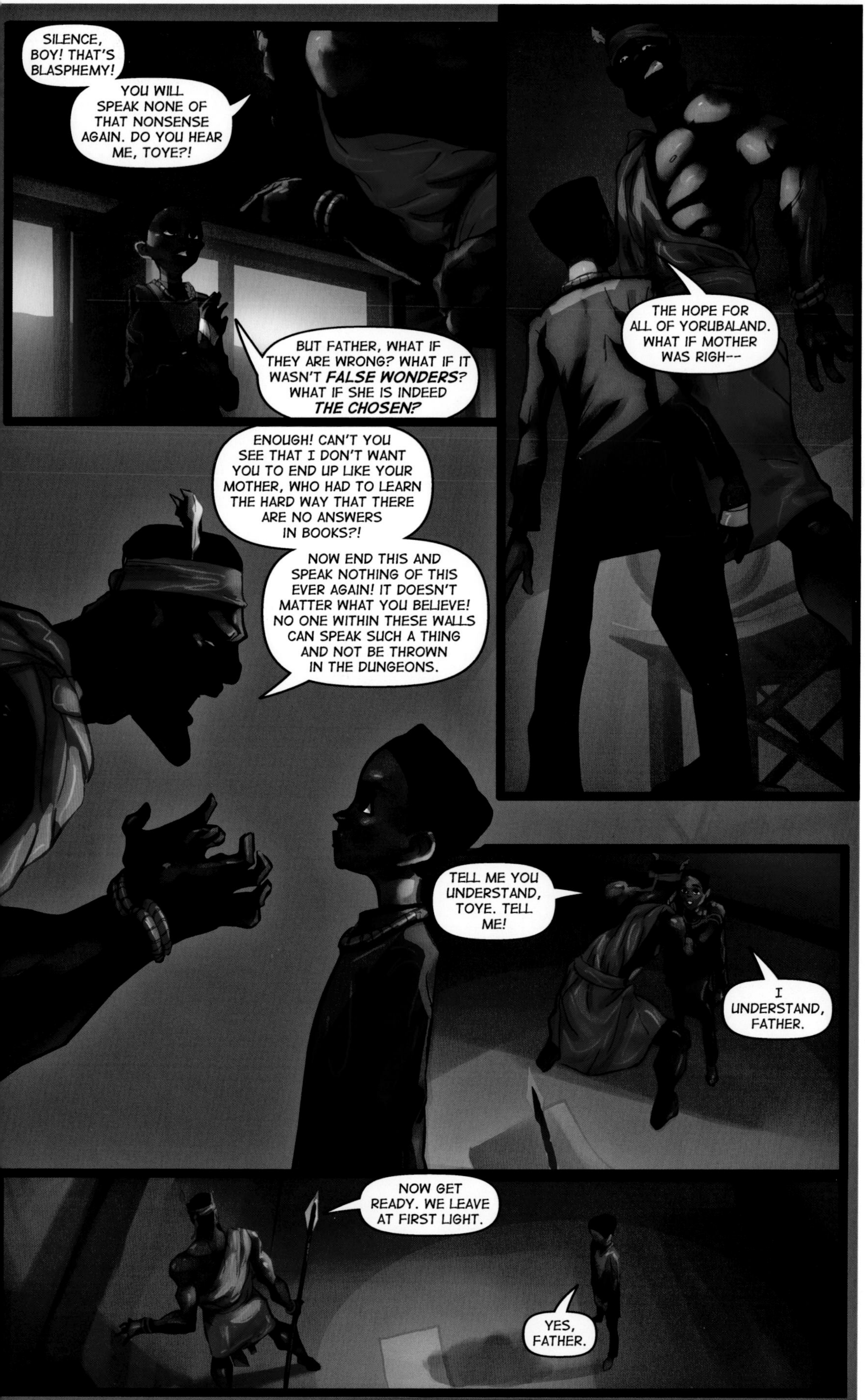

SILENCE, BOY! THAT'S BLASPHEMY!
YOU WILL SPEAK NONE OF THAT NONSENSE AGAIN. DO YOU HEAR ME, TOYE?!
BUT FATHER, WHAT IF THEY ARE WRONG? WHAT IF IT WASN'T *FALSE WONDERS*? WHAT IF SHE IS INDEED *THE CHOSEN*?
THE HOPE FOR ALL OF YORUBALAND. WHAT IF MOTHER WAS RIGH--
ENOUGH! CAN'T YOU SEE THAT I DON'T WANT YOU TO END UP LIKE YOUR MOTHER, WHO HAD TO LEARN THE HARD WAY THAT THERE ARE NO ANSWERS IN BOOKS?!
NOW END THIS AND SPEAK NOTHING OF THIS EVER AGAIN! IT DOESN'T MATTER WHAT YOU BELIEVE! NO ONE WITHIN THESE WALLS CAN SPEAK SUCH A THING AND NOT BE THROWN IN THE DUNGEONS.
TELL ME YOU UNDERSTAND, TOYE. TELL ME!
I UNDERSTAND, FATHER.
NOW GET READY. WE LEAVE AT FIRST LIGHT.
YES, FATHER.

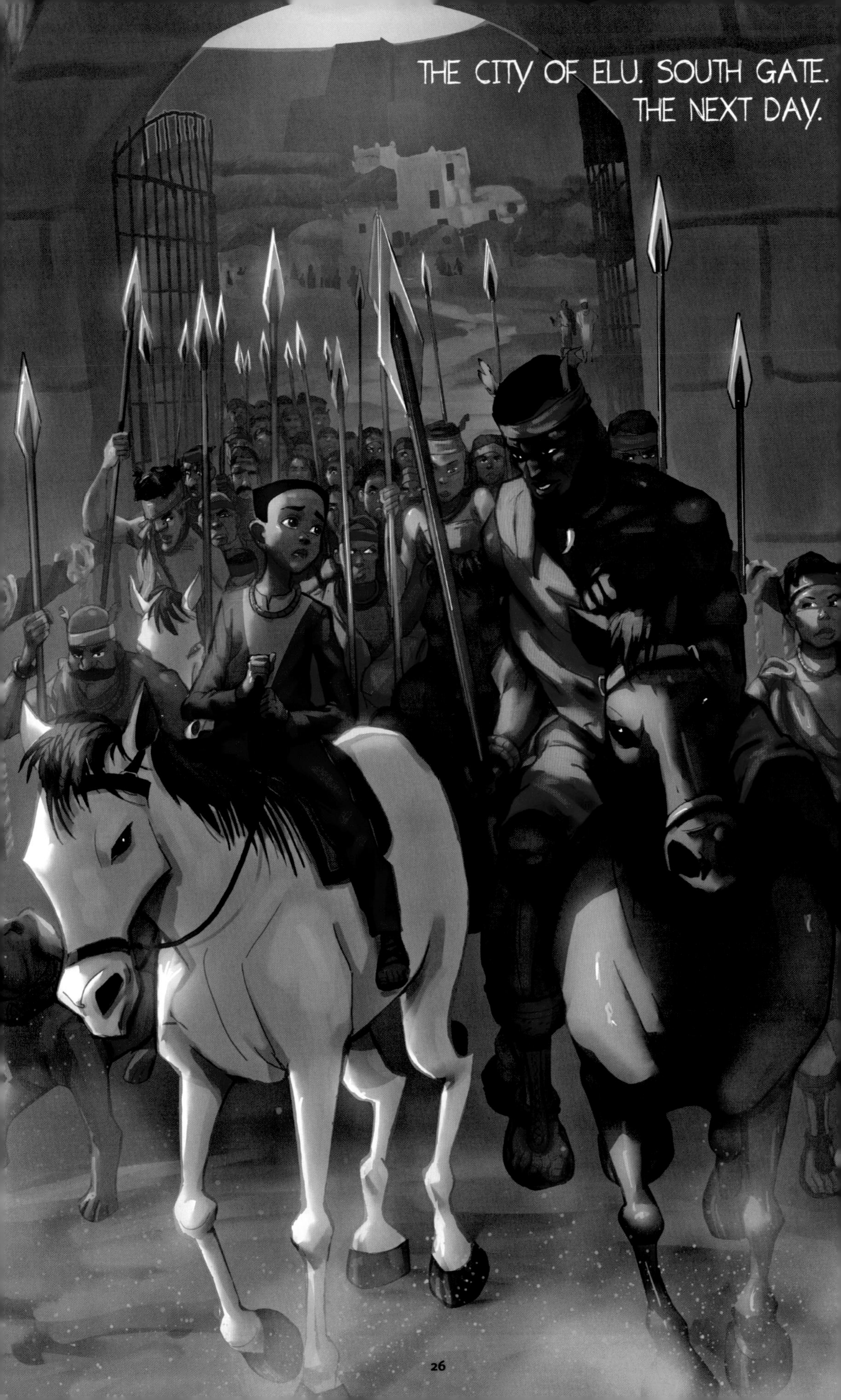
THE CITY OF ELU. SOUTH GATE.
THE NEXT DAY.

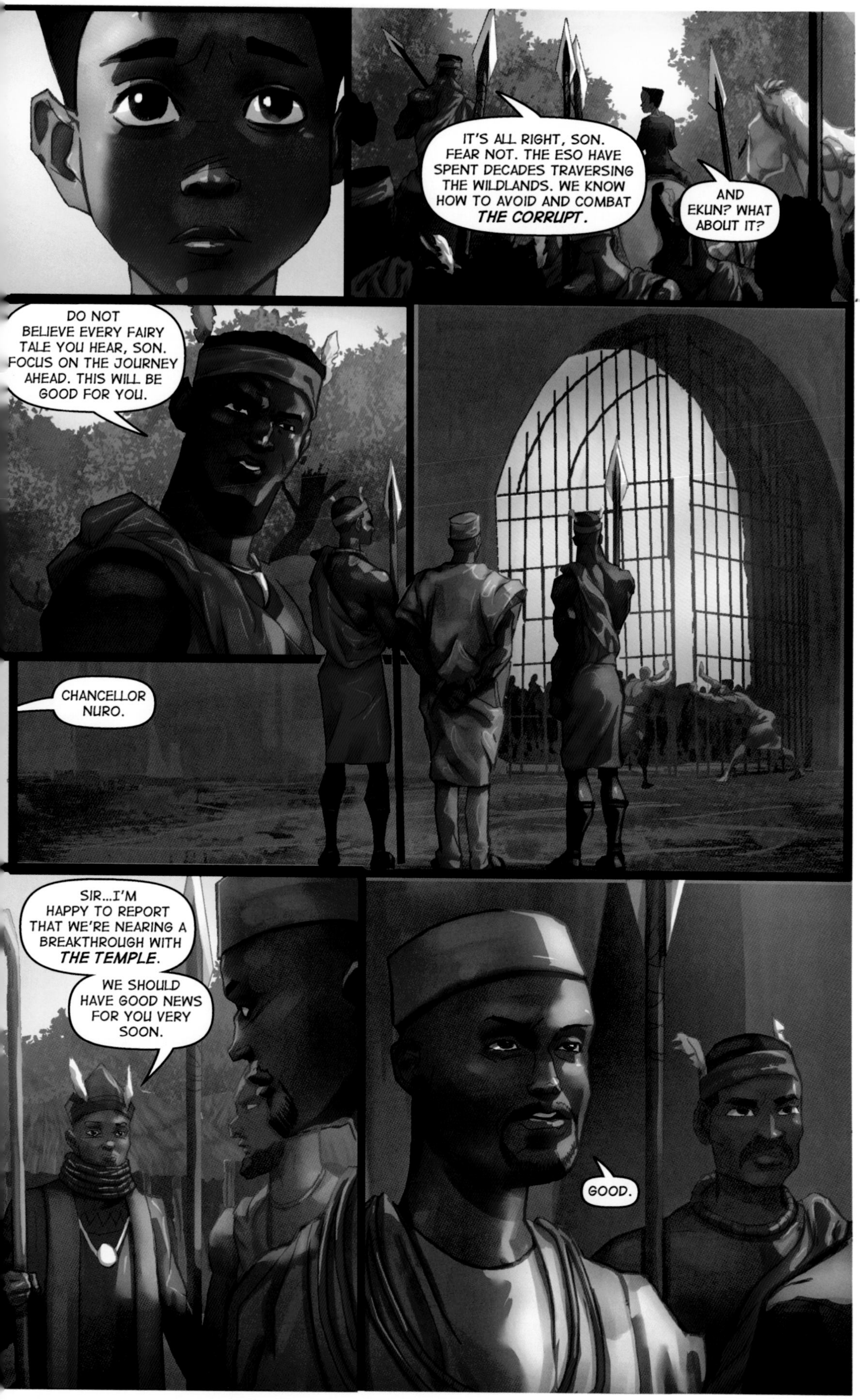
IT'S ALL RIGHT, SON. FEAR NOT. THE ESO HAVE SPENT DECADES TRAVERSING THE WILDLANDS. WE KNOW HOW TO AVOID AND COMBAT *THE CORRUPT*.
AND EKUN? WHAT ABOUT IT?
DO NOT BELIEVE EVERY FAIRY TALE YOU HEAR, SON. FOCUS ON THE JOURNEY AHEAD. THIS WILL BE GOOD FOR YOU.
CHANCELLOR NURO.
SIR...I'M HAPPY TO REPORT THAT WE'RE NEARING A BREAKTHROUGH WITH *THE TEMPLE*.
WE SHOULD HAVE GOOD NEWS FOR YOU VERY SOON.
GOOD.

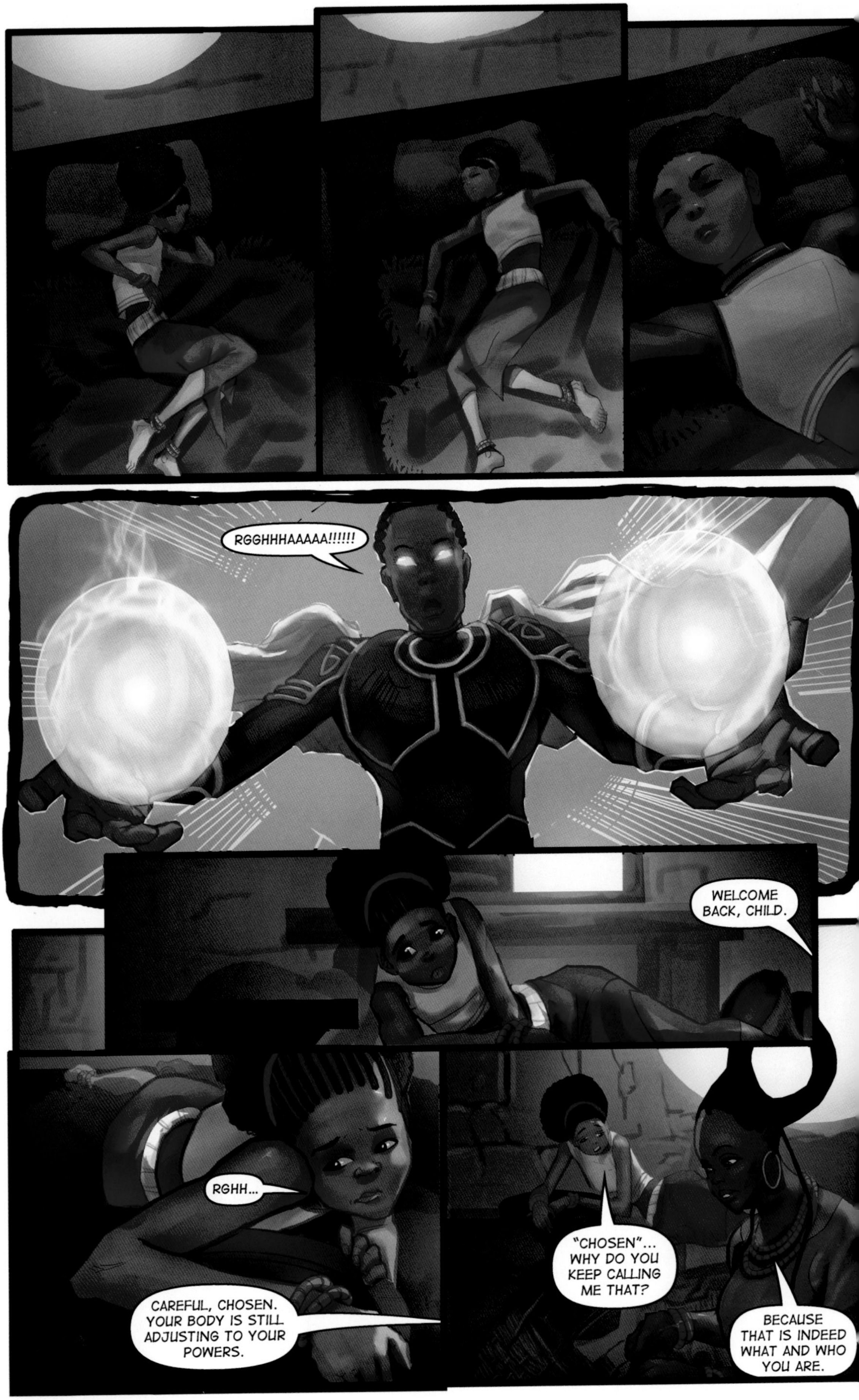
RGGHHHAAAAA!!!!!!
WELCOME BACK, CHILD.
RGHH...
CAREFUL, CHOSEN. YOUR BODY IS STILL ADJUSTING TO YOUR POWERS.
"CHOSEN"... WHY DO YOU KEEP CALLING ME THAT?
BECAUSE THAT IS INDEED WHAT AND WHO YOU ARE.

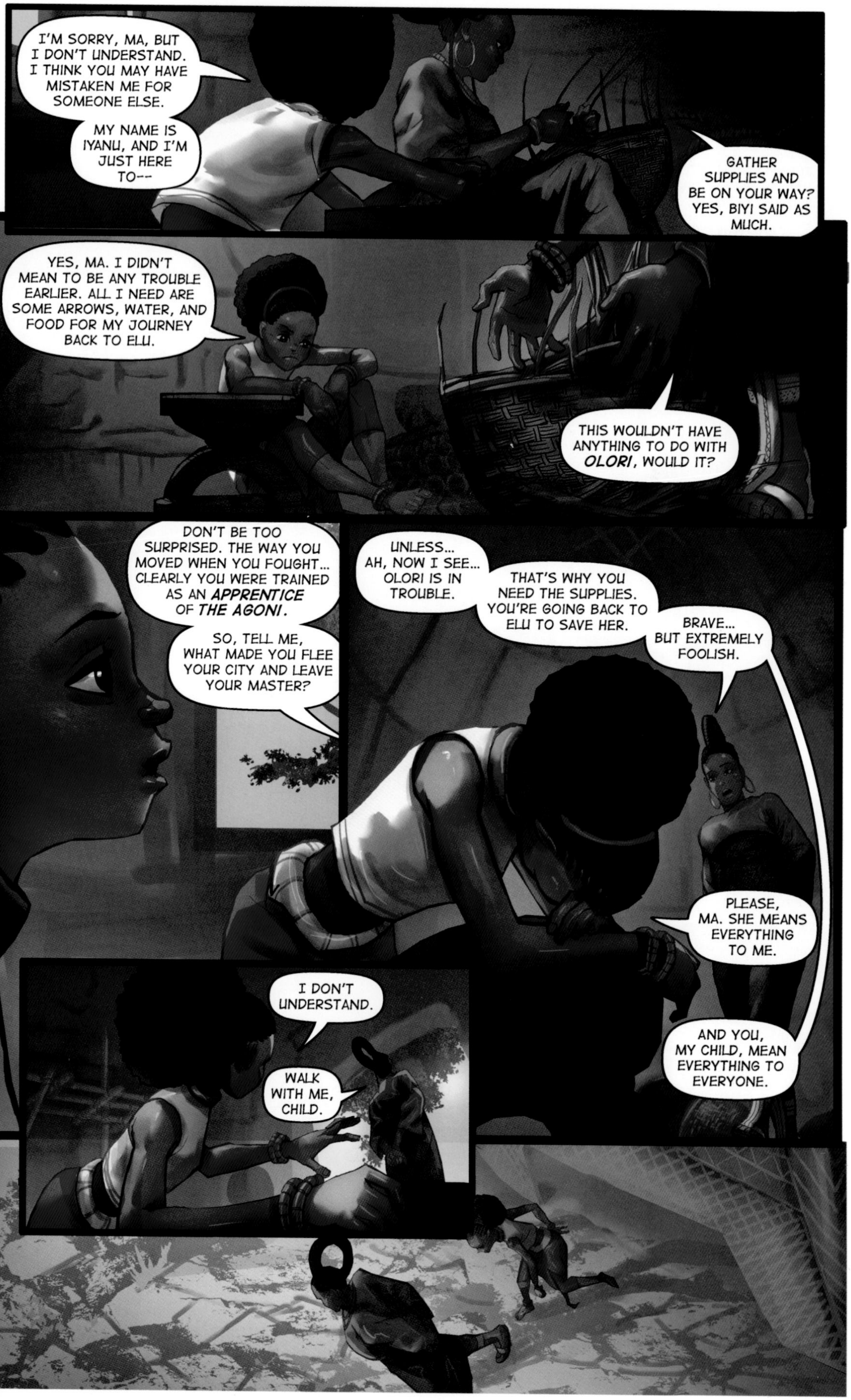
I'M SORRY, MA, BUT I DON'T UNDERSTAND. I THINK YOU MAY HAVE MISTAKEN ME FOR SOMEONE ELSE.
MY NAME IS IYANU, AND I'M JUST HERE TO--
GATHER SUPPLIES AND BE ON YOUR WAY? YES, BIYI SAID AS MUCH.
YES, MA. I DIDN'T MEAN TO BE ANY TROUBLE EARLIER. ALL I NEED ARE SOME ARROWS, WATER, AND FOOD FOR MY JOURNEY BACK TO ELU.
THIS WOULDN'T HAVE ANYTHING TO DO WITH OLORI, WOULD IT?
DON'T BE TOO SURPRISED. THE WAY YOU MOVED WHEN YOU FOUGHT... CLEARLY YOU WERE TRAINED AS AN APPRENTICE OF THE AGONI.
SO, TELL ME, WHAT MADE YOU FLEE YOUR CITY AND LEAVE YOUR MASTER?
UNLESS... AH, NOW I SEE... OLORI IS IN TROUBLE.
THAT'S WHY YOU NEED THE SUPPLIES. YOU'RE GOING BACK TO ELU TO SAVE HER.
BRAVE... BUT EXTREMELY FOOLISH.
PLEASE, MA. SHE MEANS EVERYTHING TO ME.
AND YOU, MY CHILD, MEAN EVERYTHING TO EVERYONE.
I DON'T UNDERSTAND.
WALK WITH ME, CHILD.

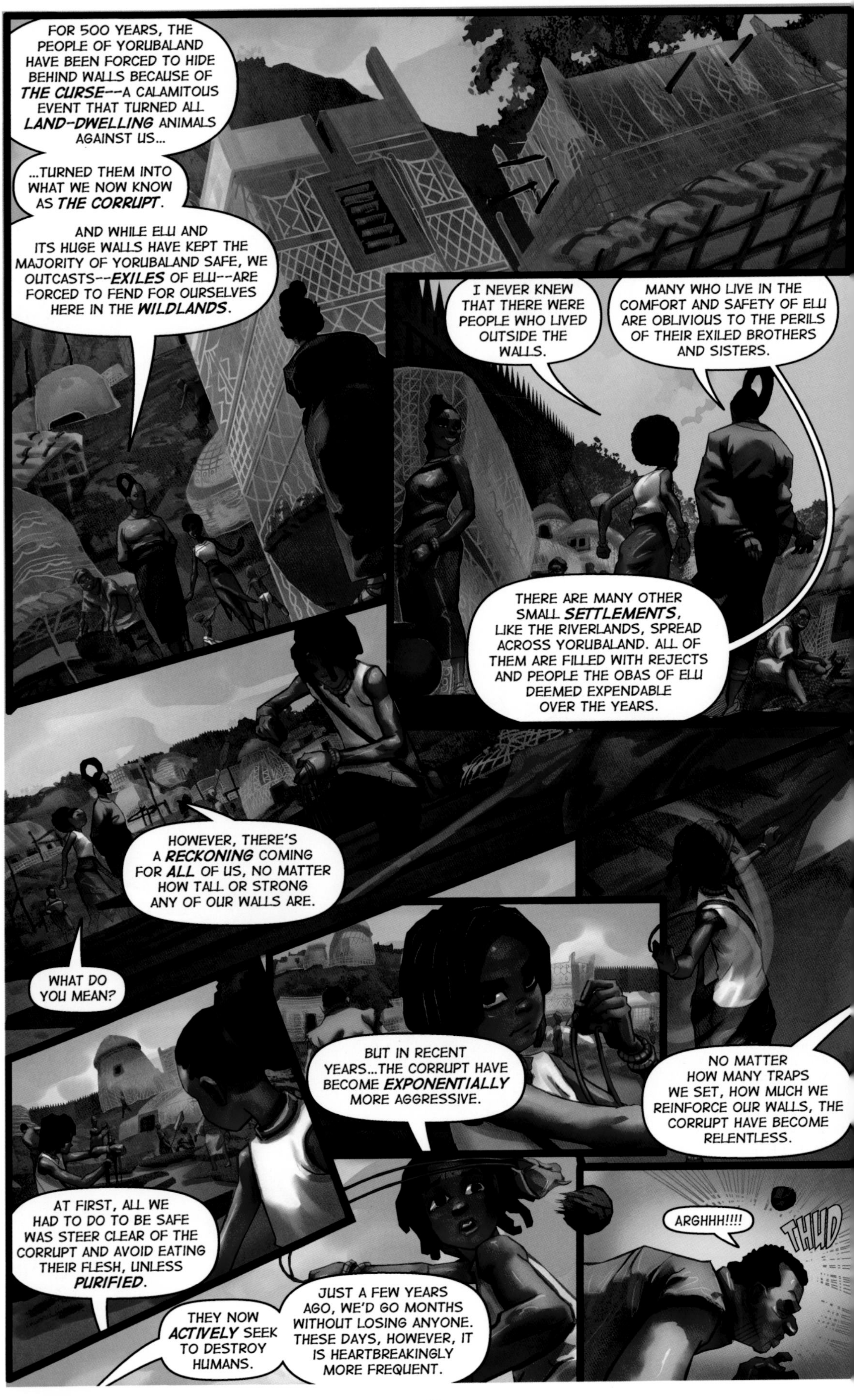
FOR 500 YEARS, THE PEOPLE OF YORUBALAND HAVE BEEN FORCED TO HIDE BEHIND WALLS BECAUSE OF THE CURSE--A CALAMITOUS EVENT THAT TURNED ALL LAND-DWELLING ANIMALS AGAINST US...
...TURNED THEM INTO WHAT WE NOW KNOW AS THE CORRUPT.
AND WHILE ELU AND ITS HUGE WALLS HAVE KEPT THE MAJORITY OF YORUBALAND SAFE, WE OUTCASTS--EXILES OF ELU--ARE FORCED TO FEND FOR OURSELVES HERE IN THE WILDLANDS.
I NEVER KNEW THAT THERE WERE PEOPLE WHO LIVED OUTSIDE THE WALLS.
MANY WHO LIVE IN THE COMFORT AND SAFETY OF ELU ARE OBLIVIOUS TO THE PERILS OF THEIR EXILED BROTHERS AND SISTERS.
THERE ARE MANY OTHER SMALL SETTLEMENTS, LIKE THE RIVERLANDS, SPREAD ACROSS YORUBALAND. ALL OF THEM ARE FILLED WITH REJECTS AND PEOPLE THE OBAS OF ELU DEEMED EXPENDABLE OVER THE YEARS.
HOWEVER, THERE'S A RECKONING COMING FOR ALL OF US, NO MATTER HOW TALL OR STRONG ANY OF OUR WALLS ARE.
WHAT DO YOU MEAN?
BUT IN RECENT YEARS...THE CORRUPT HAVE BECOME EXPONENTIALLY MORE AGGRESSIVE.
NO MATTER HOW MANY TRAPS WE SET, HOW MUCH WE REINFORCE OUR WALLS, THE CORRUPT HAVE BECOME RELENTLESS.
AT FIRST, ALL WE HAD TO DO TO BE SAFE WAS STEER CLEAR OF THE CORRUPT AND AVOID EATING THEIR FLESH, UNLESS PURIFIED.
THEY NOW ACTIVELY SEEK TO DESTROY HUMANS.
JUST A FEW YEARS AGO, WE'D GO MONTHS WITHOUT LOSING ANYONE. THESE DAYS, HOWEVER, IT IS HEARTBREAKINGLY MORE FREQUENT.
ARGHHH!!!!
THUD

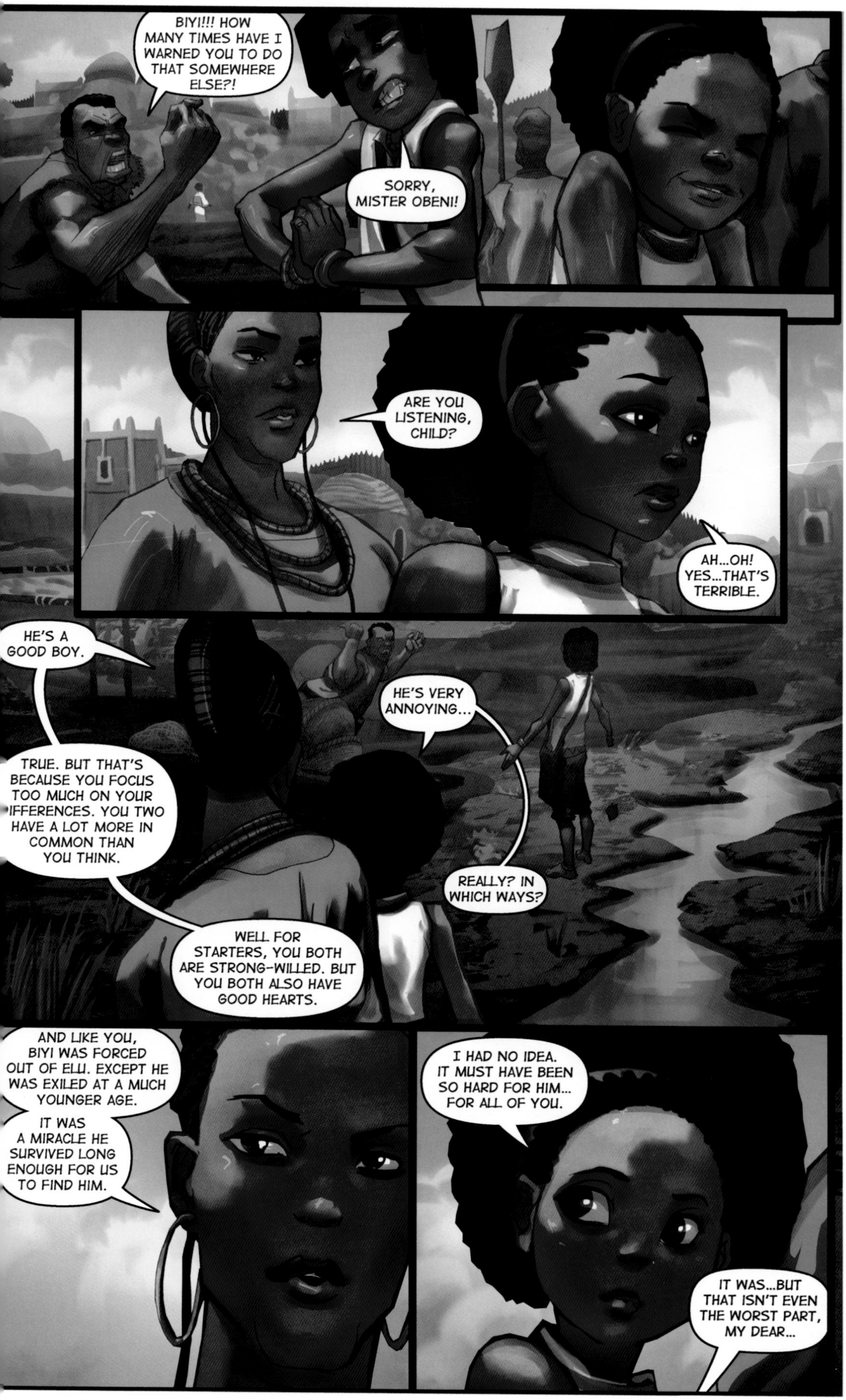
BIYI!!! HOW MANY TIMES HAVE I WARNED YOU TO DO THAT SOMEWHERE ELSE?!
SORRY, MISTER OBENI!
ARE YOU LISTENING, CHILD?
AH...OH! YES...THAT'S TERRIBLE.
HE'S A GOOD BOY.
HE'S VERY ANNOYING...
TRUE. BUT THAT'S BECAUSE YOU FOCUS TOO MUCH ON YOUR IFFERENCES. YOU TWO HAVE A LOT MORE IN COMMON THAN YOU THINK.
REALLY? IN WHICH WAYS?
WELL FOR STARTERS, YOU BOTH ARE STRONG-WILLED. BUT YOU BOTH ALSO HAVE GOOD HEARTS.
AND LIKE YOU, BIYI WAS FORCED OUT OF ELU. EXCEPT HE WAS EXILED AT A MUCH YOUNGER AGE.
IT WAS A MIRACLE HE SURVIVED LONG ENOUGH FOR US TO FIND HIM.
I HAD NO IDEA. IT MUST HAVE BEEN SO HARD FOR HIM... FOR ALL OF YOU.
IT WAS...BUT THAT ISN'T EVEN THE WORST PART, MY DEAR...

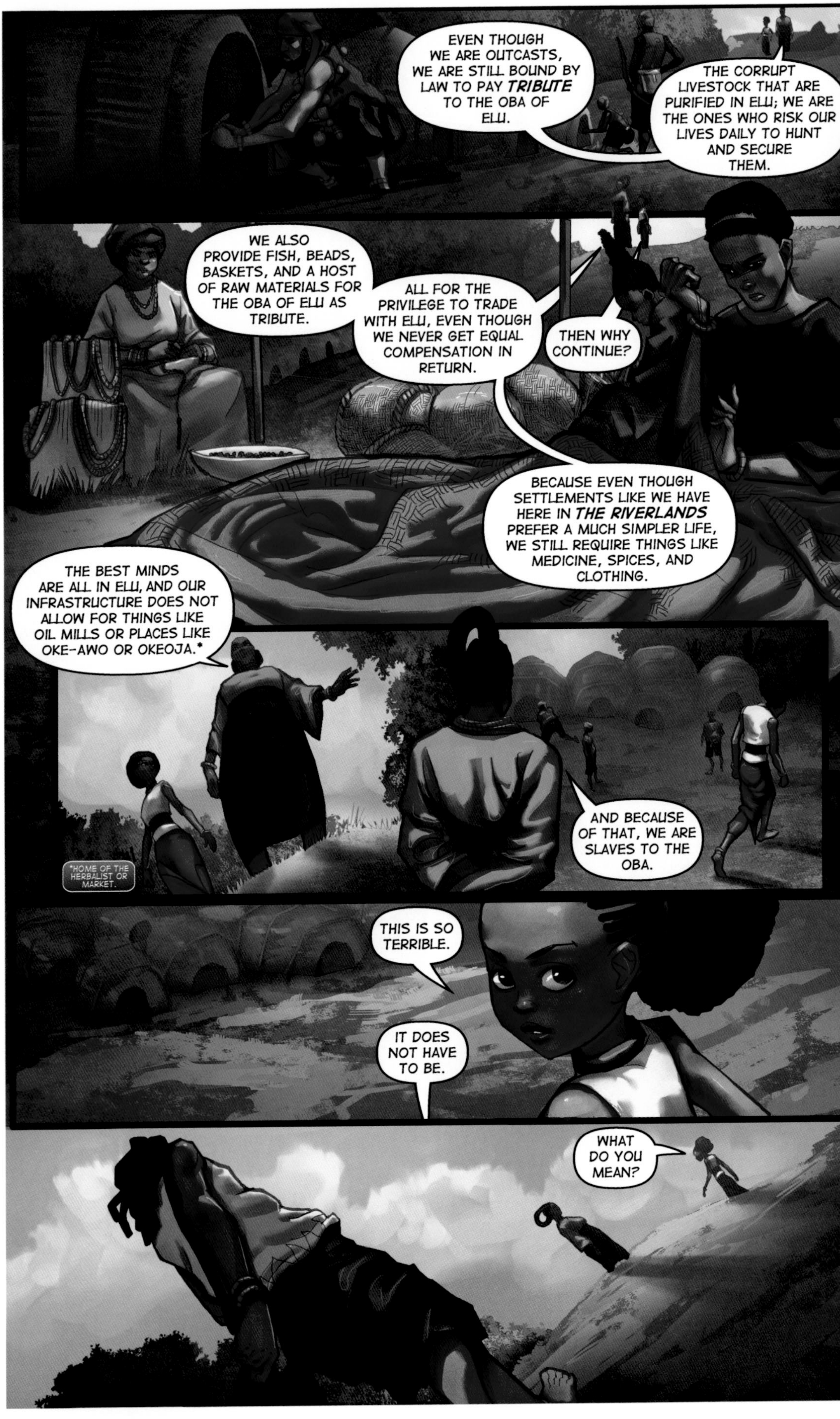
EVEN THOUGH WE ARE OUTCASTS, WE ARE STILL BOUND BY LAW TO PAY *TRIBUTE* TO THE OBA OF ELU.
THE CORRUPT LIVESTOCK THAT ARE PURIFIED IN ELU; WE ARE THE ONES WHO RISK OUR LIVES DAILY TO HUNT AND SECURE THEM.
WE ALSO PROVIDE FISH, BEADS, BASKETS, AND A HOST OF RAW MATERIALS FOR THE OBA OF ELU AS TRIBUTE.
ALL FOR THE PRIVILEGE TO TRADE WITH ELU, EVEN THOUGH WE NEVER GET EQUAL COMPENSATION IN RETURN.
THEN WHY CONTINUE?
BECAUSE EVEN THOUGH SETTLEMENTS LIKE WE HAVE HERE IN *THE RIVERLANDS* PREFER A MUCH SIMPLER LIFE, WE STILL REQUIRE THINGS LIKE MEDICINE, SPICES, AND CLOTHING.
THE BEST MINDS ARE ALL IN ELU, AND OUR INFRASTRUCTURE DOES NOT ALLOW FOR THINGS LIKE OIL MILLS OR PLACES LIKE OKE-AWO OR OKEOJA.*
AND BECAUSE OF THAT, WE ARE SLAVES TO THE OBA.
*HOME OF THE HERBALIST OR MARKET.
THIS IS SO TERRIBLE.
IT DOES NOT HAVE TO BE.
WHAT DO YOU MEAN?

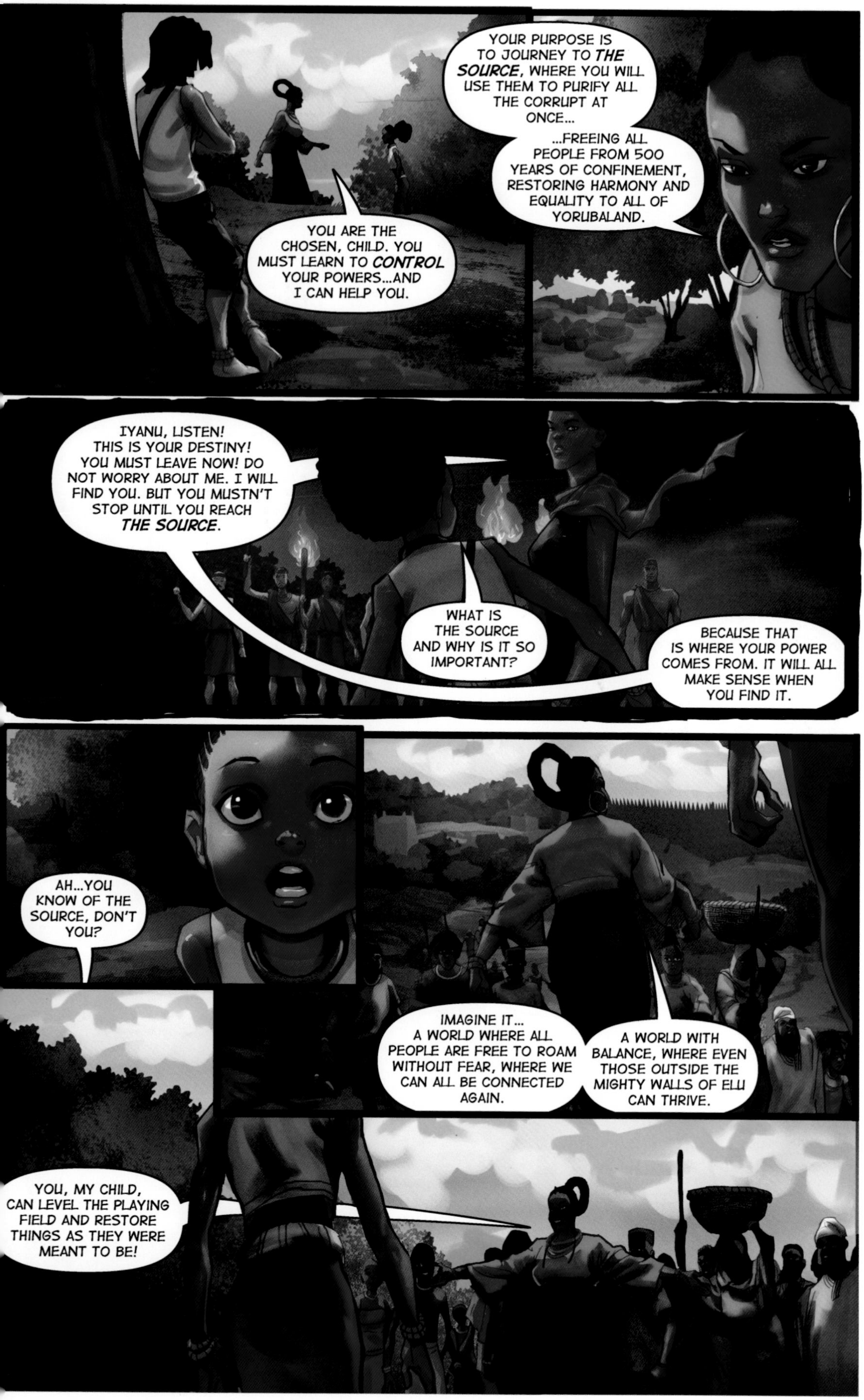
YOUR PURPOSE IS TO JOURNEY TO THE SOURCE, WHERE YOU WILL USE THEM TO PURIFY ALL THE CORRUPT AT ONCE...
...FREEING ALL PEOPLE FROM 500 YEARS OF CONFINEMENT, RESTORING HARMONY AND EQUALITY TO ALL OF YORUBALAND.
YOU ARE THE CHOSEN, CHILD. YOU MUST LEARN TO CONTROL YOUR POWERS...AND I CAN HELP YOU.
IYANU, LISTEN! THIS IS YOUR DESTINY! YOU MUST LEAVE NOW! DO NOT WORRY ABOUT ME. I WILL FIND YOU. BUT YOU MUSTN'T STOP UNTIL YOU REACH THE SOURCE.
WHAT IS THE SOURCE AND WHY IS IT SO IMPORTANT?
BECAUSE THAT IS WHERE YOUR POWER COMES FROM. IT WILL ALL MAKE SENSE WHEN YOU FIND IT.
AH...YOU KNOW OF THE SOURCE, DON'T YOU?
IMAGINE IT... A WORLD WHERE ALL PEOPLE ARE FREE TO ROAM WITHOUT FEAR, WHERE WE CAN ALL BE CONNECTED AGAIN.
A WORLD WITH BALANCE, WHERE EVEN THOSE OUTSIDE THE MIGHTY WALLS OF ELU CAN THRIVE.
YOU, MY CHILD, CAN LEVEL THE PLAYING FIELD AND RESTORE THINGS AS THEY WERE MEANT TO BE!

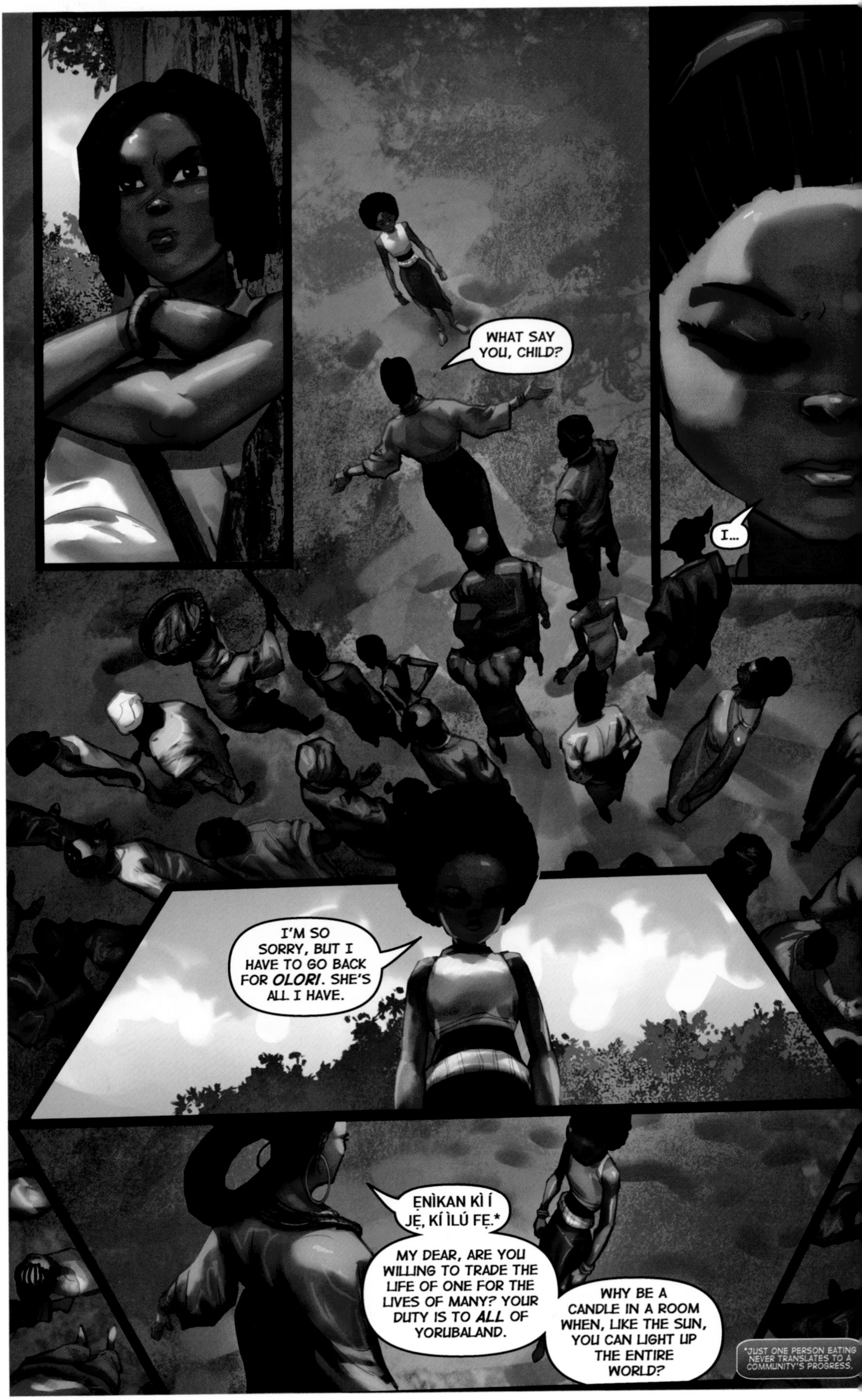
WHAT SAY YOU, CHILD?
I...
I'M SO SORRY, BUT I HAVE TO GO BACK FOR *OLORI*. SHE'S ALL I HAVE.
ẸNÌKAN KÌ Í JẸ, KÍ ÌLÚ FẸ.*
MY DEAR, ARE YOU WILLING TO TRADE THE LIFE OF ONE FOR THE LIVES OF MANY? YOUR DUTY IS TO *ALL* OF YORUBALAND.
WHY BE A CANDLE IN A ROOM WHEN, LIKE THE SUN, YOU CAN LIGHT UP THE ENTIRE WORLD?
*JUST ONE PERSON EATING NEVER TRANSLATES TO A COMMUNITY'S PROGRESS.

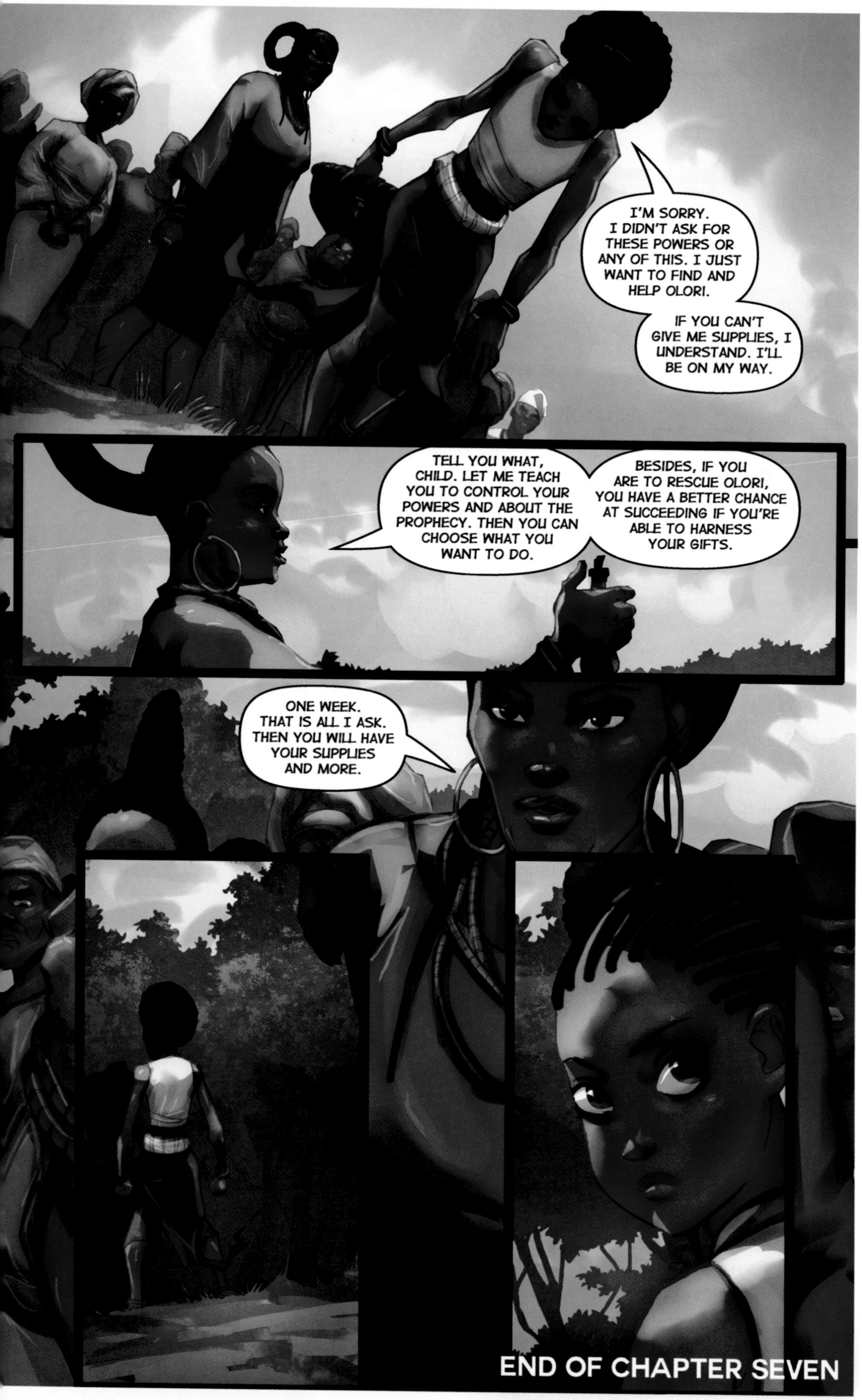
I'M SORRY. I DIDN'T ASK FOR THESE POWERS OR ANY OF THIS. I JUST WANT TO FIND AND HELP OLORI.
IF YOU CAN'T GIVE ME SUPPLIES, I UNDERSTAND. I'LL BE ON MY WAY.
TELL YOU WHAT, CHILD. LET ME TEACH YOU TO CONTROL YOUR POWERS AND ABOUT THE PROPHECY. THEN YOU CAN CHOOSE WHAT YOU WANT TO DO.
BESIDES, IF YOU ARE TO RESCUE OLORI, YOU HAVE A BETTER CHANCE AT SUCCEEDING IF YOU'RE ABLE TO HARNESS YOUR GIFTS.
ONE WEEK. THAT IS ALL I ASK. THEN YOU WILL HAVE YOUR SUPPLIES AND MORE.
END OF CHAPTER SEVEN

CHAPTER EIGHT

The Eso

The Eso are the elite military men and women of Elu. They are the only ones permitted to venture outside the walls. The Eso have three primary responsibilities. First and foremost is to protect the citizens of Elu. Second, to maintain law and order within the walls. And third, to venture outside Elu with the king's emissaries to collect tribute from exiled settlements. In exchange for their tribute, some of the Eso are stationed outside the walls to serve as extra protection for the exiled settlements from the corrupt. They are led by the Eso of Esos: Kanfo.

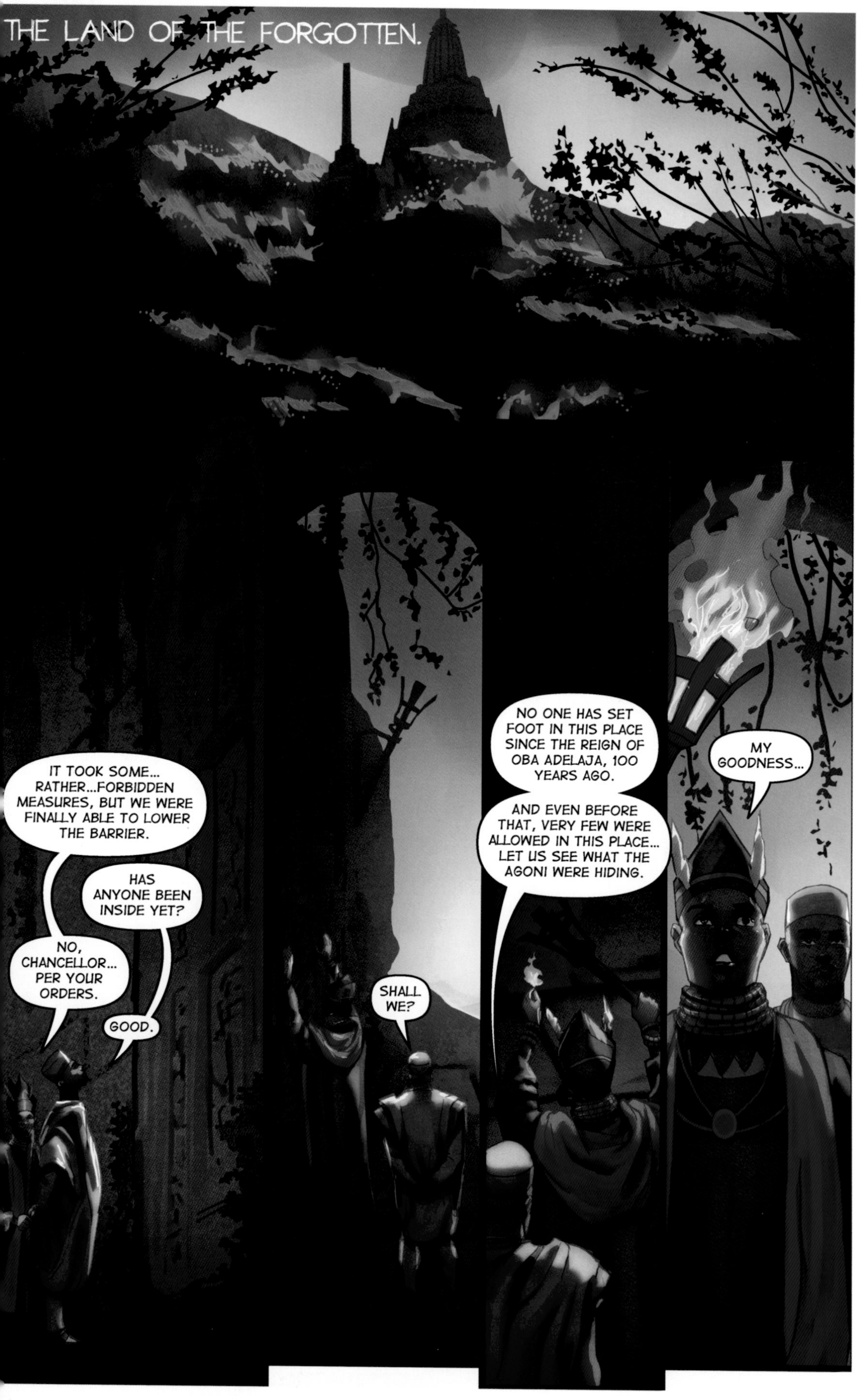
THE LAND OF THE FORGOTTEN.
IT TOOK SOME... RATHER...FORBIDDEN MEASURES, BUT WE WERE FINALLY ABLE TO LOWER THE BARRIER.
HAS ANYONE BEEN INSIDE YET?
NO, CHANCELLOR... PER YOUR ORDERS.
GOOD.
SHALL WE?
NO ONE HAS SET FOOT IN THIS PLACE SINCE THE REIGN OF OBA ADELAJA, 100 YEARS AGO.
AND EVEN BEFORE THAT, VERY FEW WERE ALLOWED IN THIS PLACE... LET US SEE WHAT THE AGONI WERE HIDING.
MY GOODNESS...

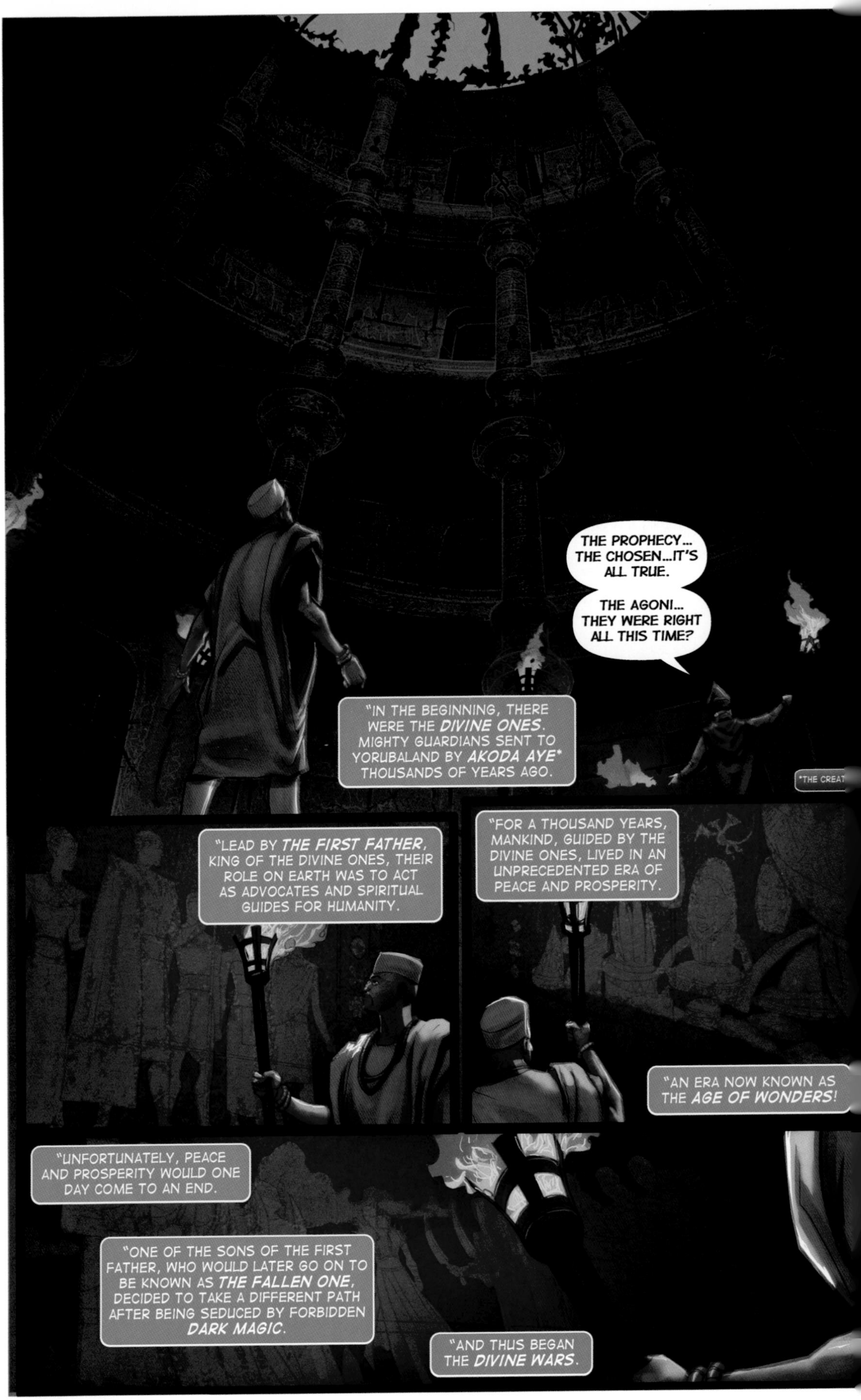
THE PROPHECY... THE CHOSEN...IT'S ALL TRUE.
THE AGONI... THEY WERE RIGHT ALL THIS TIME?
"IN THE BEGINNING, THERE WERE THE *DIVINE ONES*. MIGHTY GUARDIANS SENT TO YORUBALAND BY *AKODA AYE** THOUSANDS OF YEARS AGO.
*THE CREAT
"LEAD BY *THE FIRST FATHER*, KING OF THE DIVINE ONES, THEIR ROLE ON EARTH WAS TO ACT AS ADVOCATES AND SPIRITUAL GUIDES FOR HUMANITY.
"FOR A THOUSAND YEARS, MANKIND, GUIDED BY THE DIVINE ONES, LIVED IN AN UNPRECEDENTED ERA OF PEACE AND PROSPERITY.
"AN ERA NOW KNOWN AS THE *AGE OF WONDERS*!
"UNFORTUNATELY, PEACE AND PROSPERITY WOULD ONE DAY COME TO AN END.
"ONE OF THE SONS OF THE FIRST FATHER, WHO WOULD LATER GO ON TO BE KNOWN AS *THE FALLEN ONE*, DECIDED TO TAKE A DIFFERENT PATH AFTER BEING SEDUCED BY FORBIDDEN *DARK MAGIC*.
"AND THUS BEGAN THE *DIVINE WARS*.

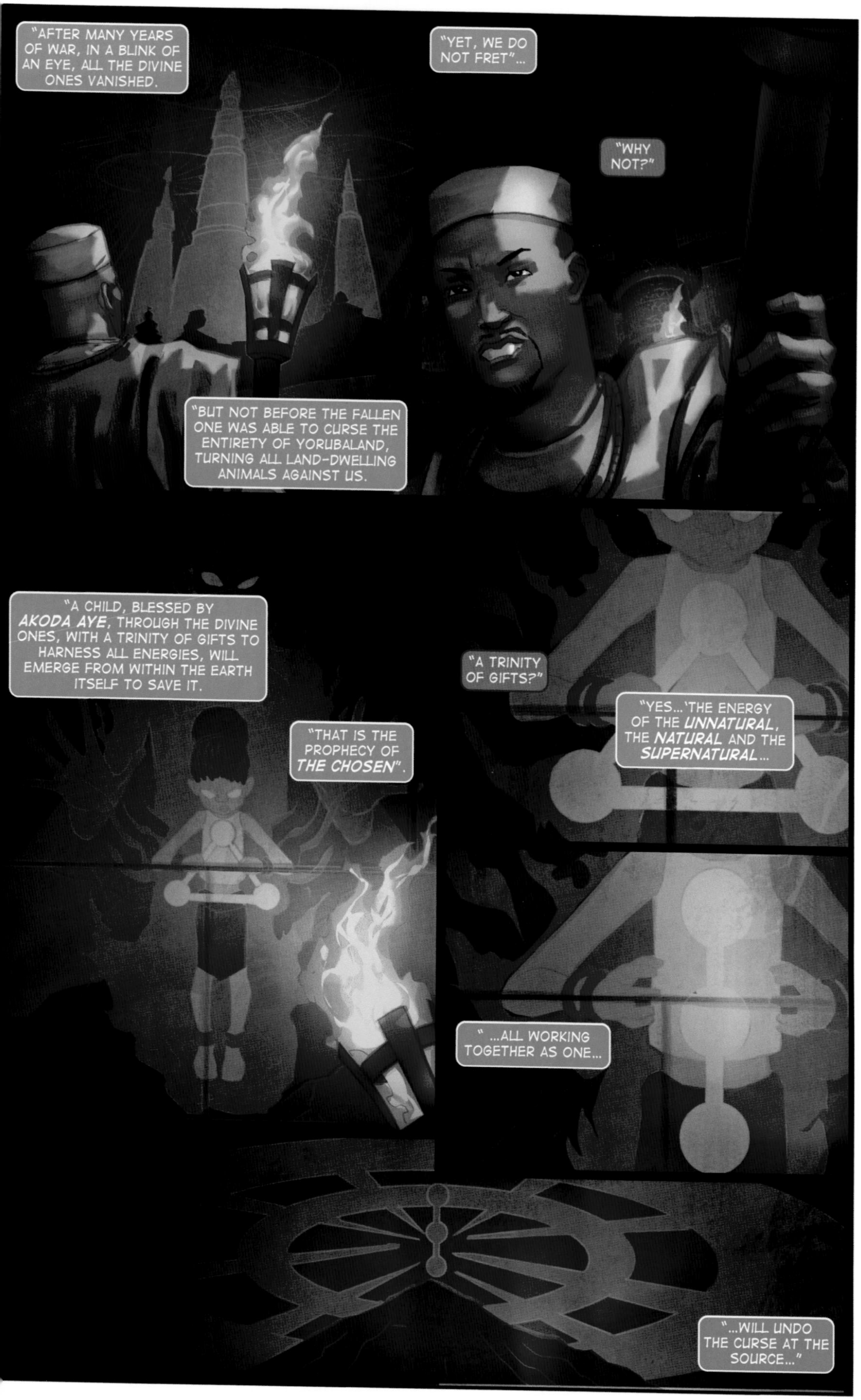
"AFTER MANY YEARS OF WAR, IN A BLINK OF AN EYE, ALL THE DIVINE ONES VANISHED.
"BUT NOT BEFORE THE FALLEN ONE WAS ABLE TO CURSE THE ENTIRETY OF YORUBALAND, TURNING ALL LAND-DWELLING ANIMALS AGAINST US.
"YET, WE DO NOT FRET"...
"WHY NOT?"
"A CHILD, BLESSED BY **AKODA AYE**, THROUGH THE DIVINE ONES, WITH A TRINITY OF GIFTS TO HARNESS ALL ENERGIES, WILL EMERGE FROM WITHIN THE EARTH ITSELF TO SAVE IT.
"THAT IS THE PROPHECY OF ***THE CHOSEN***".
"A TRINITY OF GIFTS?"
"YES...'THE ENERGY OF THE ***UNNATURAL***, THE ***NATURAL*** AND THE ***SUPERNATURAL***...
" ...ALL WORKING TOGETHER AS ONE...
"...WILL UNDO THE CURSE AT THE SOURCE..."

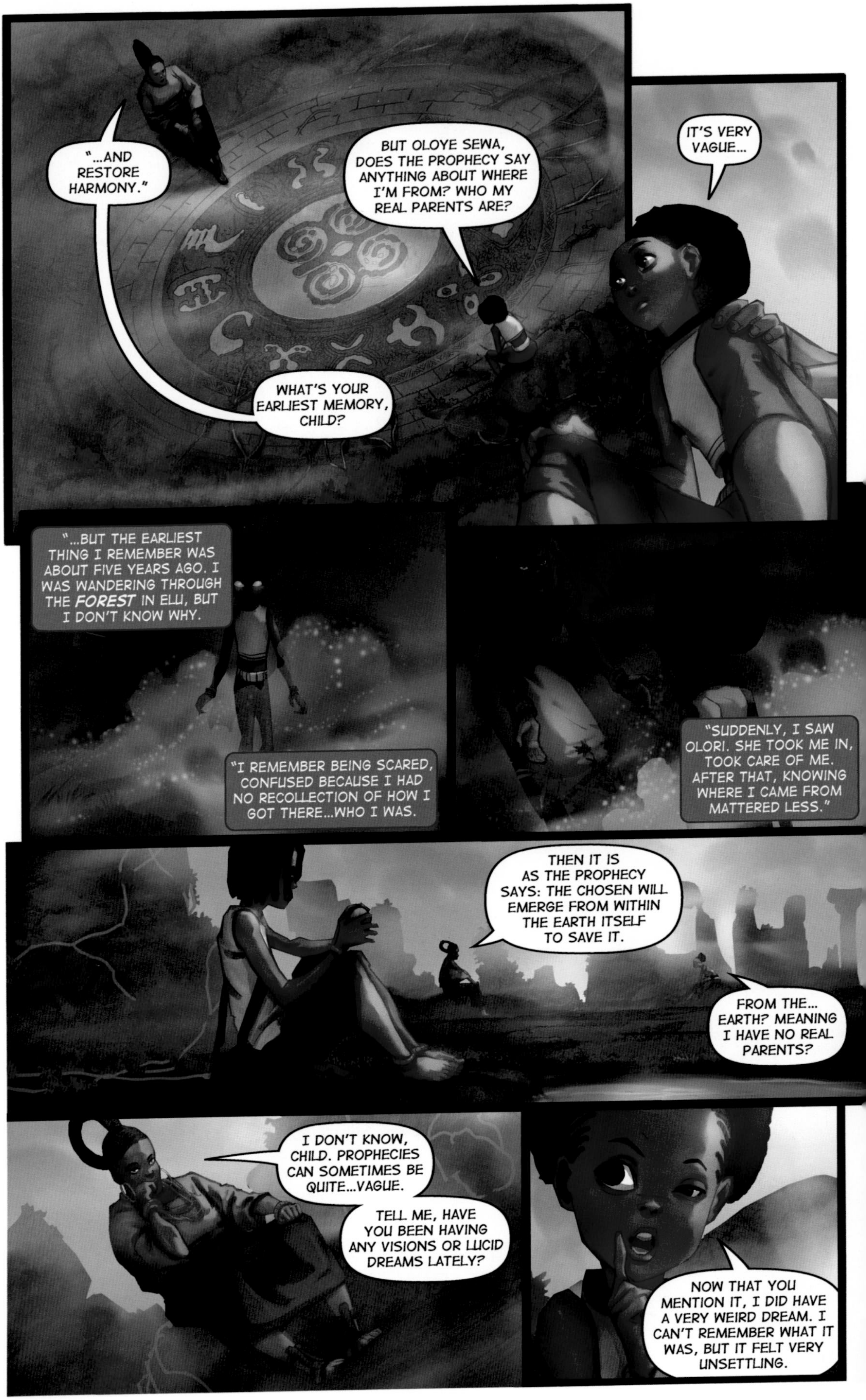
"...AND RESTORE HARMONY."
BUT OLOYE SEWA, DOES THE PROPHECY SAY ANYTHING ABOUT WHERE I'M FROM? WHO MY REAL PARENTS ARE?
IT'S VERY VAGUE...
WHAT'S YOUR EARLIEST MEMORY, CHILD?
"...BUT THE EARLIEST THING I REMEMBER WAS ABOUT FIVE YEARS AGO. I WAS WANDERING THROUGH THE FOREST IN ELU, BUT I DON'T KNOW WHY.
"I REMEMBER BEING SCARED, CONFUSED BECAUSE I HAD NO RECOLLECTION OF HOW I GOT THERE...WHO I WAS.
"SUDDENLY, I SAW OLORI. SHE TOOK ME IN, TOOK CARE OF ME. AFTER THAT, KNOWING WHERE I CAME FROM MATTERED LESS."
THEN IT IS AS THE PROPHECY SAYS: THE CHOSEN WILL EMERGE FROM WITHIN THE EARTH ITSELF TO SAVE IT.
FROM THE... EARTH? MEANING I HAVE NO REAL PARENTS?
I DON'T KNOW, CHILD. PROPHECIES CAN SOMETIMES BE QUITE...VAGUE.
TELL ME, HAVE YOU BEEN HAVING ANY VISIONS OR LUCID DREAMS LATELY?
NOW THAT YOU MENTION IT, I DID HAVE A VERY WEIRD DREAM. I CAN'T REMEMBER WHAT IT WAS, BUT IT FELT VERY UNSETTLING.

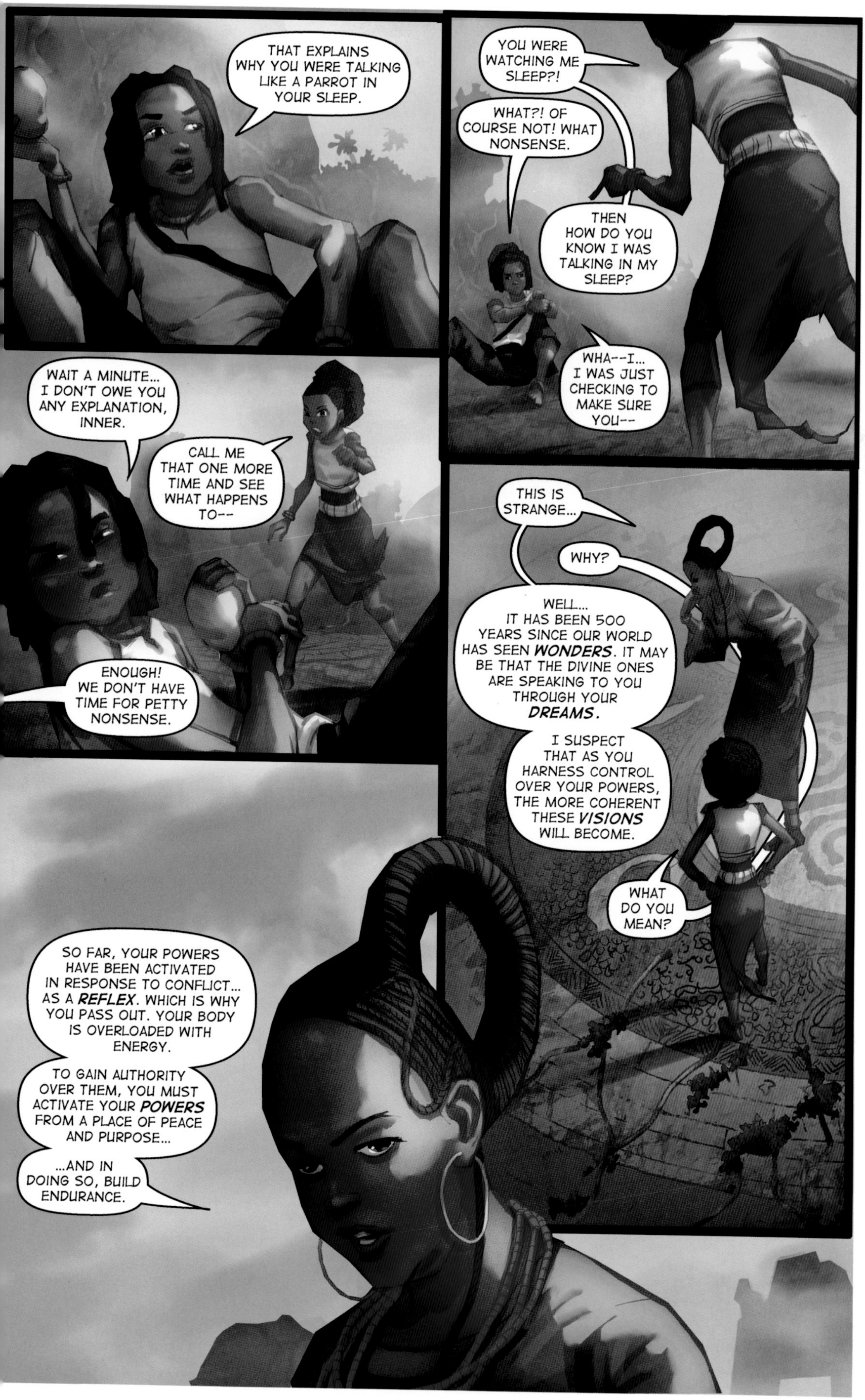
THAT EXPLAINS WHY YOU WERE TALKING LIKE A PARROT IN YOUR SLEEP.
YOU WERE WATCHING ME SLEEP?!
WHAT?! OF COURSE NOT! WHAT NONSENSE.
THEN HOW DO YOU KNOW I WAS TALKING IN MY SLEEP?
WHA--I... I WAS JUST CHECKING TO MAKE SURE YOU--
WAIT A MINUTE... I DON'T OWE YOU ANY EXPLANATION, INNER.
CALL ME THAT ONE MORE TIME AND SEE WHAT HAPPENS TO--
ENOUGH! WE DON'T HAVE TIME FOR PETTY NONSENSE.
THIS IS STRANGE...
WHY?
WELL... IT HAS BEEN 500 YEARS SINCE OUR WORLD HAS SEEN ***WONDERS***. IT MAY BE THAT THE DIVINE ONES ARE SPEAKING TO YOU THROUGH YOUR ***DREAMS***.
I SUSPECT THAT AS YOU HARNESS CONTROL OVER YOUR POWERS, THE MORE COHERENT THESE ***VISIONS*** WILL BECOME.
WHAT DO YOU MEAN?
SO FAR, YOUR POWERS HAVE BEEN ACTIVATED IN RESPONSE TO CONFLICT... AS A ***REFLEX***. WHICH IS WHY YOU PASS OUT. YOUR BODY IS OVERLOADED WITH ENERGY.
TO GAIN AUTHORITY OVER THEM, YOU MUST ACTIVATE YOUR ***POWERS*** FROM A PLACE OF PEACE AND PURPOSE...
...AND IN DOING SO, BUILD ENDURANCE.

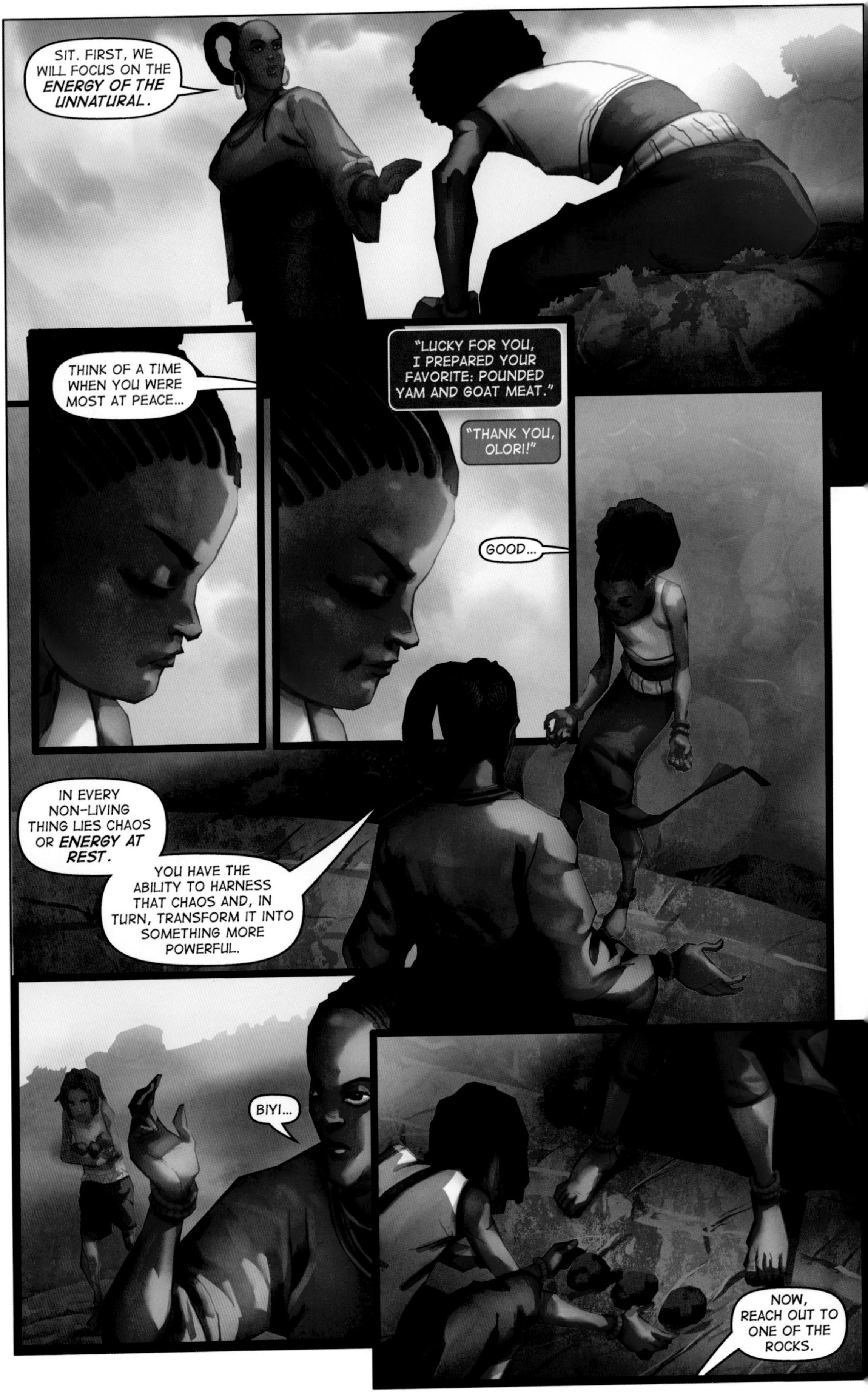
SIT. FIRST, WE WILL FOCUS ON THE ENERGY OF THE UNNATURAL.
THINK OF A TIME WHEN YOU WERE MOST AT PEACE...
"LUCKY FOR YOU, I PREPARED YOUR FAVORITE: POUNDED YAM AND GOAT MEAT."
"THANK YOU, OLORI!"
GOOD...
IN EVERY NON-LIVING THING LIES CHAOS OR ENERGY AT REST.
YOU HAVE THE ABILITY TO HARNESS THAT CHAOS AND, IN TURN, TRANSFORM IT INTO SOMETHING MORE POWERFUL.
BIYI...
NOW, REACH OUT TO ONE OF THE ROCKS.

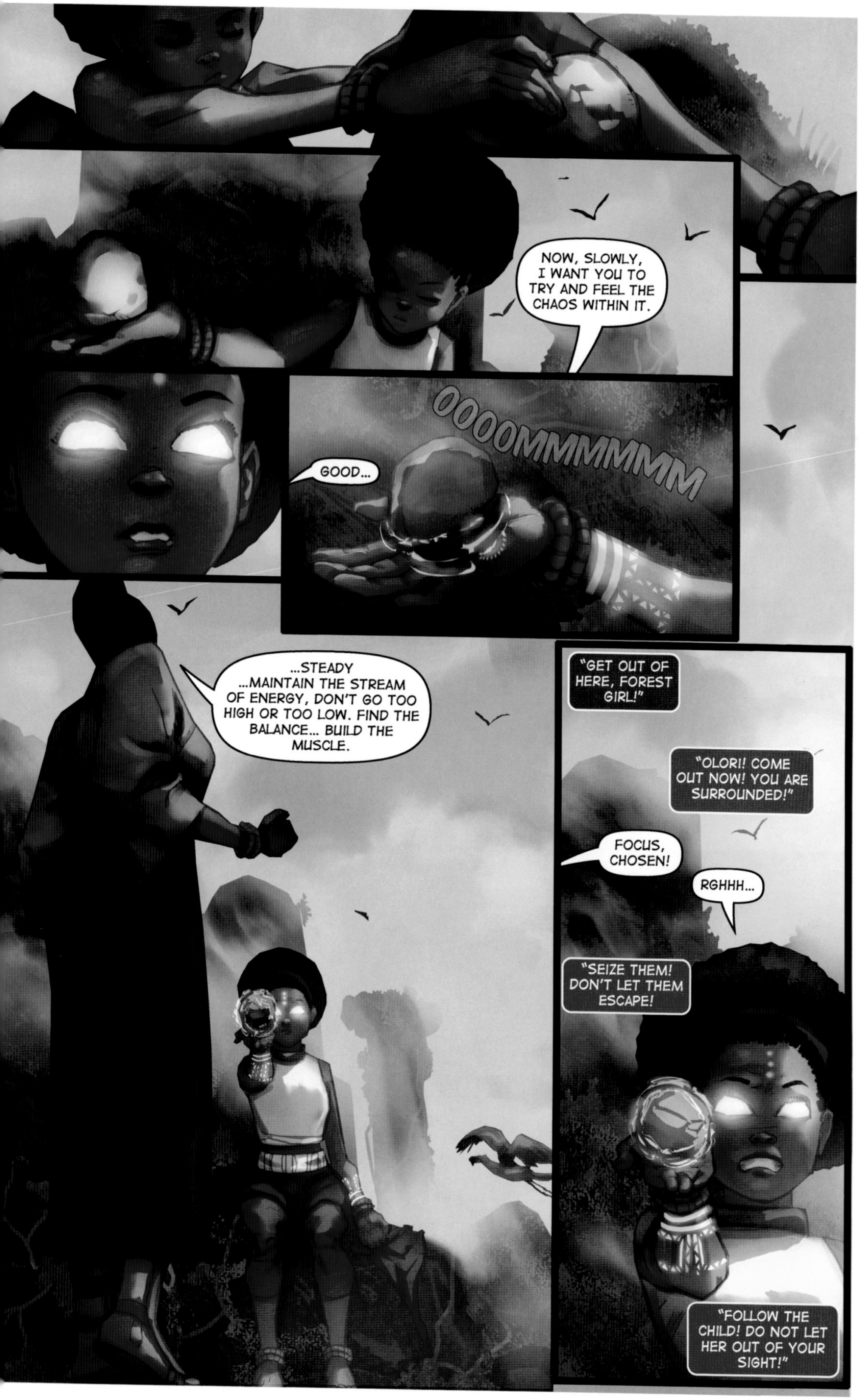
NOW, SLOWLY, I WANT YOU TO TRY AND FEEL THE CHAOS WITHIN IT.
OOOOMMMMMMM
GOOD...
...STEADY ...MAINTAIN THE STREAM OF ENERGY, DON'T GO TOO HIGH OR TOO LOW. FIND THE BALANCE... BUILD THE MUSCLE.
"GET OUT OF HERE, FOREST GIRL!"
"OLORI! COME OUT NOW! YOU ARE SURROUNDED!"
FOCUS, CHOSEN!
RGHHH...
"SEIZE THEM! DON'T LET THEM ESCAPE!
"FOLLOW THE CHILD! DO NOT LET HER OUT OF YOUR SIGHT!"

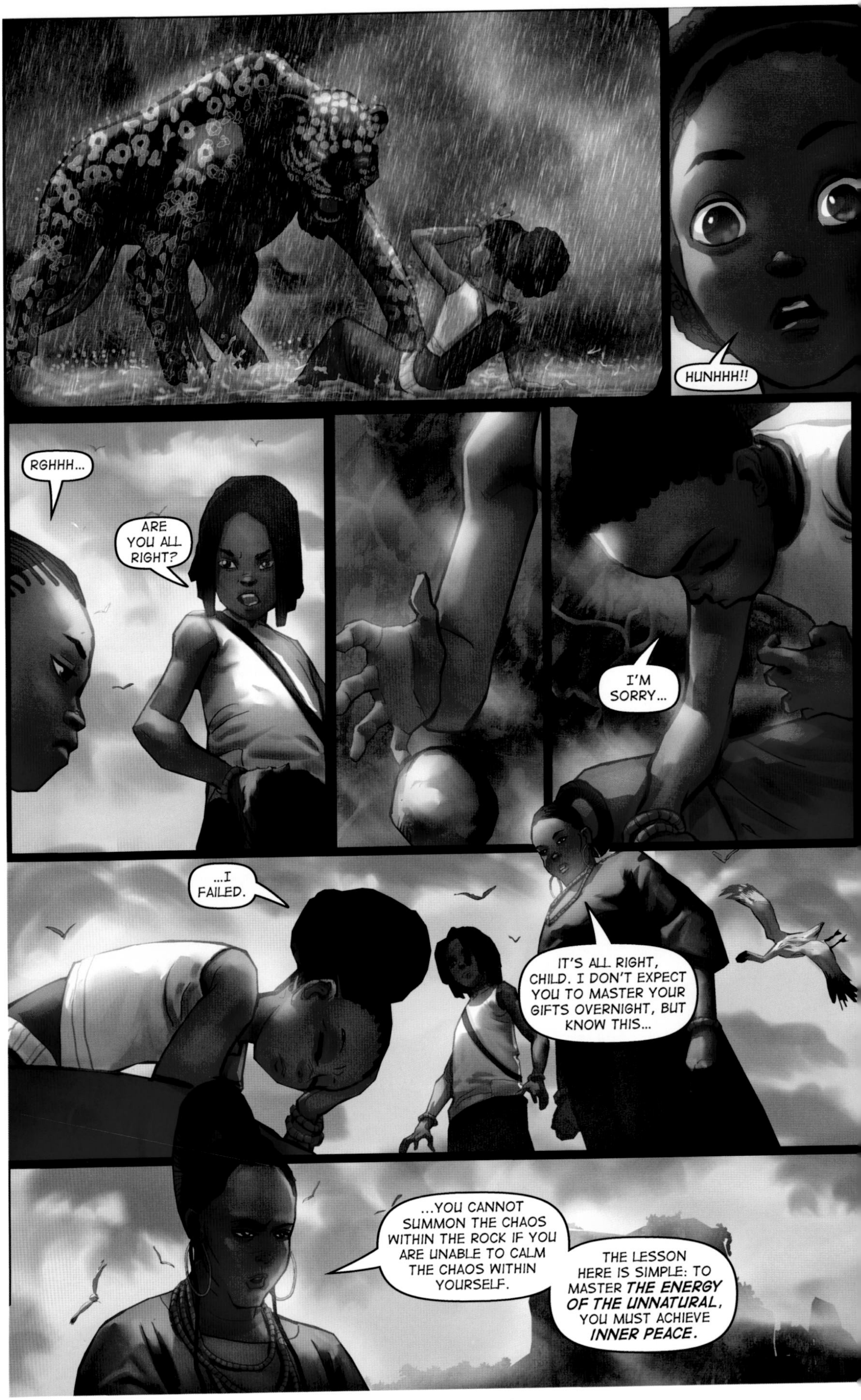
HUNHHH!!
RGHHH...
ARE YOU ALL RIGHT?
I'M SORRY...
...I FAILED.
IT'S ALL RIGHT, CHILD. I DON'T EXPECT YOU TO MASTER YOUR GIFTS OVERNIGHT, BUT KNOW THIS...
...YOU CANNOT SUMMON THE CHAOS WITHIN THE ROCK IF YOU ARE UNABLE TO CALM THE CHAOS WITHIN YOURSELF.
THE LESSON HERE IS SIMPLE: TO MASTER THE ENERGY OF THE UNNATURAL, YOU MUST ACHIEVE INNER PEACE.

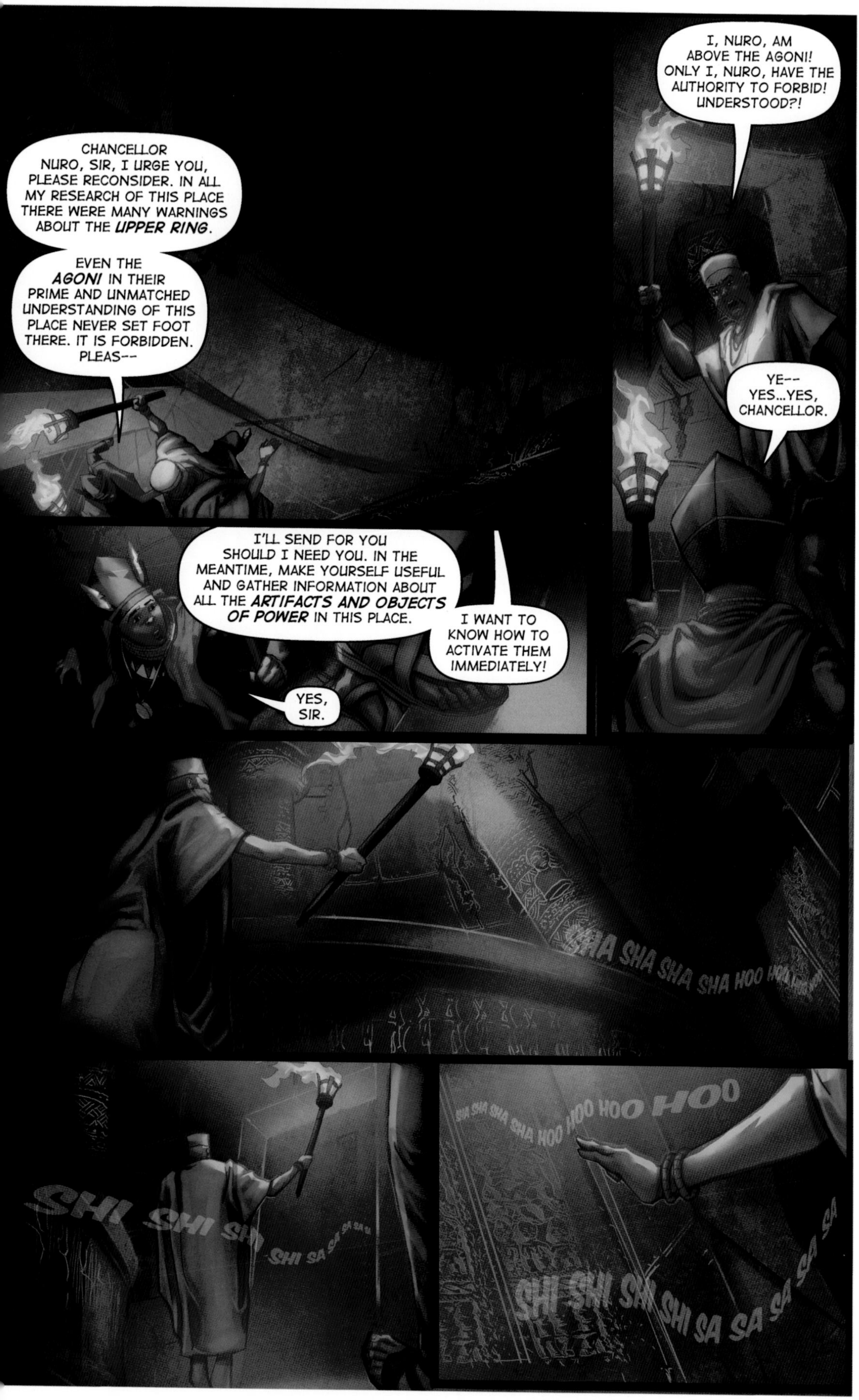
CHANCELLOR NURO, SIR, I URGE YOU, PLEASE RECONSIDER. IN ALL MY RESEARCH OF THIS PLACE THERE WERE MANY WARNINGS ABOUT THE UPPER RING.
EVEN THE AGONI IN THEIR PRIME AND UNMATCHED UNDERSTANDING OF THIS PLACE NEVER SET FOOT THERE. IT IS FORBIDDEN. PLEAS--
I, NURO, AM ABOVE THE AGONI! ONLY I, NURO, HAVE THE AUTHORITY TO FORBID! UNDERSTOOD?!
YE-- YES...YES, CHANCELLOR.
I'LL SEND FOR YOU SHOULD I NEED YOU. IN THE MEANTIME, MAKE YOURSELF USEFUL AND GATHER INFORMATION ABOUT ALL THE ARTIFACTS AND OBJECTS OF POWER IN THIS PLACE.
I WANT TO KNOW HOW TO ACTIVATE THEM IMMEDIATELY!
YES, SIR.
SHA SHA SHA SHA HOO HOO
SHI SHI SHI SHI SA SA SA
SHA SHA SHA SHA HOO HOO HOO HOO HOO
SHI SHI SHI SHI SA SA SA SA SA

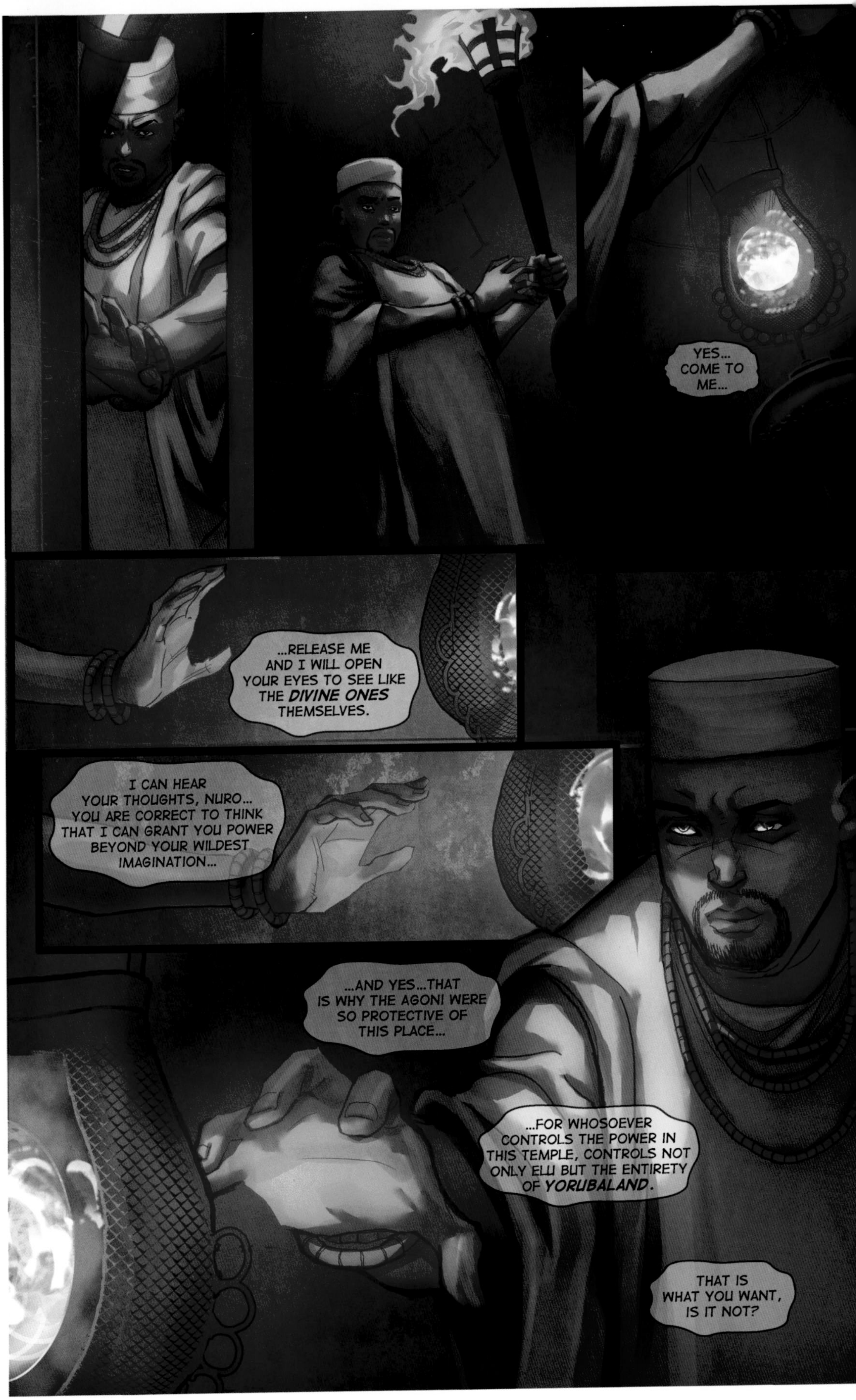
YES... COME TO ME...
...RELEASE ME AND I WILL OPEN YOUR EYES TO SEE LIKE THE *DIVINE ONES* THEMSELVES.
I CAN HEAR YOUR THOUGHTS, NURO... YOU ARE CORRECT TO THINK THAT I CAN GRANT YOU POWER BEYOND YOUR WILDEST IMAGINATION...
...AND YES...THAT IS WHY THE AGONI WERE SO PROTECTIVE OF THIS PLACE...
...FOR WHOSOEVER CONTROLS THE POWER IN THIS TEMPLE, CONTROLS NOT ONLY ELU BUT THE ENTIRETY OF *YORUBALAND*.
THAT IS WHAT YOU WANT, IS IT NOT?

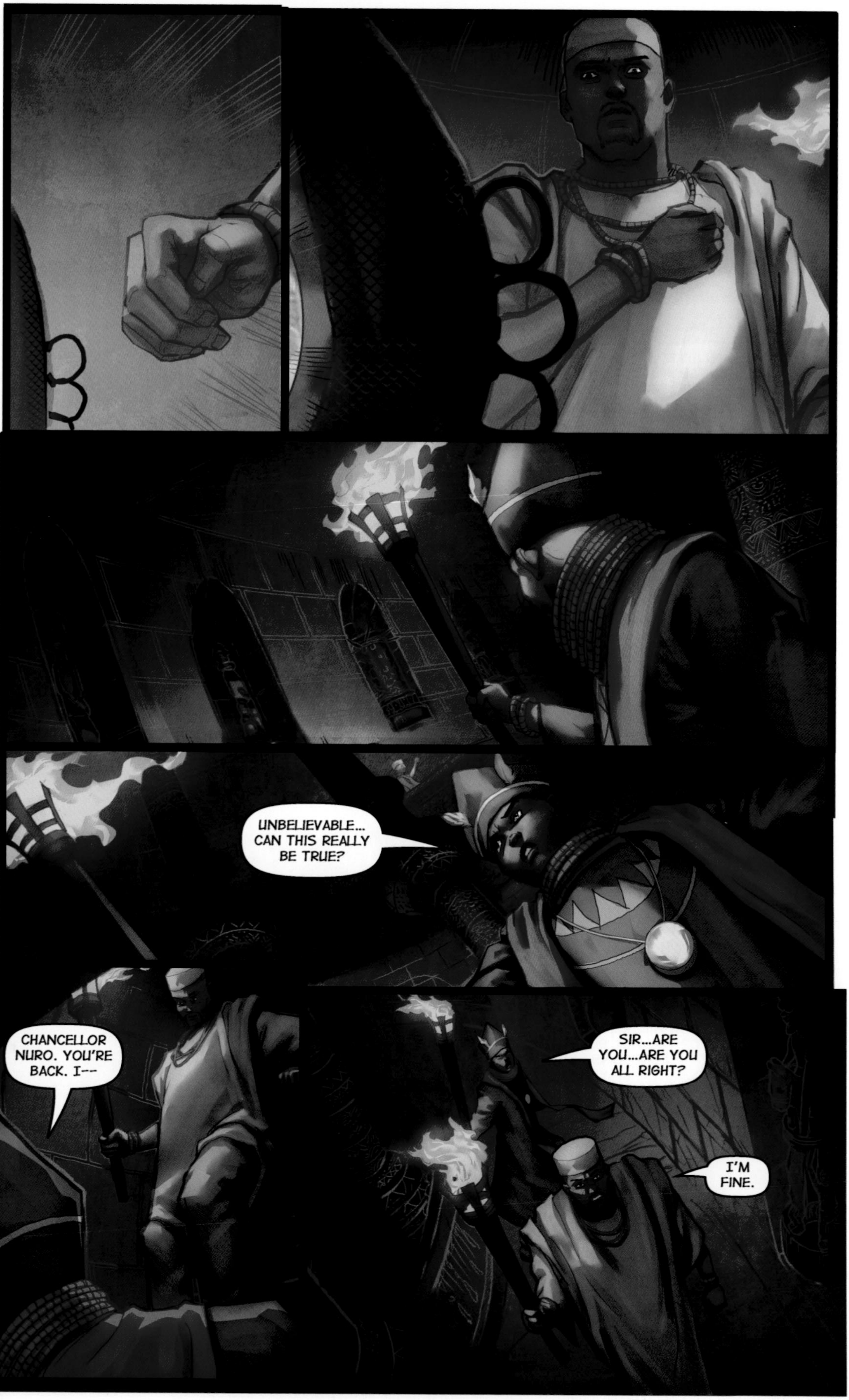
UNBELIEVABLE... CAN THIS REALLY BE TRUE?
CHANCELLOR NURO. YOU'RE BACK. I--
SIR...ARE YOU...ARE YOU ALL RIGHT?
I'M FINE.

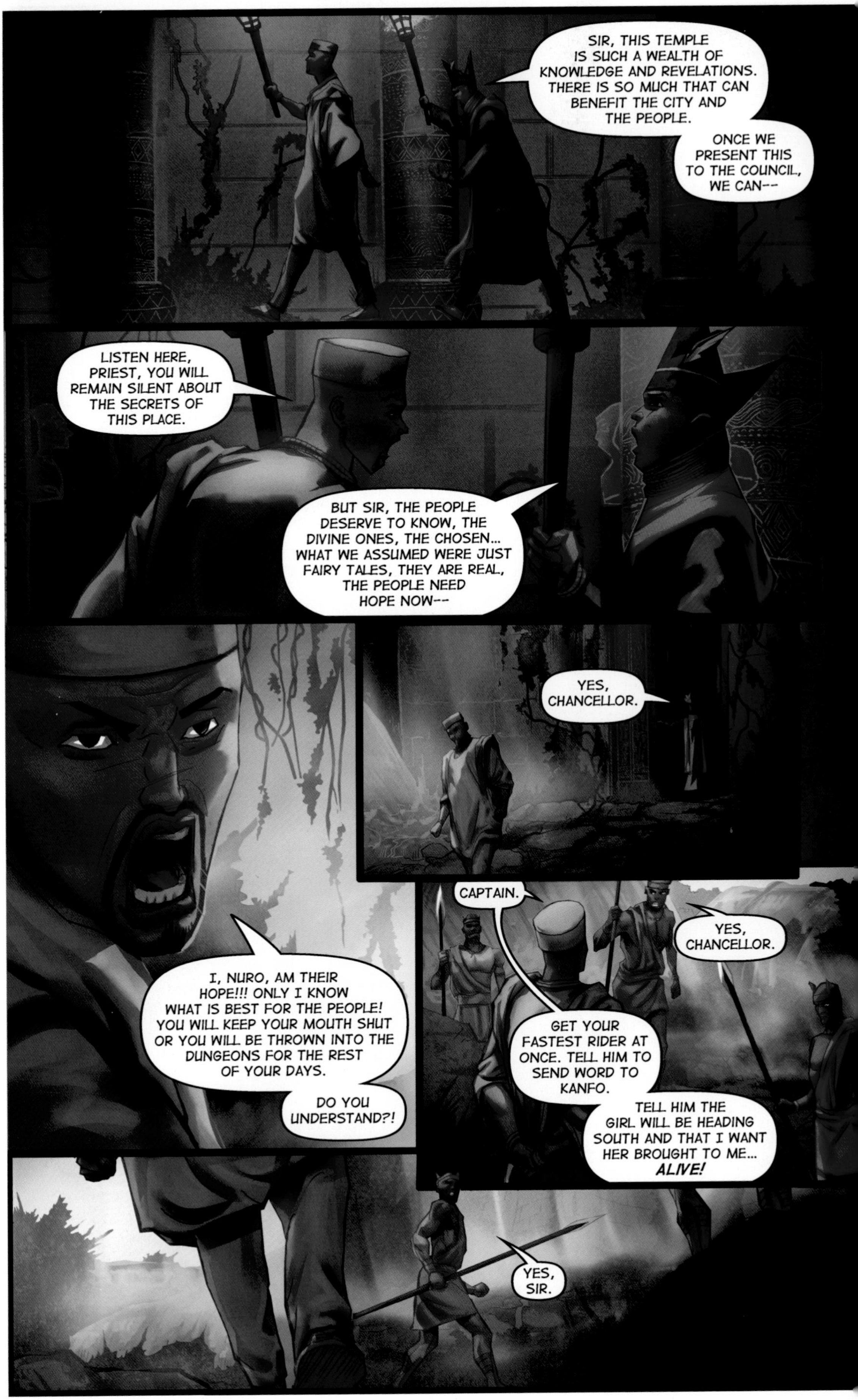
SIR, THIS TEMPLE IS SUCH A WEALTH OF KNOWLEDGE AND REVELATIONS. THERE IS SO MUCH THAT CAN BENEFIT THE CITY AND THE PEOPLE.
ONCE WE PRESENT THIS TO THE COUNCIL, WE CAN--
LISTEN HERE, PRIEST, YOU WILL REMAIN SILENT ABOUT THE SECRETS OF THIS PLACE.
BUT SIR, THE PEOPLE DESERVE TO KNOW, THE DIVINE ONES, THE CHOSEN... WHAT WE ASSUMED WERE JUST FAIRY TALES, THEY ARE REAL, THE PEOPLE NEED HOPE NOW--
I, NURO, AM THEIR HOPE!!! ONLY I KNOW WHAT IS BEST FOR THE PEOPLE! YOU WILL KEEP YOUR MOUTH SHUT OR YOU WILL BE THROWN INTO THE DUNGEONS FOR THE REST OF YOUR DAYS.
DO YOU UNDERSTAND?!
YES, CHANCELLOR.
CAPTAIN.
YES, CHANCELLOR.
GET YOUR FASTEST RIDER AT ONCE. TELL HIM TO SEND WORD TO KANFO.
TELL HIM THE GIRL WILL BE HEADING SOUTH AND THAT I WANT HER BROUGHT TO ME... ***ALIVE!***
YES, SIR.

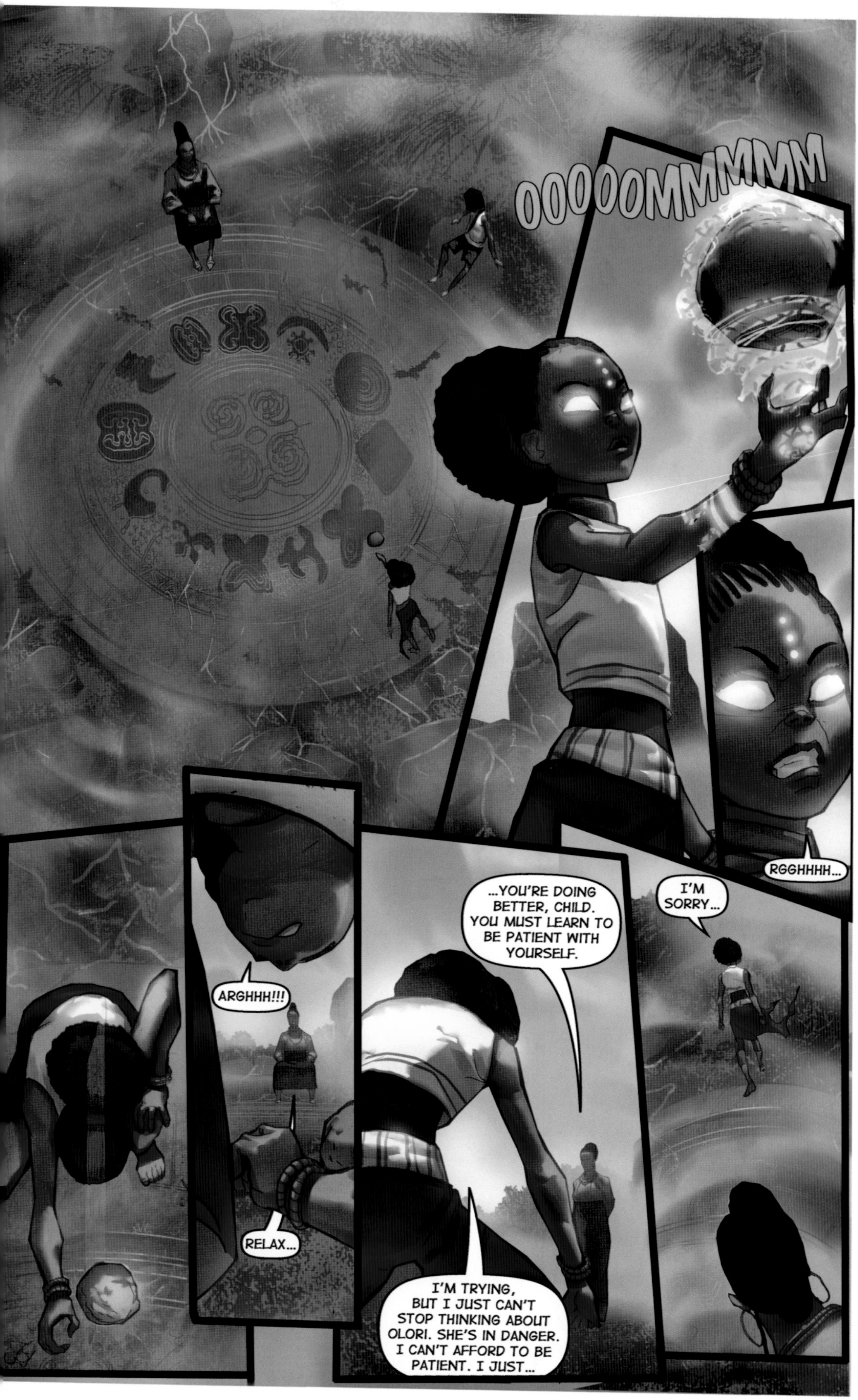
OOOOOMMMMMM
RGGHHHH...
ARGHHH!!!
RELAX...
...YOU'RE DOING BETTER, CHILD. YOU MUST LEARN TO BE PATIENT WITH YOURSELF.
I'M TRYING, BUT I JUST CAN'T STOP THINKING ABOUT OLORI. SHE'S IN DANGER. I CAN'T AFFORD TO BE PATIENT. I JUST...
I'M SORRY...

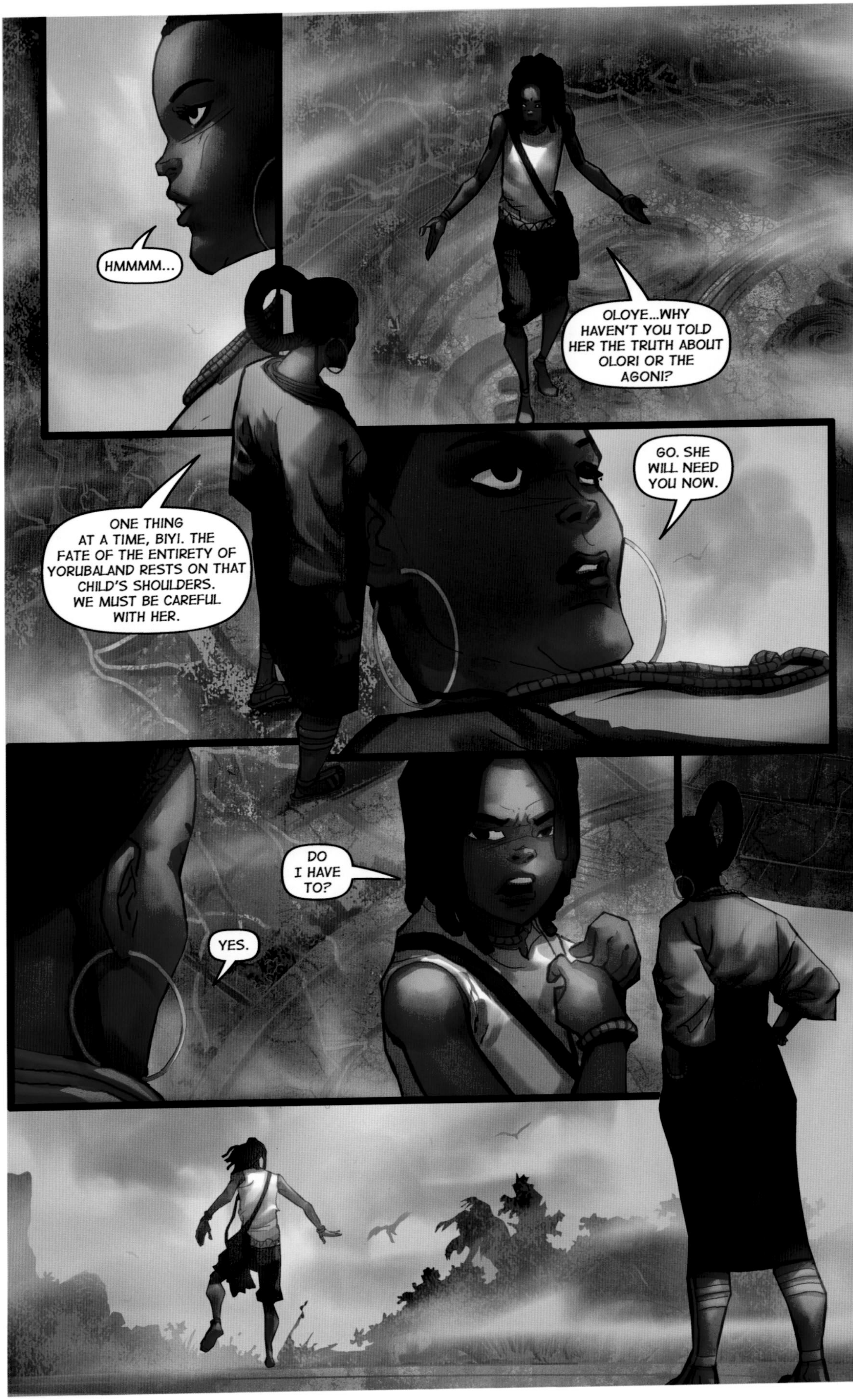
HMMMM...
OLOYE...WHY HAVEN'T YOU TOLD HER THE TRUTH ABOUT OLORI OR THE AGONI?
ONE THING AT A TIME, BIYI. THE FATE OF THE ENTIRETY OF YORUBALAND RESTS ON THAT CHILD'S SHOULDERS. WE MUST BE CAREFUL WITH HER.
GO. SHE WILL NEED YOU NOW.
DO I HAVE TO?
YES.

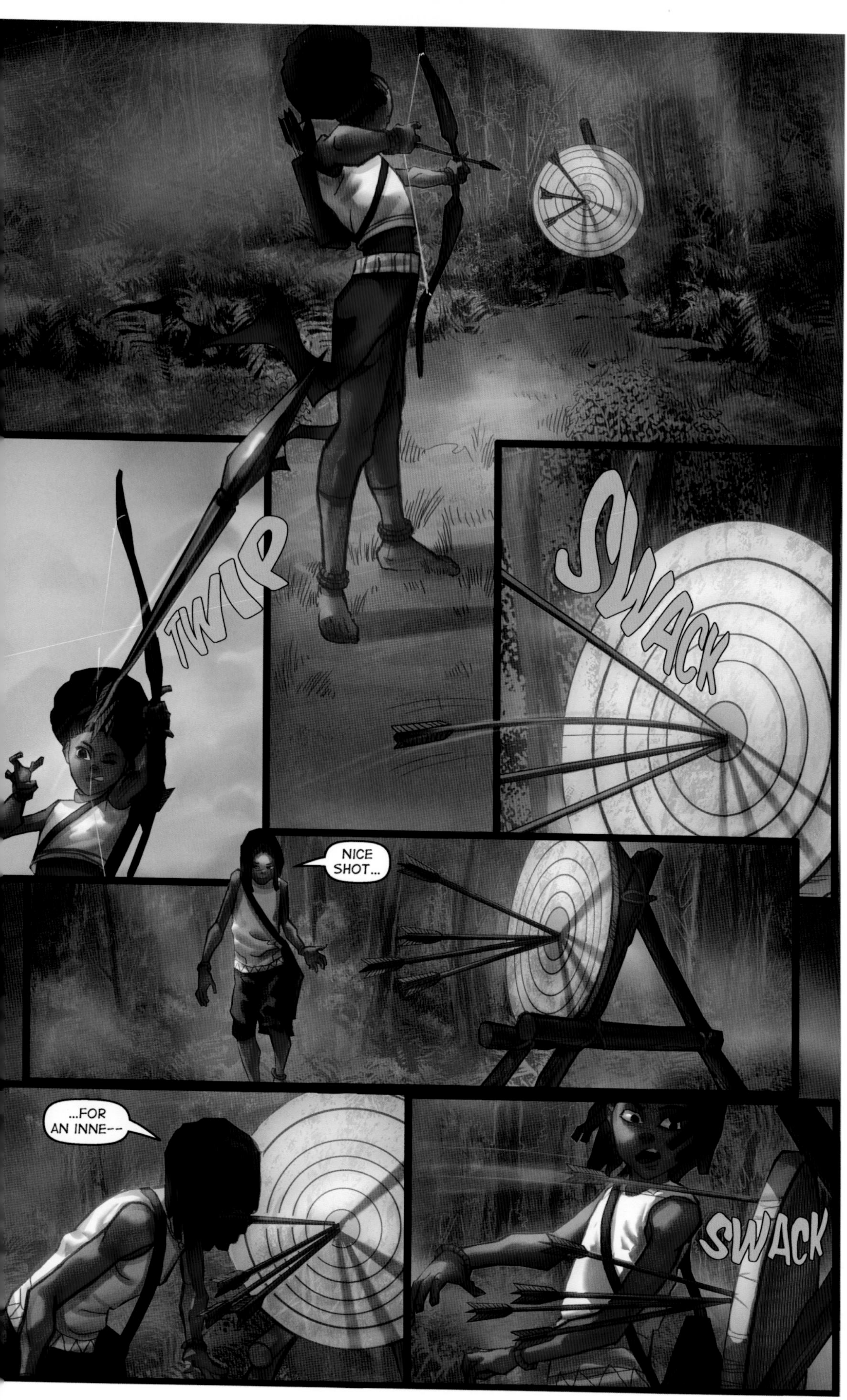
TWIP
SWACK
NICE SHOT...
...FOR AN INNE--
SWACK

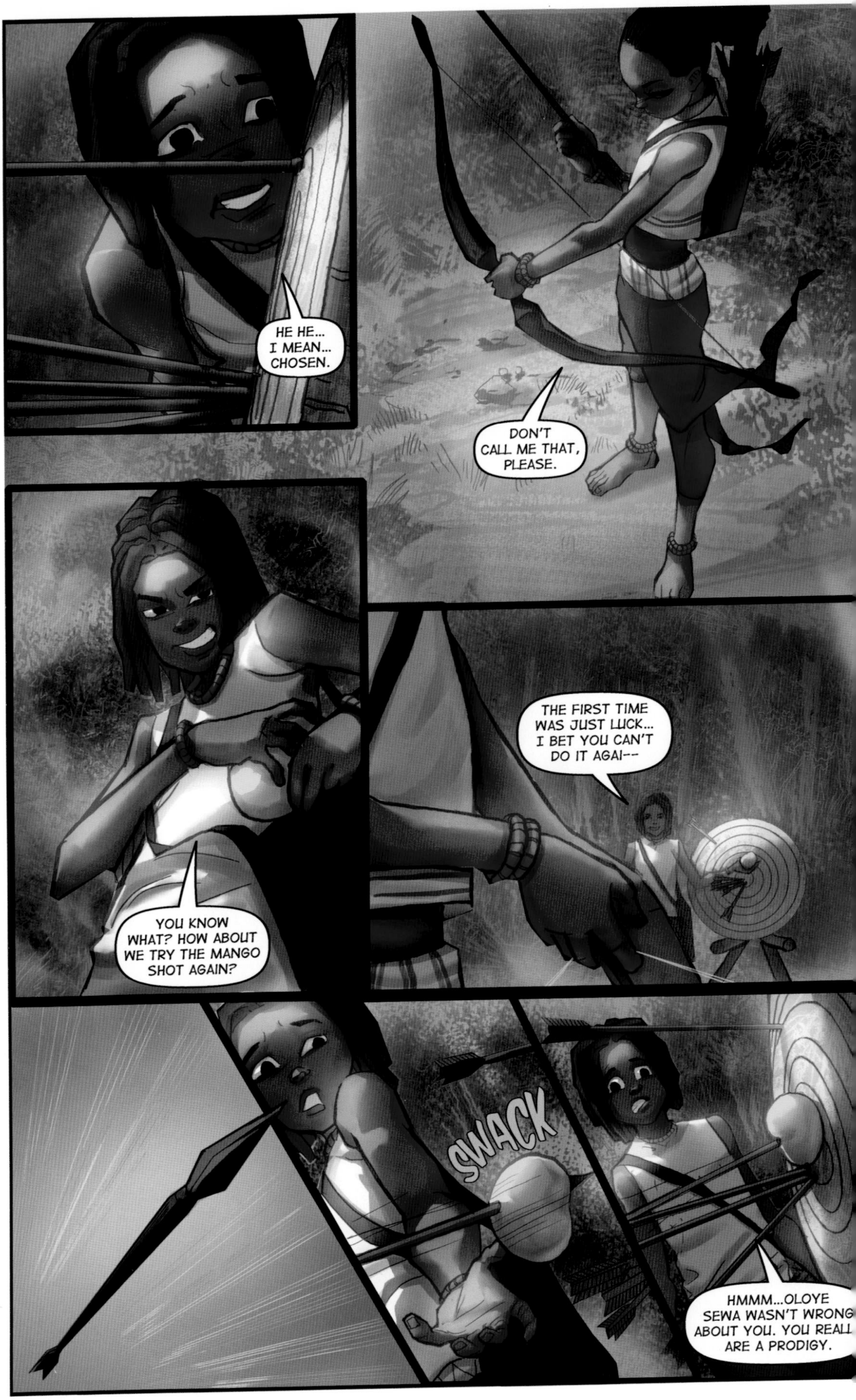
HE HE... I MEAN... CHOSEN.
DON'T CALL ME THAT, PLEASE.
YOU KNOW WHAT? HOW ABOUT WE TRY THE MANGO SHOT AGAIN?
THE FIRST TIME WAS JUST LUCK... I BET YOU CAN'T DO IT AGAI--
SWACK
HMMM...OLOYE SEWA WASN'T WRONG ABOUT YOU. YOU REALL ARE A PRODIGY.

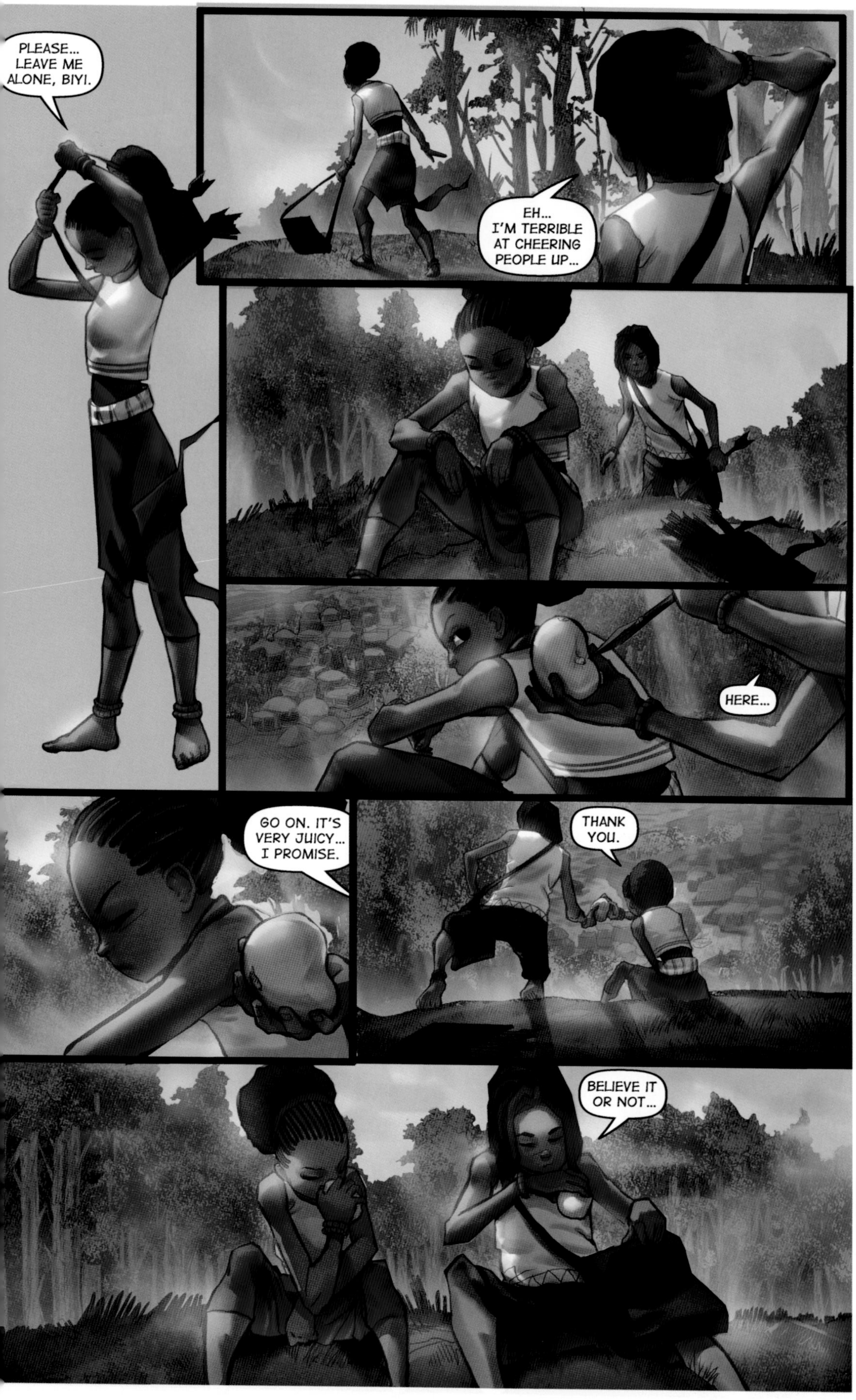
PLEASE... LEAVE ME ALONE, BIYI.
EH... I'M TERRIBLE AT CHEERING PEOPLE UP...
HERE...
GO ON. IT'S VERY JUICY... I PROMISE.
THANK YOU.
BELIEVE IT OR NOT...

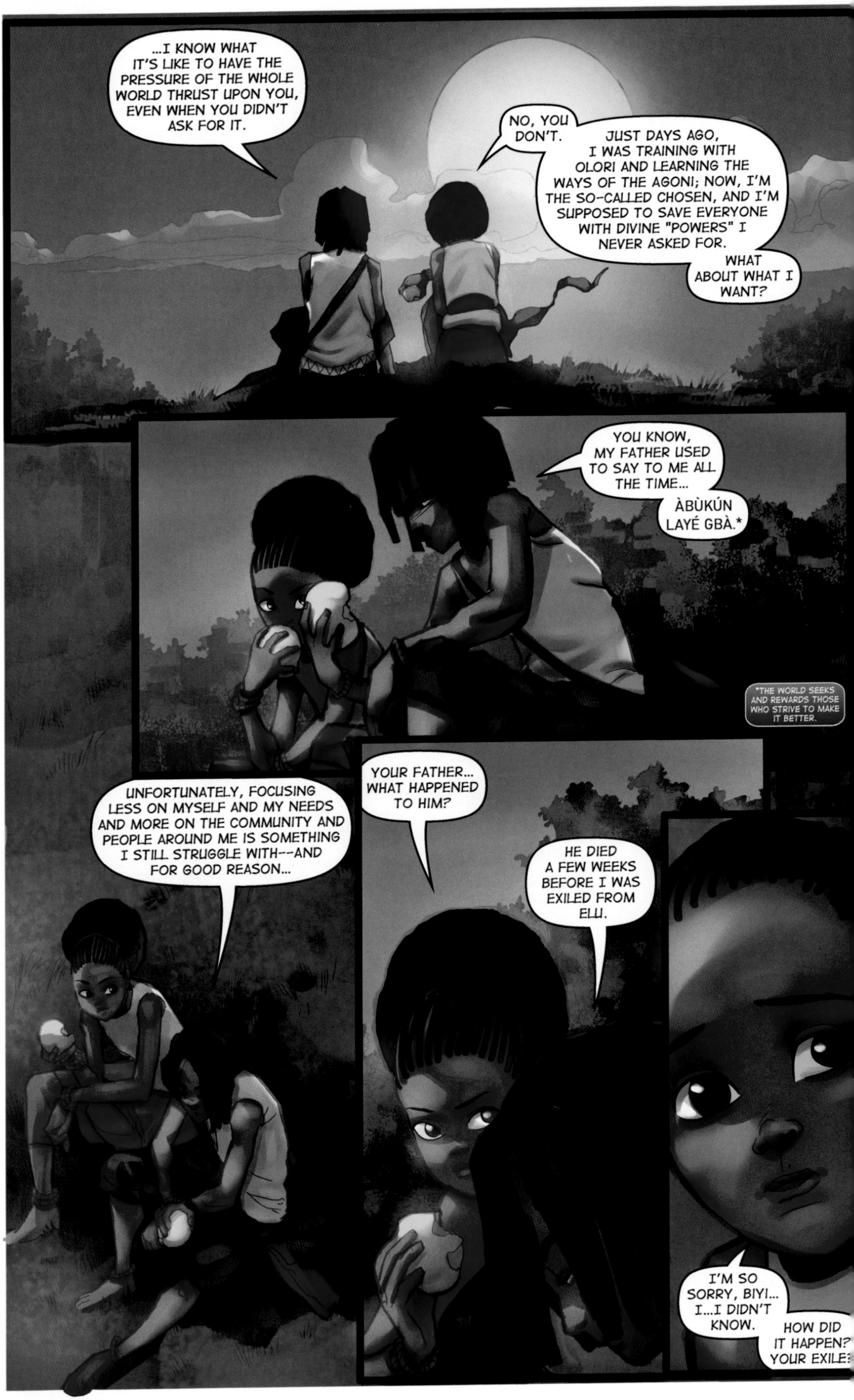
...I KNOW WHAT IT'S LIKE TO HAVE THE PRESSURE OF THE WHOLE WORLD THRUST UPON YOU, EVEN WHEN YOU DIDN'T ASK FOR IT.
NO, YOU DON'T.
JUST DAYS AGO, I WAS TRAINING WITH OLORI AND LEARNING THE WAYS OF THE AGONI; NOW, I'M THE SO-CALLED CHOSEN, AND I'M SUPPOSED TO SAVE EVERYONE WITH DIVINE "POWERS" I NEVER ASKED FOR.
WHAT ABOUT WHAT I WANT?
YOU KNOW, MY FATHER USED TO SAY TO ME ALL THE TIME...
ÀBÙKÚN LAYÉ GBÀ.*
*THE WORLD SEEKS AND REWARDS THOSE WHO STRIVE TO MAKE IT BETTER.
UNFORTUNATELY, FOCUSING LESS ON MYSELF AND MY NEEDS AND MORE ON THE COMMUNITY AND PEOPLE AROUND ME IS SOMETHING I STILL STRUGGLE WITH--AND FOR GOOD REASON...
YOUR FATHER... WHAT HAPPENED TO HIM?
HE DIED A FEW WEEKS BEFORE I WAS EXILED FROM ELU.
I'M SO SORRY, BIYI... I...I DIDN'T KNOW.
HOW DID IT HAPPEN? YOUR EXILE?

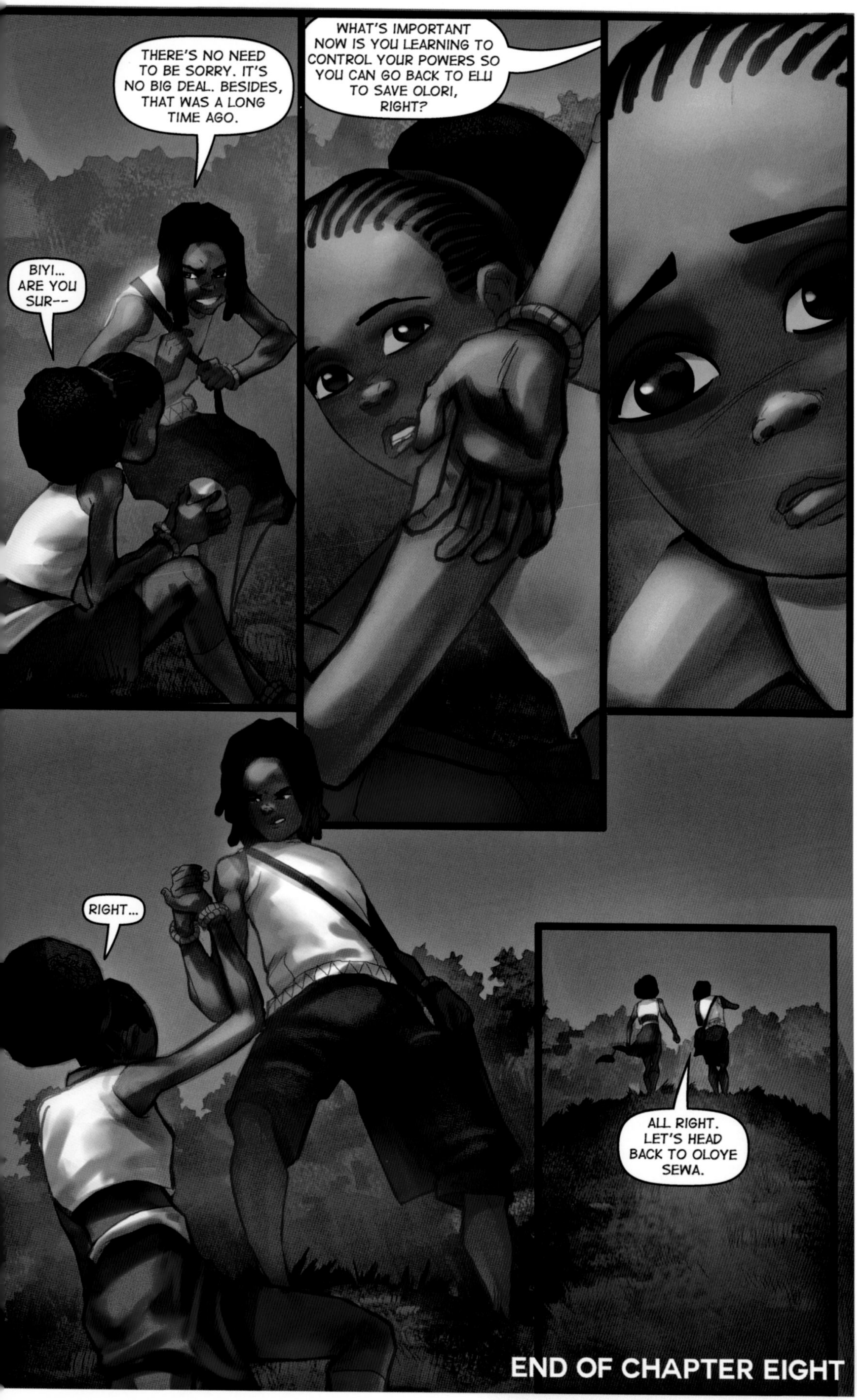
THERE'S NO NEED TO BE SORRY. IT'S NO BIG DEAL. BESIDES, THAT WAS A LONG TIME AGO.
BIYI... ARE YOU SUR--
WHAT'S IMPORTANT NOW IS YOU LEARNING TO CONTROL YOUR POWERS SO YOU CAN GO BACK TO ELU TO SAVE OLORI, RIGHT?
RIGHT...
ALL RIGHT. LET'S HEAD BACK TO OLOYE SEWA.
END OF CHAPTER EIGHT

CHAPTER NINE

The Prophecy of the Chosen

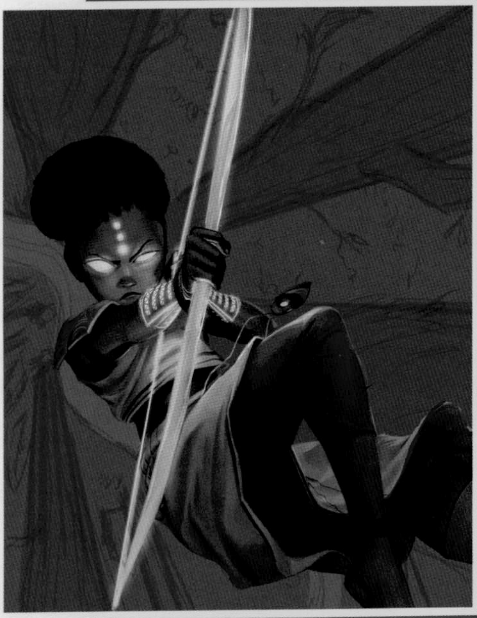

One day, the **Chosen**, a human with Innate Divine Power, would emerge to lift the curse and restore peace between people and animals in all of Yorubaland.

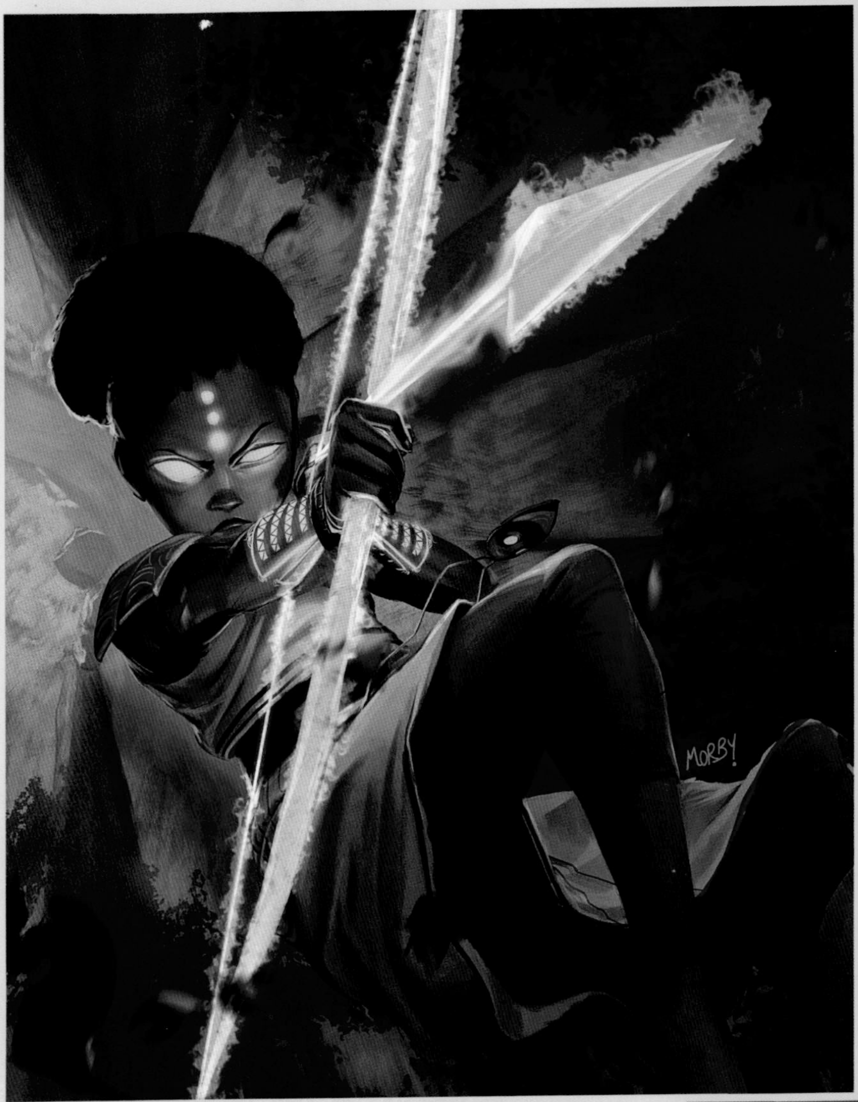
MORBY

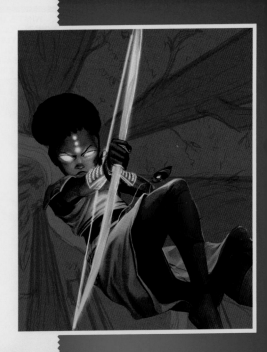

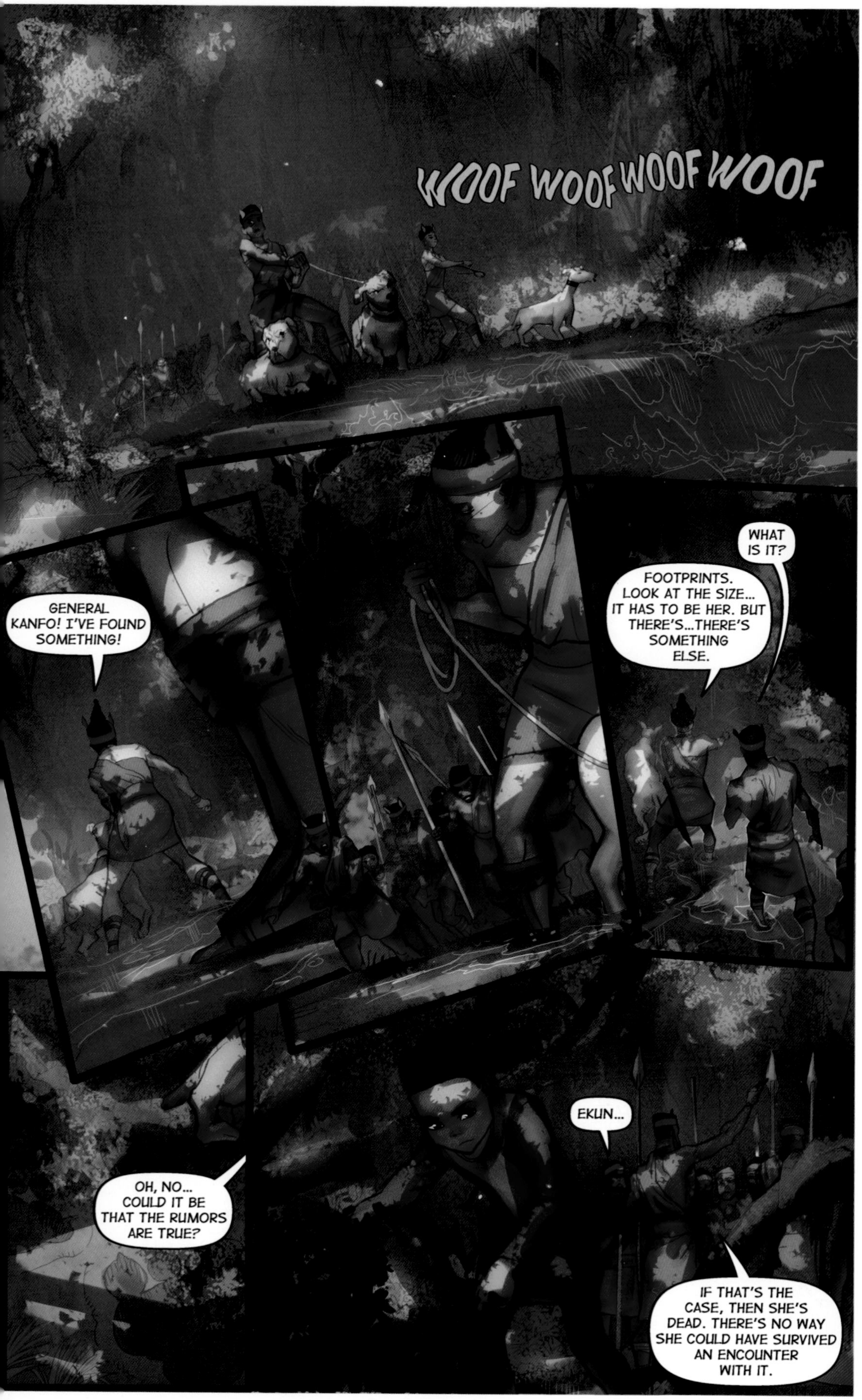
WOOF WOOF WOOF WOOF
GENERAL KANFO! I'VE FOUND SOMETHING!
WHAT IS IT?
FOOTPRINTS. LOOK AT THE SIZE... IT HAS TO BE HER. BUT THERE'S...THERE'S SOMETHING ELSE.
OH, NO... COULD IT BE THAT THE RUMORS ARE TRUE?
EKUN...
IF THAT'S THE CASE, THEN SHE'S DEAD. THERE'S NO WAY SHE COULD HAVE SURVIVED AN ENCOUNTER WITH IT.

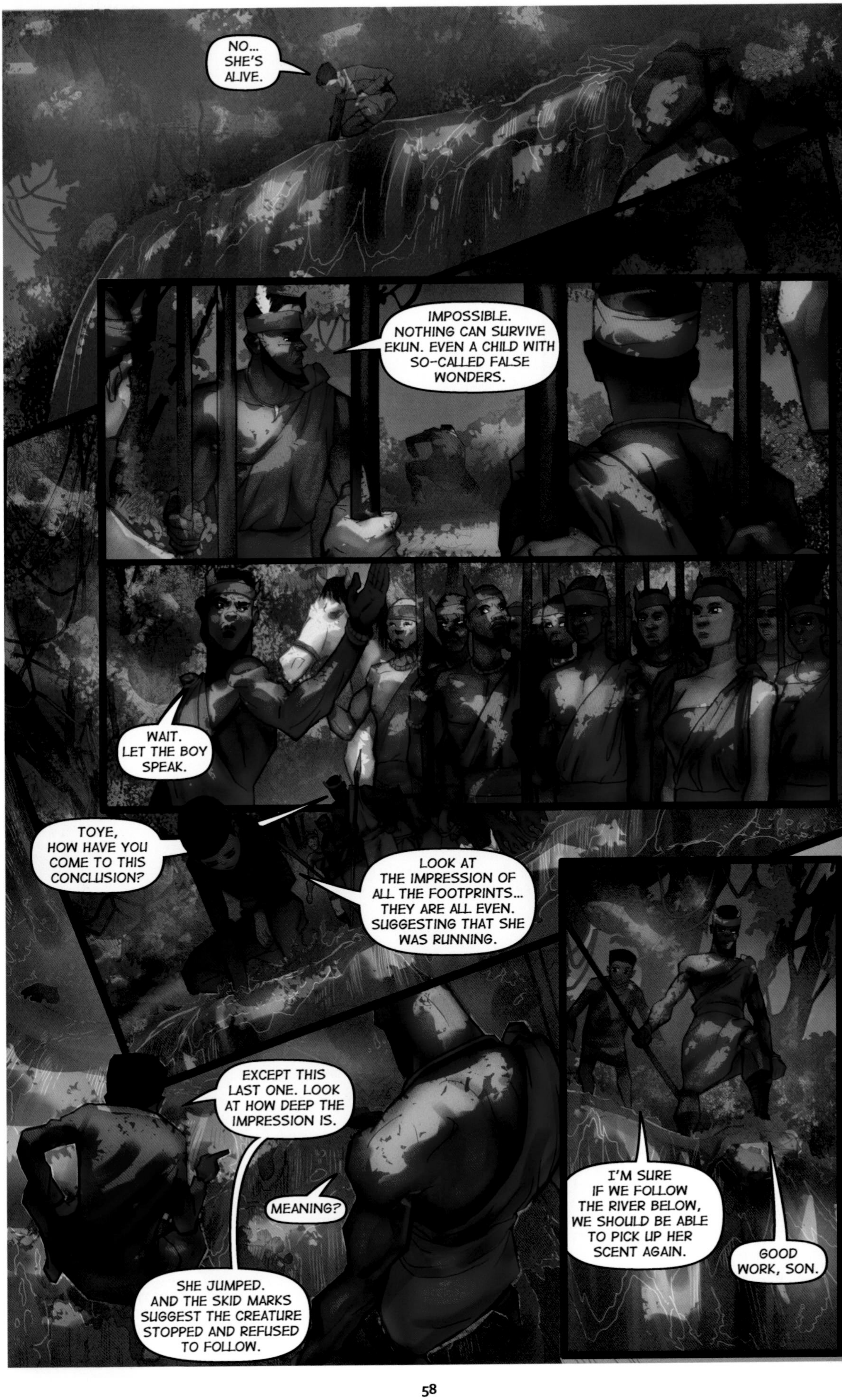
NO... SHE'S ALIVE.
IMPOSSIBLE. NOTHING CAN SURVIVE EKUN. EVEN A CHILD WITH SO-CALLED FALSE WONDERS.
WAIT. LET THE BOY SPEAK.
TOYE, HOW HAVE YOU COME TO THIS CONCLUSION?
LOOK AT THE IMPRESSION OF ALL THE FOOTPRINTS... THEY ARE ALL EVEN. SUGGESTING THAT SHE WAS RUNNING.
EXCEPT THIS LAST ONE. LOOK AT HOW DEEP THE IMPRESSION IS.
MEANING?
SHE JUMPED. AND THE SKID MARKS SUGGEST THE CREATURE STOPPED AND REFUSED TO FOLLOW.
I'M SURE IF WE FOLLOW THE RIVER BELOW, WE SHOULD BE ABLE TO PICK UP HER SCENT AGAIN.
GOOD WORK, SON.

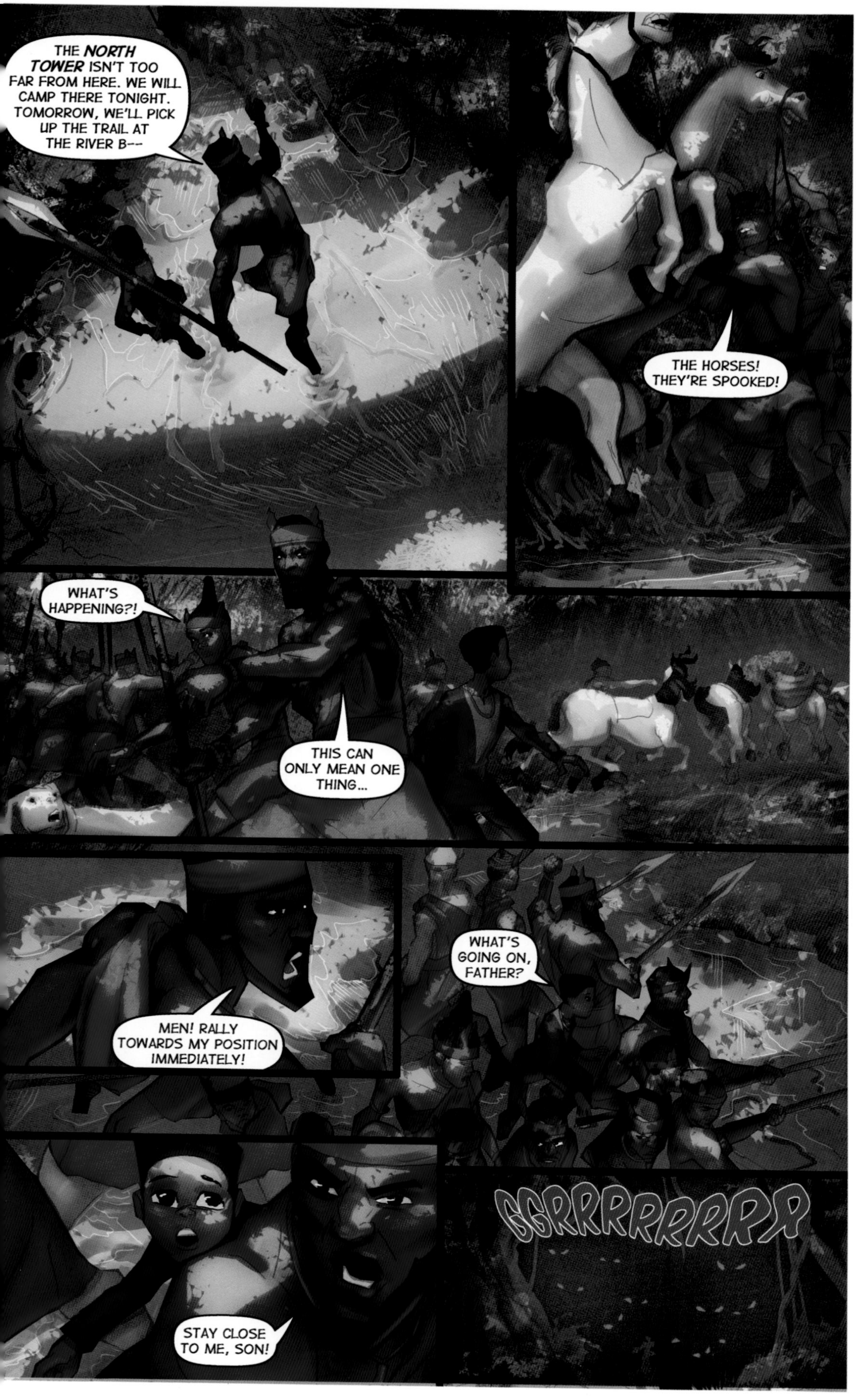
THE **NORTH TOWER** ISN'T TOO FAR FROM HERE. WE WILL CAMP THERE TONIGHT. TOMORROW, WE'LL PICK UP THE TRAIL AT THE RIVER B--
THE HORSES! THEY'RE SPOOKED!
WHAT'S HAPPENING?!
THIS CAN ONLY MEAN ONE THING...
MEN! RALLY TOWARDS MY POSITION IMMEDIATELY!
WHAT'S GOING ON, FATHER?
STAY CLOSE TO ME, SON!
GGRRRRRRRRR

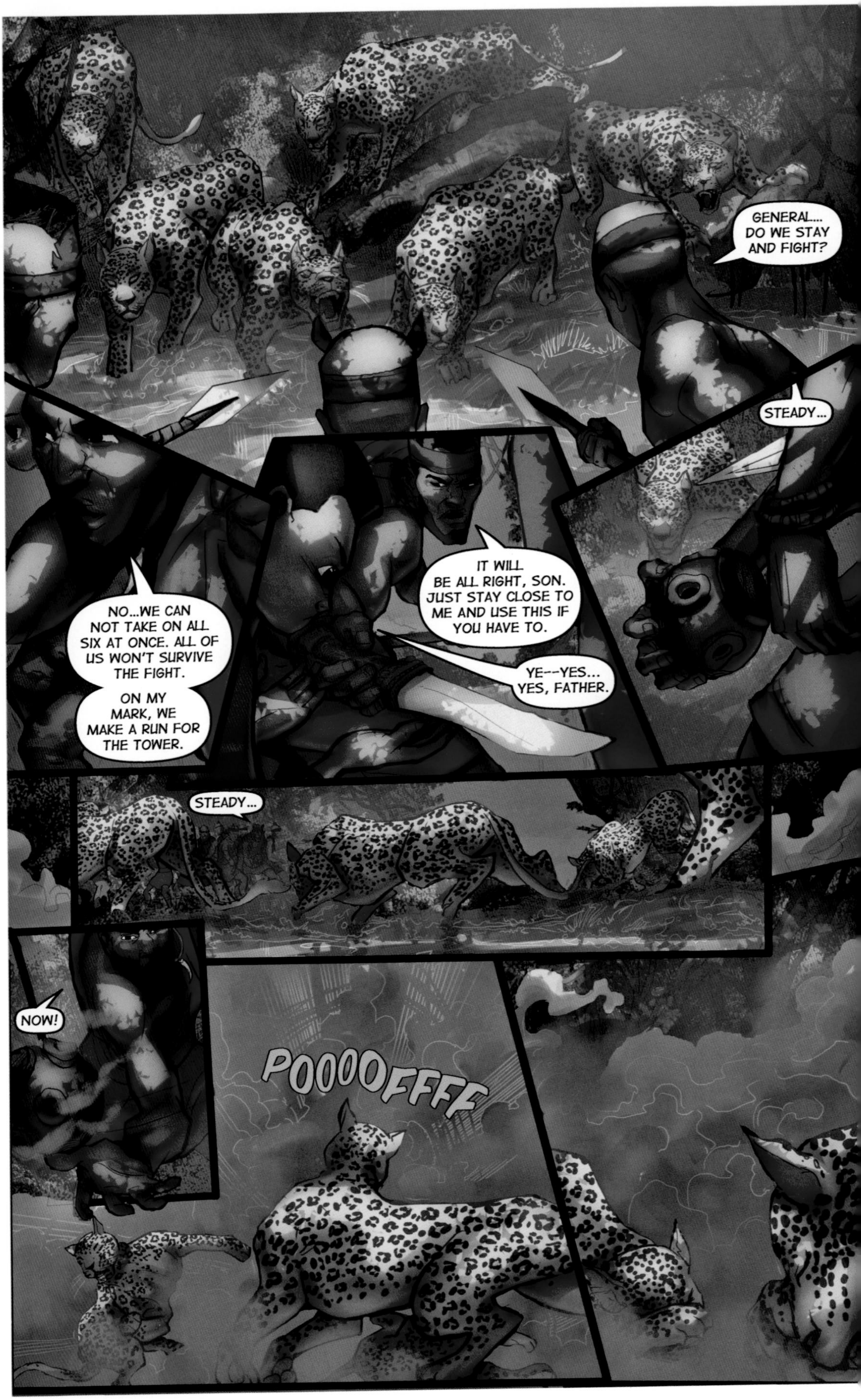
GENERAL... DO WE STAY AND FIGHT?
STEADY...
NO...WE CAN NOT TAKE ON ALL SIX AT ONCE. ALL OF US WON'T SURVIVE THE FIGHT.
ON MY MARK, WE MAKE A RUN FOR THE TOWER.
IT WILL BE ALL RIGHT, SON. JUST STAY CLOSE TO ME AND USE THIS IF YOU HAVE TO.
YE--YES... YES, FATHER.
STEADY...
NOW!
POOOOFFFF

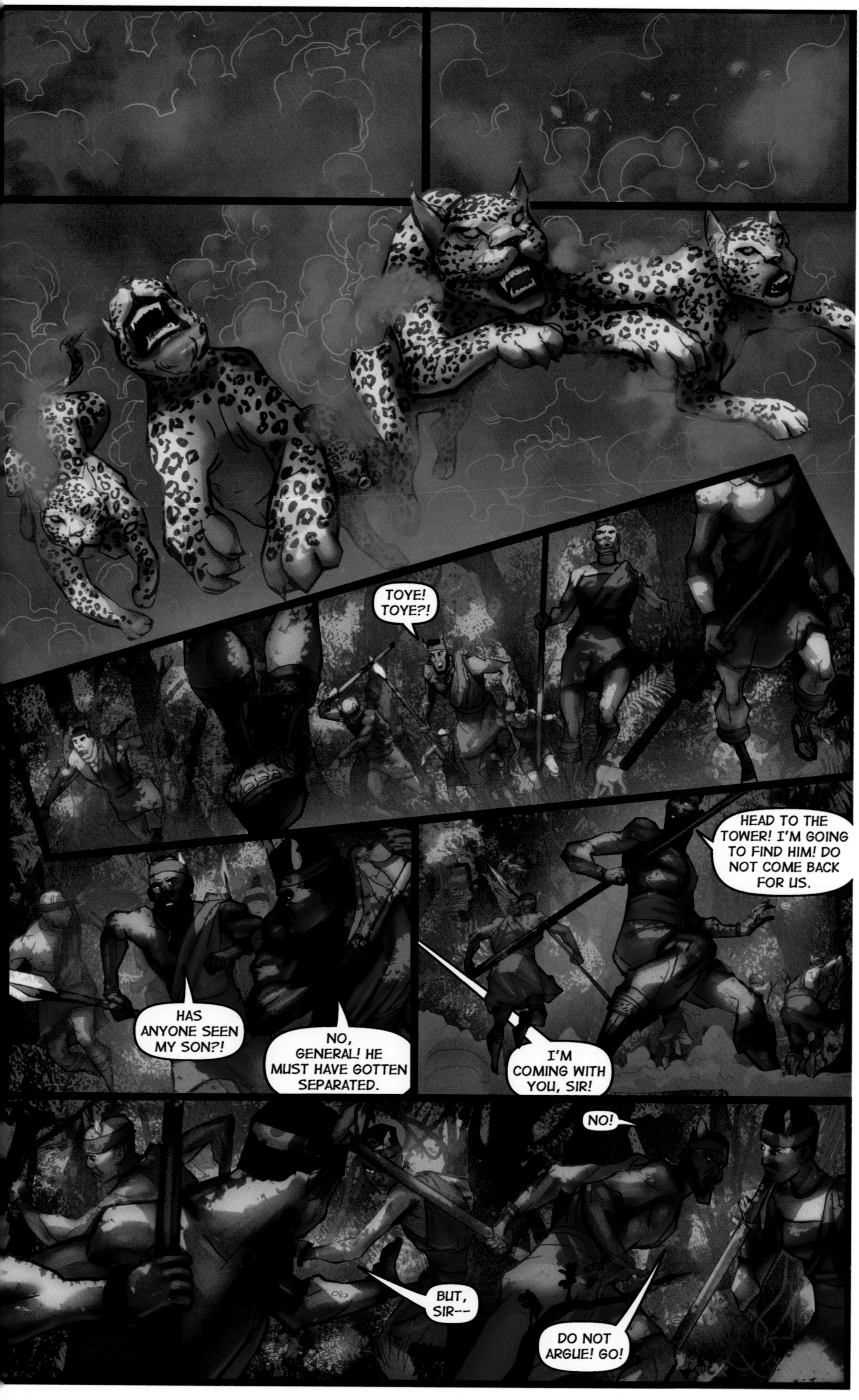
TOYE! TOYE?!
HAS ANYONE SEEN MY SON?!
NO, GENERAL! HE MUST HAVE GOTTEN SEPARATED.
HEAD TO THE TOWER! I'M GOING TO FIND HIM! DO NOT COME BACK FOR US.
I'M COMING WITH YOU, SIR!
NO!
BUT, SIR--
DO NOT ARGUE! GO!

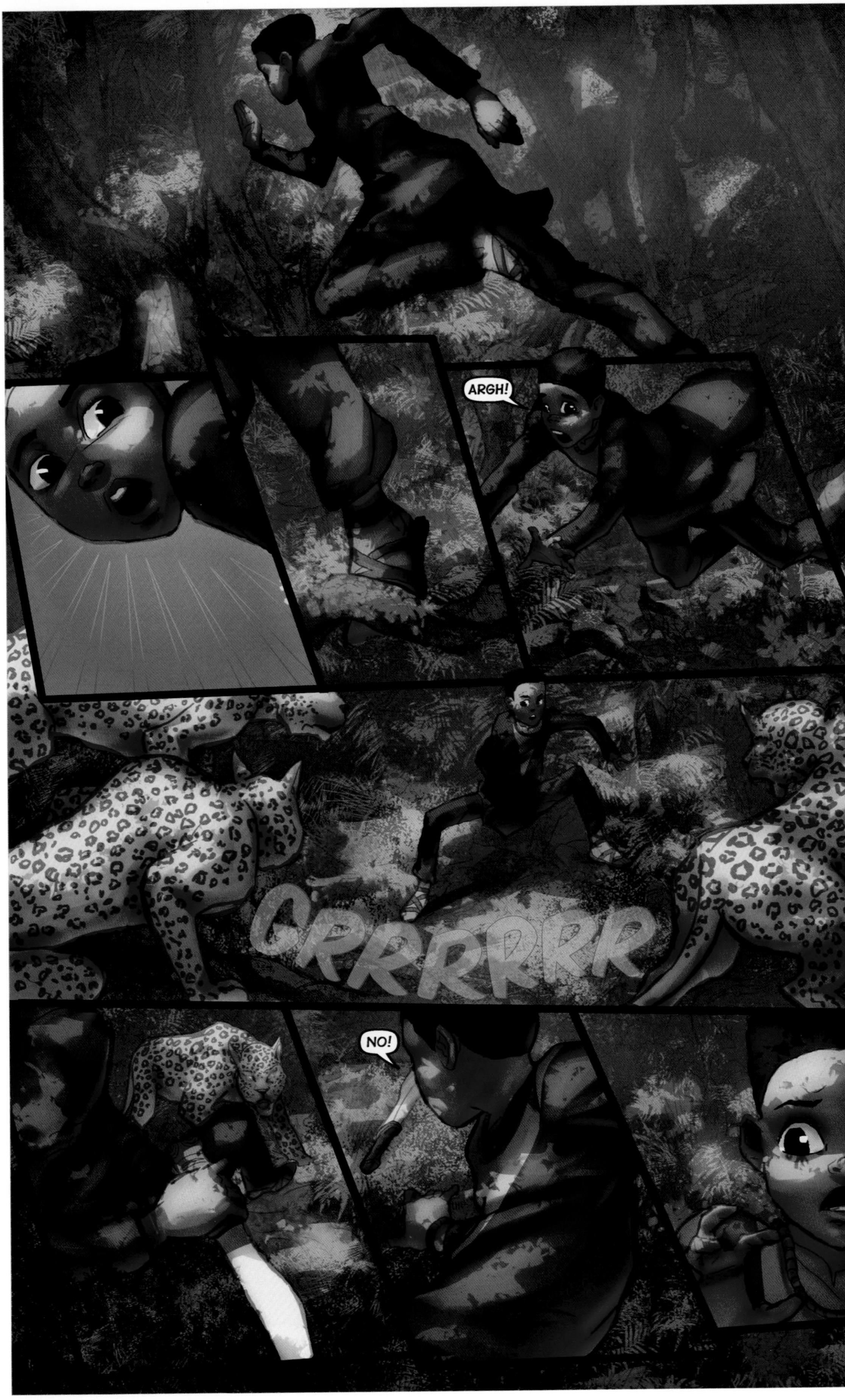
ARGH!
GRRRRRR
NO!

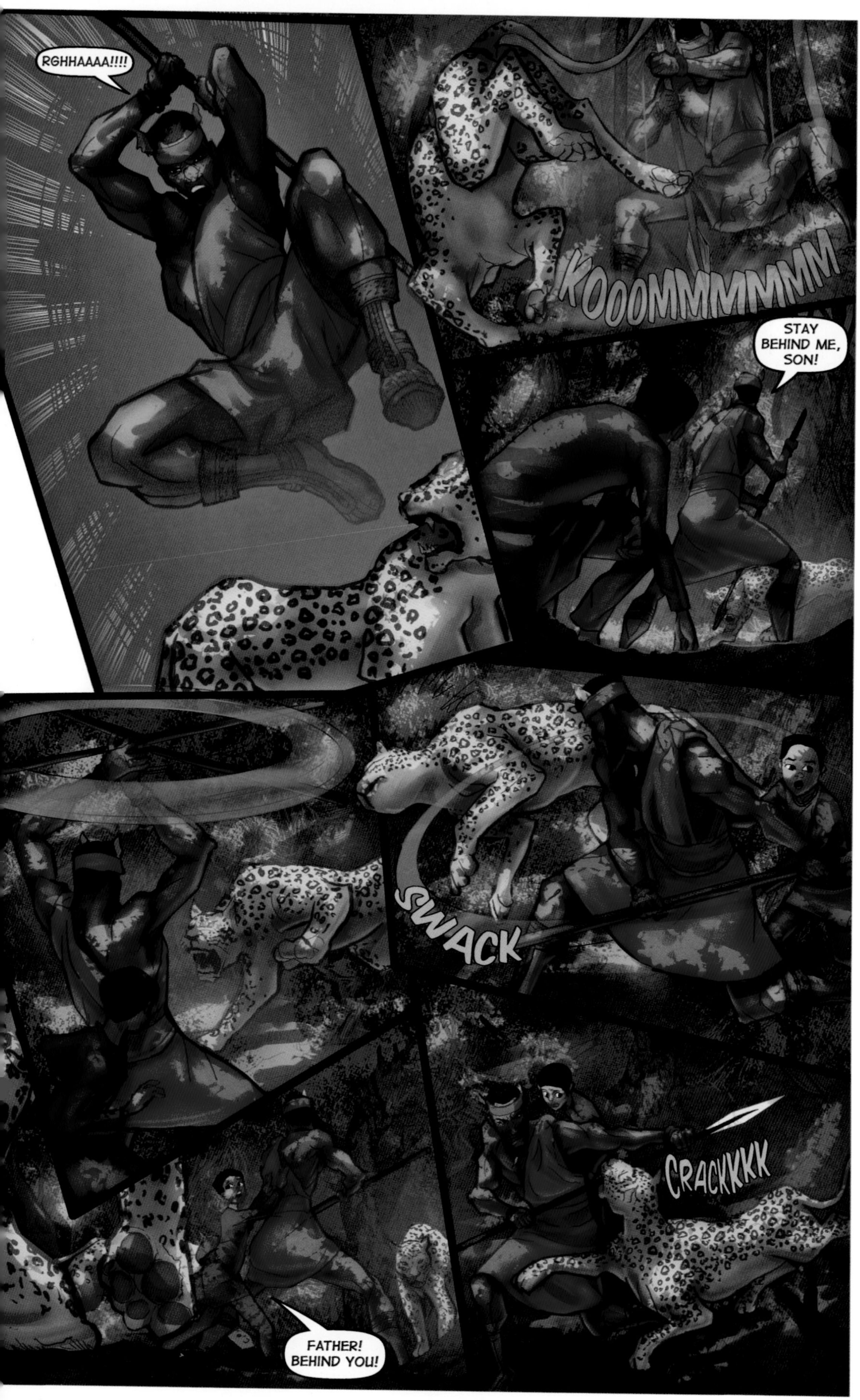
RGHHAAAA!!!!
KOOOMMMMMMM
STAY BEHIND ME, SON!
SWACK
FATHER! BEHIND YOU!
CRACKKKK

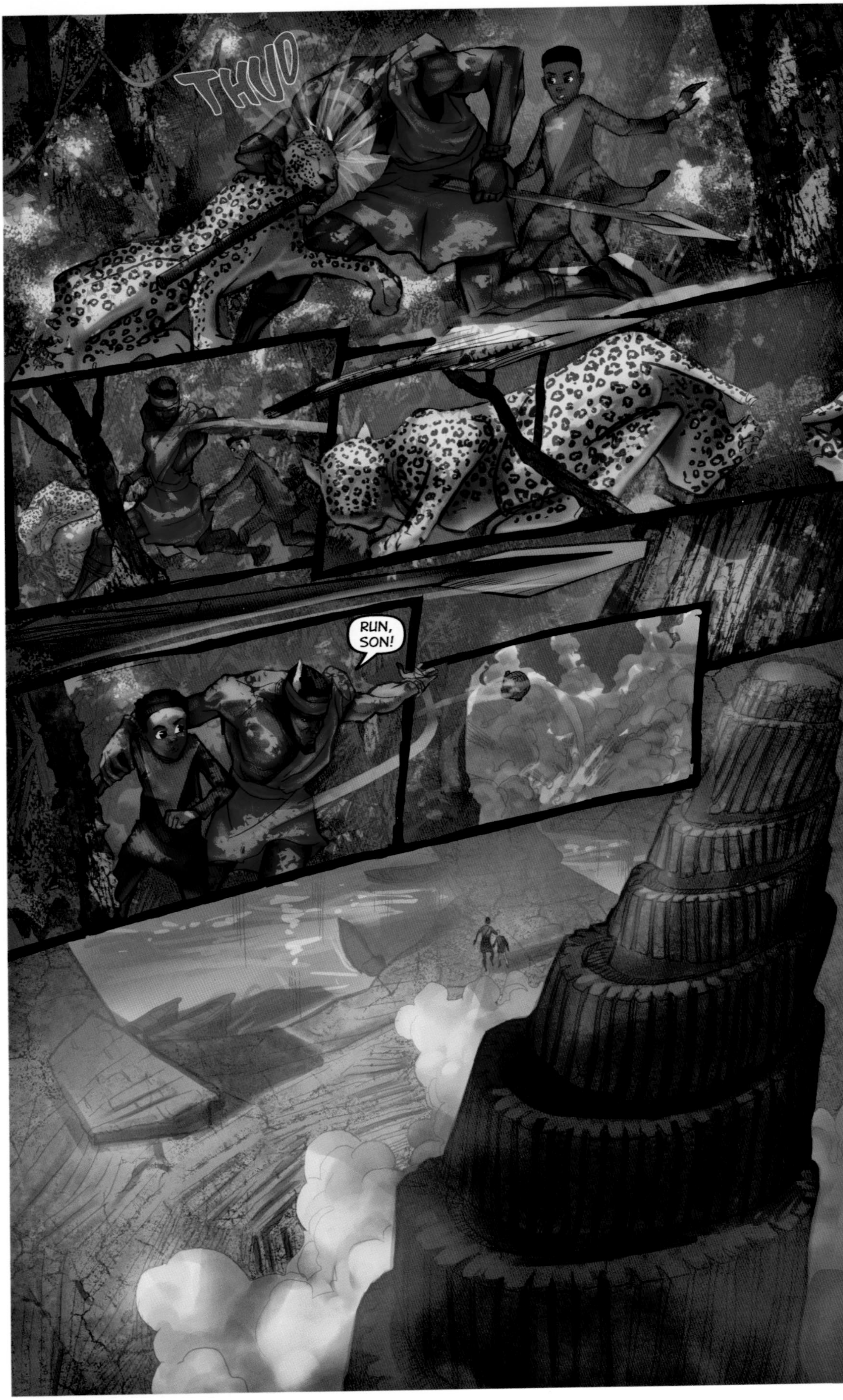
THUD
RUN, SON!

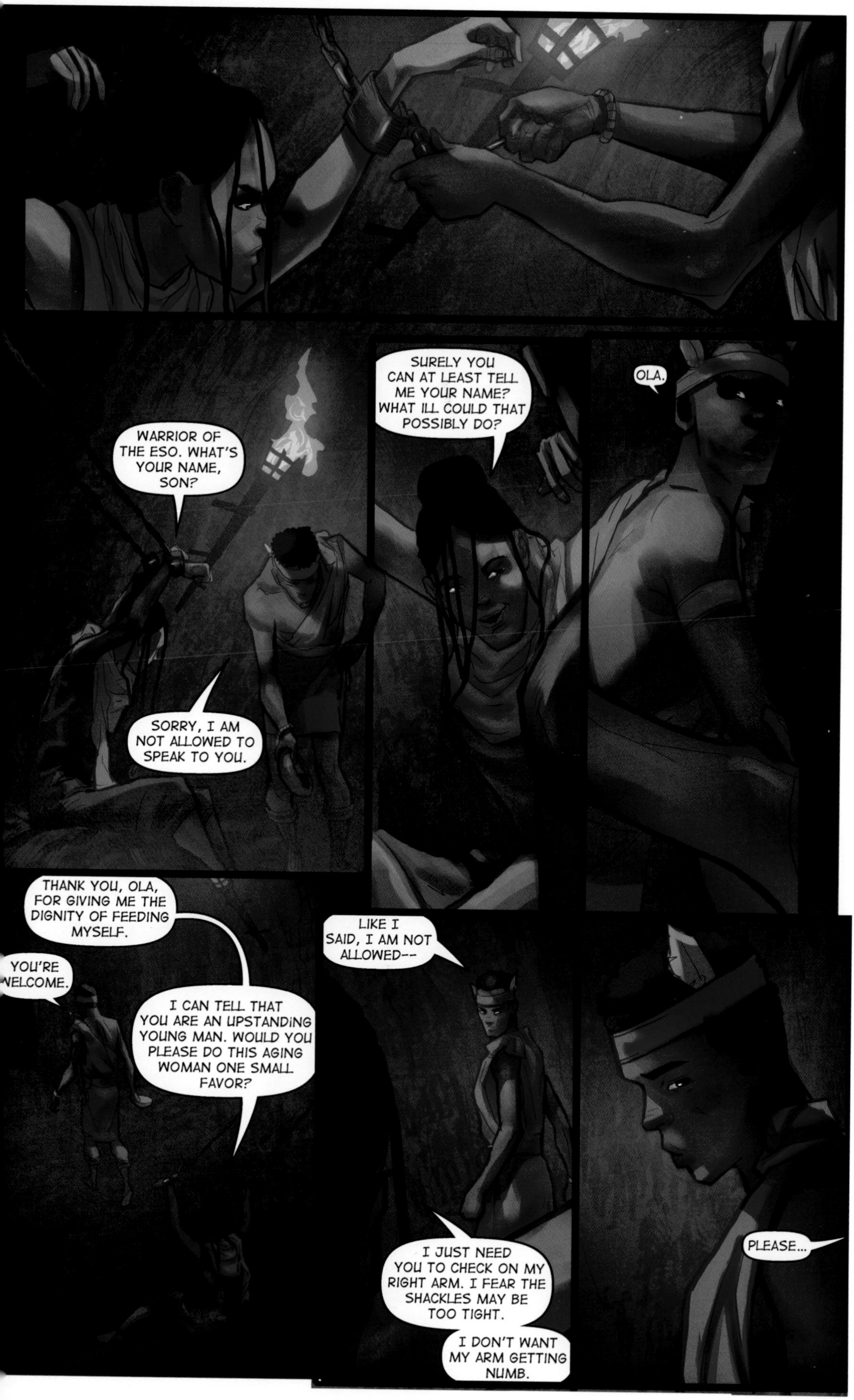
WARRIOR OF THE ESO. WHAT'S YOUR NAME, SON?
SORRY, I AM NOT ALLOWED TO SPEAK TO YOU.
SURELY YOU CAN AT LEAST TELL ME YOUR NAME? WHAT ILL COULD THAT POSSIBLY DO?
OLA.
THANK YOU, OLA, FOR GIVING ME THE DIGNITY OF FEEDING MYSELF.
YOU'RE WELCOME.
I CAN TELL THAT YOU ARE AN UPSTANDING YOUNG MAN. WOULD YOU PLEASE DO THIS AGING WOMAN ONE SMALL FAVOR?
LIKE I SAID, I AM NOT ALLOWED--
I JUST NEED YOU TO CHECK ON MY RIGHT ARM. I FEAR THE SHACKLES MAY BE TOO TIGHT.
I DON'T WANT MY ARM GETTING NUMB.
PLEASE...

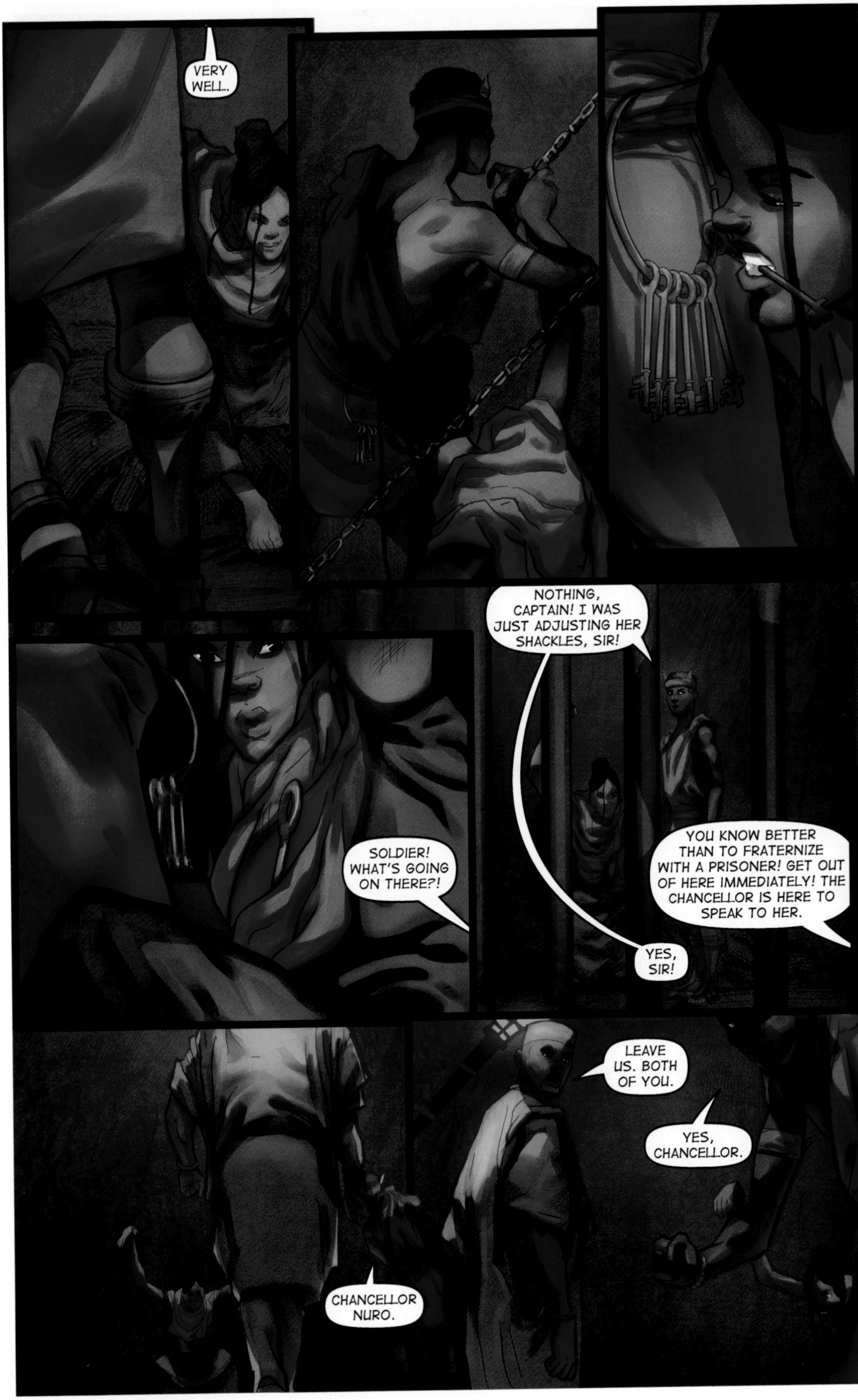
VERY WELL.
NOTHING, CAPTAIN! I WAS JUST ADJUSTING HER SHACKLES, SIR!
SOLDIER! WHAT'S GOING ON THERE?!
YOU KNOW BETTER THAN TO FRATERNIZE WITH A PRISONER! GET OUT OF HERE IMMEDIATELY! THE CHANCELLOR IS HERE TO SPEAK TO HER.
YES, SIR!
LEAVE US. BOTH OF YOU.
YES, CHANCELLOR.
CHANCELLOR NURO.

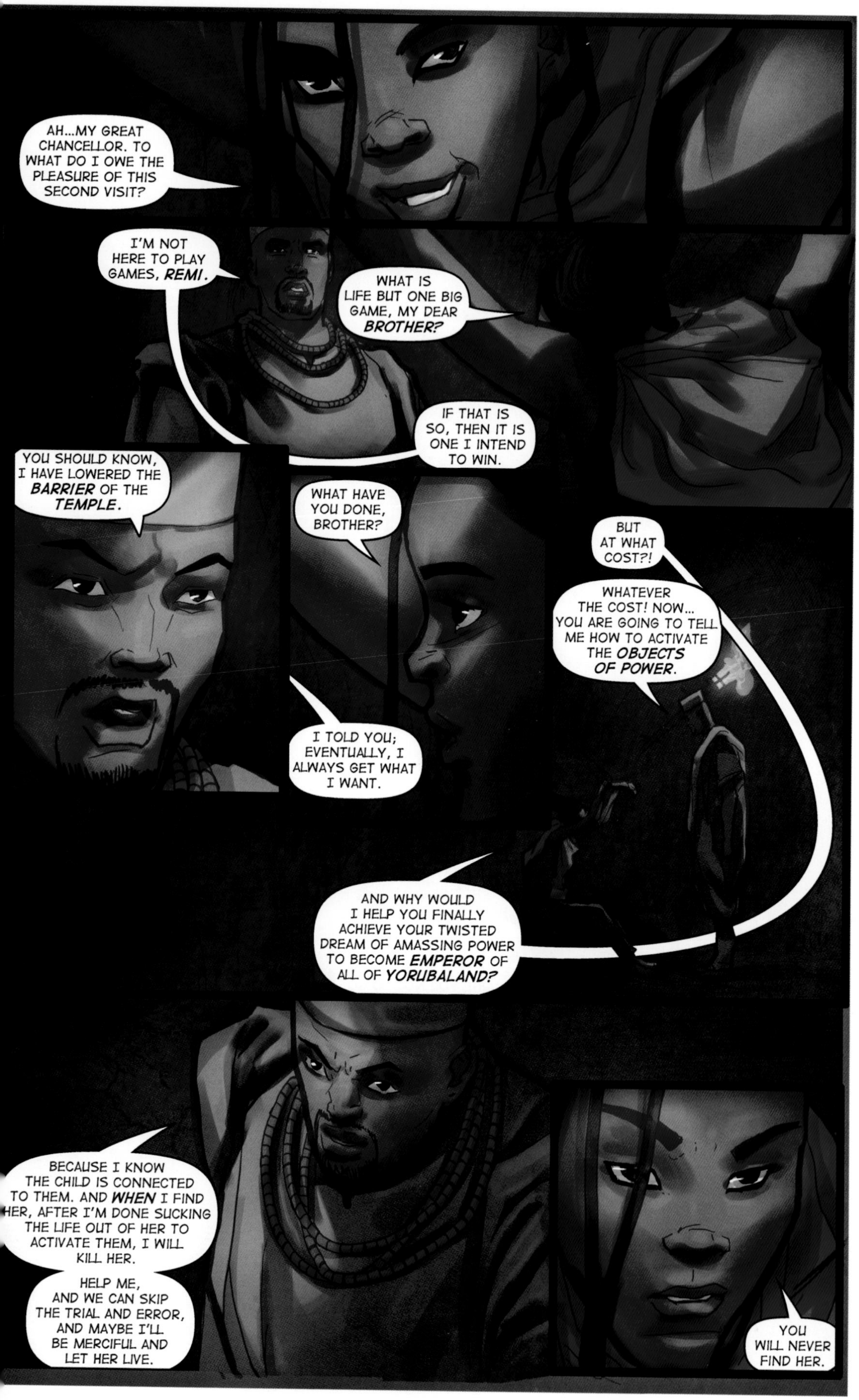
AH...MY GREAT CHANCELLOR. TO WHAT DO I OWE THE PLEASURE OF THIS SECOND VISIT?
I'M NOT HERE TO PLAY GAMES, *REMI*.
WHAT IS LIFE BUT ONE BIG GAME, MY DEAR *BROTHER?*
IF THAT IS SO, THEN IT IS ONE I INTEND TO WIN.
YOU SHOULD KNOW, I HAVE LOWERED THE *BARRIER* OF THE *TEMPLE*.
WHAT HAVE YOU DONE, BROTHER?
I TOLD YOU; EVENTUALLY, I ALWAYS GET WHAT I WANT.
BUT AT WHAT COST?!
WHATEVER THE COST! NOW... YOU ARE GOING TO TELL ME HOW TO ACTIVATE THE *OBJECTS OF POWER*.
AND WHY WOULD I HELP YOU FINALLY ACHIEVE YOUR TWISTED DREAM OF AMASSING POWER TO BECOME *EMPEROR* OF ALL OF *YORUBALAND?*
BECAUSE I KNOW THE CHILD IS CONNECTED TO THEM. AND *WHEN* I FIND HER, AFTER I'M DONE SUCKING THE LIFE OUT OF HER TO ACTIVATE THEM, I WILL KILL HER.
HELP ME, AND WE CAN SKIP THE TRIAL AND ERROR, AND MAYBE I'LL BE MERCIFUL AND LET HER LIVE.
YOU WILL NEVER FIND HER.

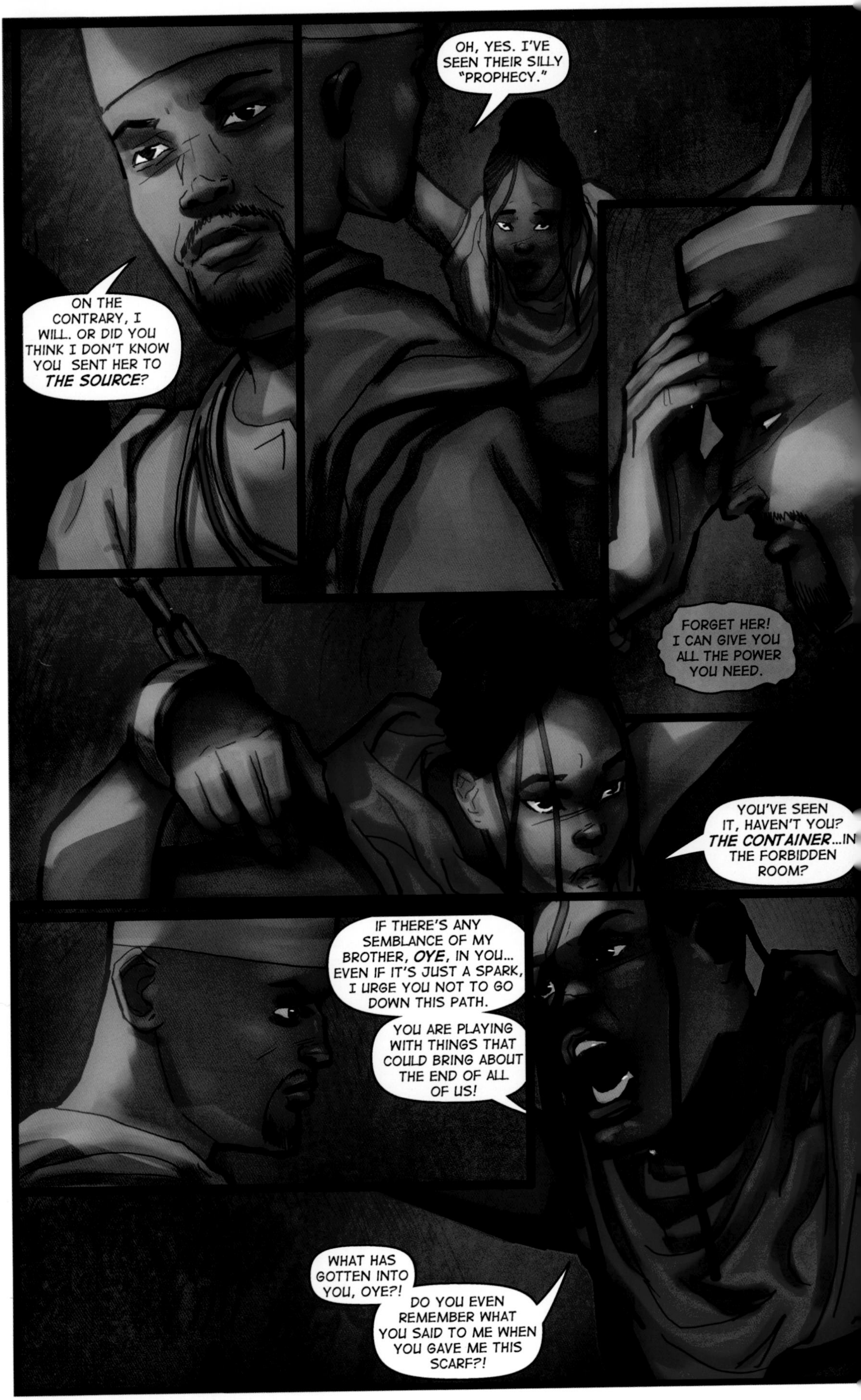

ON THE CONTRARY, I WILL. OR DID YOU THINK I DON'T KNOW YOU SENT HER TO *THE SOURCE*?
OH, YES. I'VE SEEN THEIR SILLY "PROPHECY."
FORGET HER! I CAN GIVE YOU ALL THE POWER YOU NEED.
YOU'VE SEEN IT, HAVEN'T YOU? *THE CONTAINER*...IN THE FORBIDDEN ROOM?
IF THERE'S ANY SEMBLANCE OF MY BROTHER, *OYE*, IN YOU... EVEN IF IT'S JUST A SPARK, I URGE YOU NOT TO GO DOWN THIS PATH.
YOU ARE PLAYING WITH THINGS THAT COULD BRING ABOUT THE END OF ALL OF US!
WHAT HAS GOTTEN INTO YOU, OYE?!
DO YOU EVEN REMEMBER WHAT YOU SAID TO ME WHEN YOU GAVE ME THIS SCARF?!

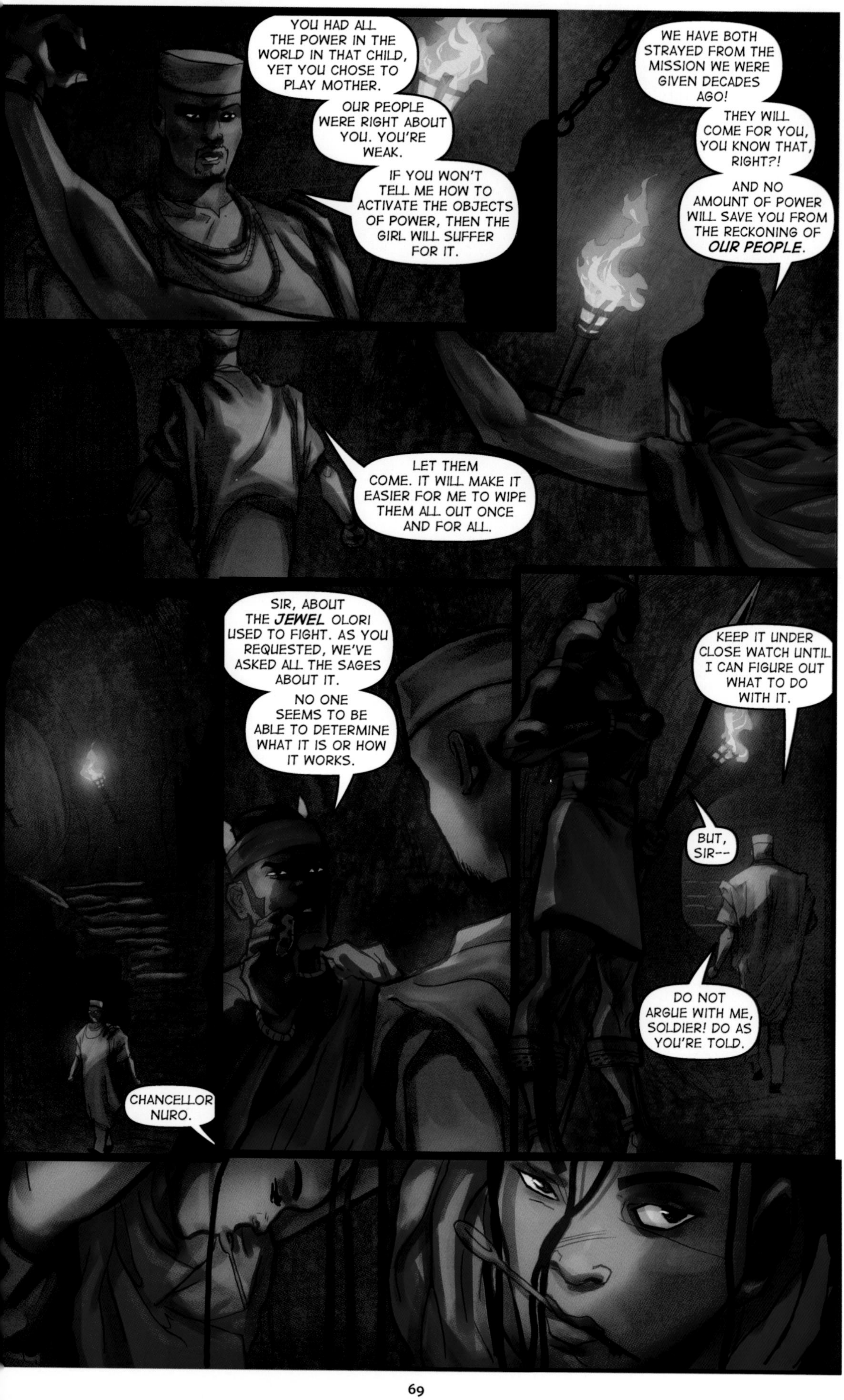
YOU HAD ALL THE POWER IN THE WORLD IN THAT CHILD, YET YOU CHOSE TO PLAY MOTHER.
OUR PEOPLE WERE RIGHT ABOUT YOU. YOU'RE WEAK.
IF YOU WON'T TELL ME HOW TO ACTIVATE THE OBJECTS OF POWER, THEN THE GIRL WILL SUFFER FOR IT.
WE HAVE BOTH STRAYED FROM THE MISSION WE WERE GIVEN DECADES AGO!
THEY WILL COME FOR YOU, YOU KNOW THAT, RIGHT?!
AND NO AMOUNT OF POWER WILL SAVE YOU FROM THE RECKONING OF *OUR PEOPLE*.
LET THEM COME. IT WILL MAKE IT EASIER FOR ME TO WIPE THEM ALL OUT ONCE AND FOR ALL.
CHANCELLOR NURO.
SIR, ABOUT THE *JEWEL* OLORI USED TO FIGHT. AS YOU REQUESTED, WE'VE ASKED ALL THE SAGES ABOUT IT.
NO ONE SEEMS TO BE ABLE TO DETERMINE WHAT IT IS OR HOW IT WORKS.
KEEP IT UNDER CLOSE WATCH UNTIL I CAN FIGURE OUT WHAT TO DO WITH IT.
BUT, SIR--
DO NOT ARGUE WITH ME, SOLDIER! DO AS YOU'RE TOLD.

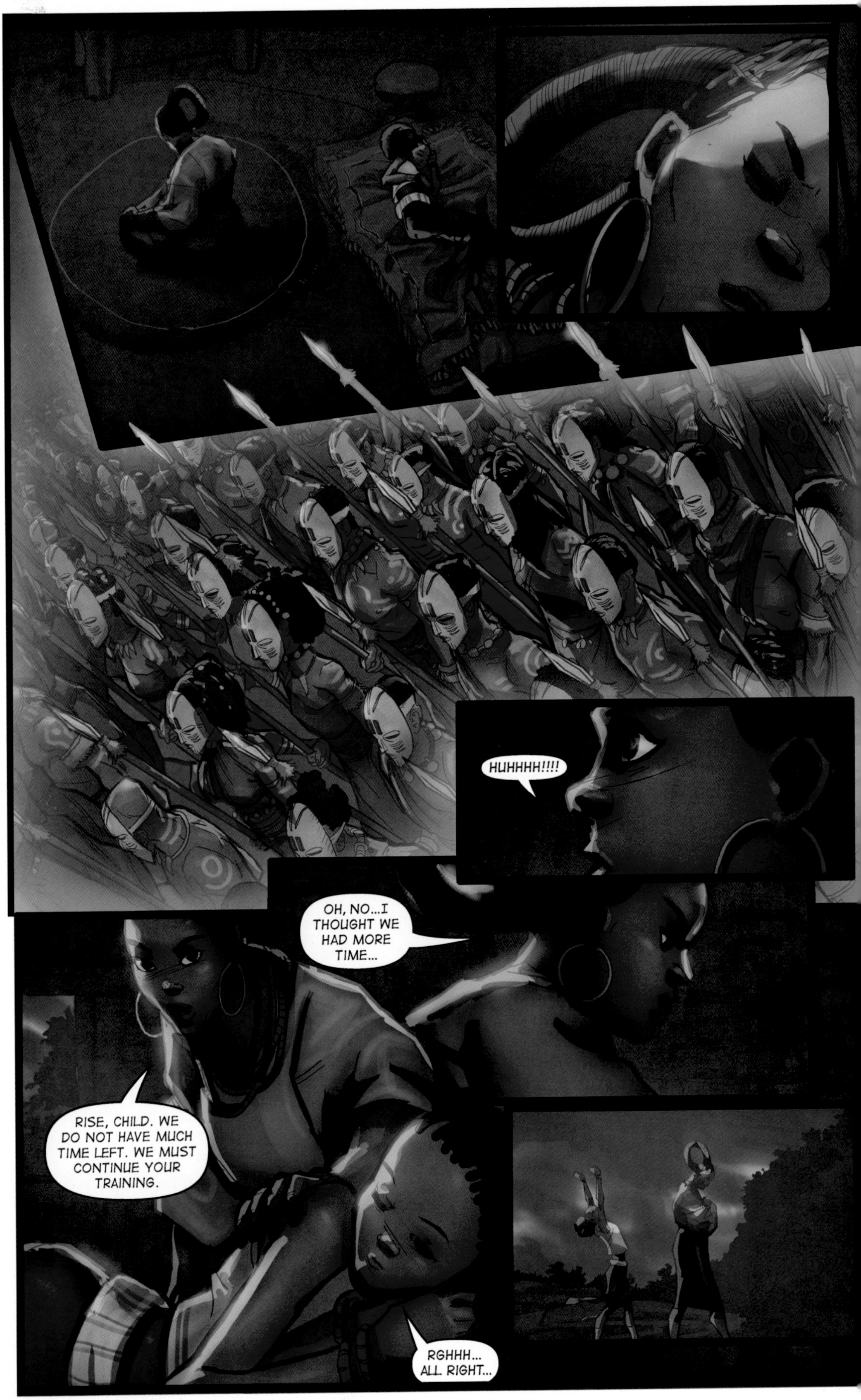
HUHHHH!!!!
OH, NO...I THOUGHT WE HAD MORE TIME...
RISE, CHILD. WE DO NOT HAVE MUCH TIME LEFT. WE MUST CONTINUE YOUR TRAINING.
RGHHH... ALL RIGHT...

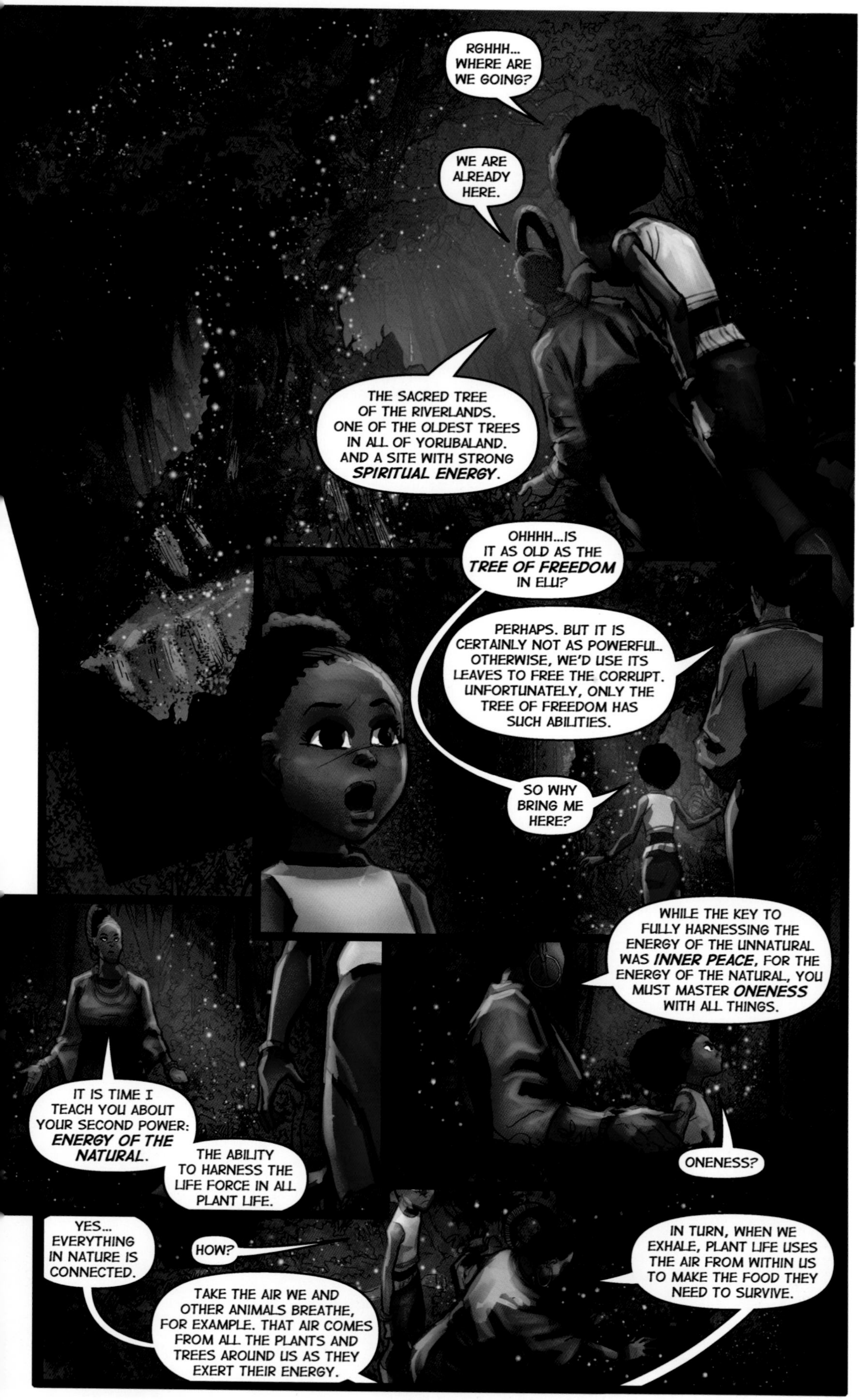
RGHHH... WHERE ARE WE GOING?
WE ARE ALREADY HERE.
THE SACRED TREE OF THE RIVERLANDS. ONE OF THE OLDEST TREES IN ALL OF YORUBALAND. AND A SITE WITH STRONG SPIRITUAL ENERGY.
OHHHH...IS IT AS OLD AS THE TREE OF FREEDOM IN ELU?
PERHAPS. BUT IT IS CERTAINLY NOT AS POWERFUL. OTHERWISE, WE'D USE ITS LEAVES TO FREE THE CORRUPT. UNFORTUNATELY, ONLY THE TREE OF FREEDOM HAS SUCH ABILITIES.
SO WHY BRING ME HERE?
IT IS TIME I TEACH YOU ABOUT YOUR SECOND POWER: ENERGY OF THE NATURAL.
THE ABILITY TO HARNESS THE LIFE FORCE IN ALL PLANT LIFE.
WHILE THE KEY TO FULLY HARNESSING THE ENERGY OF THE UNNATURAL WAS INNER PEACE, FOR THE ENERGY OF THE NATURAL, YOU MUST MASTER ONENESS WITH ALL THINGS.
ONENESS?
YES... EVERYTHING IN NATURE IS CONNECTED.
HOW?
TAKE THE AIR WE AND OTHER ANIMALS BREATHE, FOR EXAMPLE. THAT AIR COMES FROM ALL THE PLANTS AND TREES AROUND US AS THEY EXERT THEIR ENERGY.
IN TURN, WHEN WE EXHALE, PLANT LIFE USES THE AIR FROM WITHIN US TO MAKE THE FOOD THEY NEED TO SURVIVE.

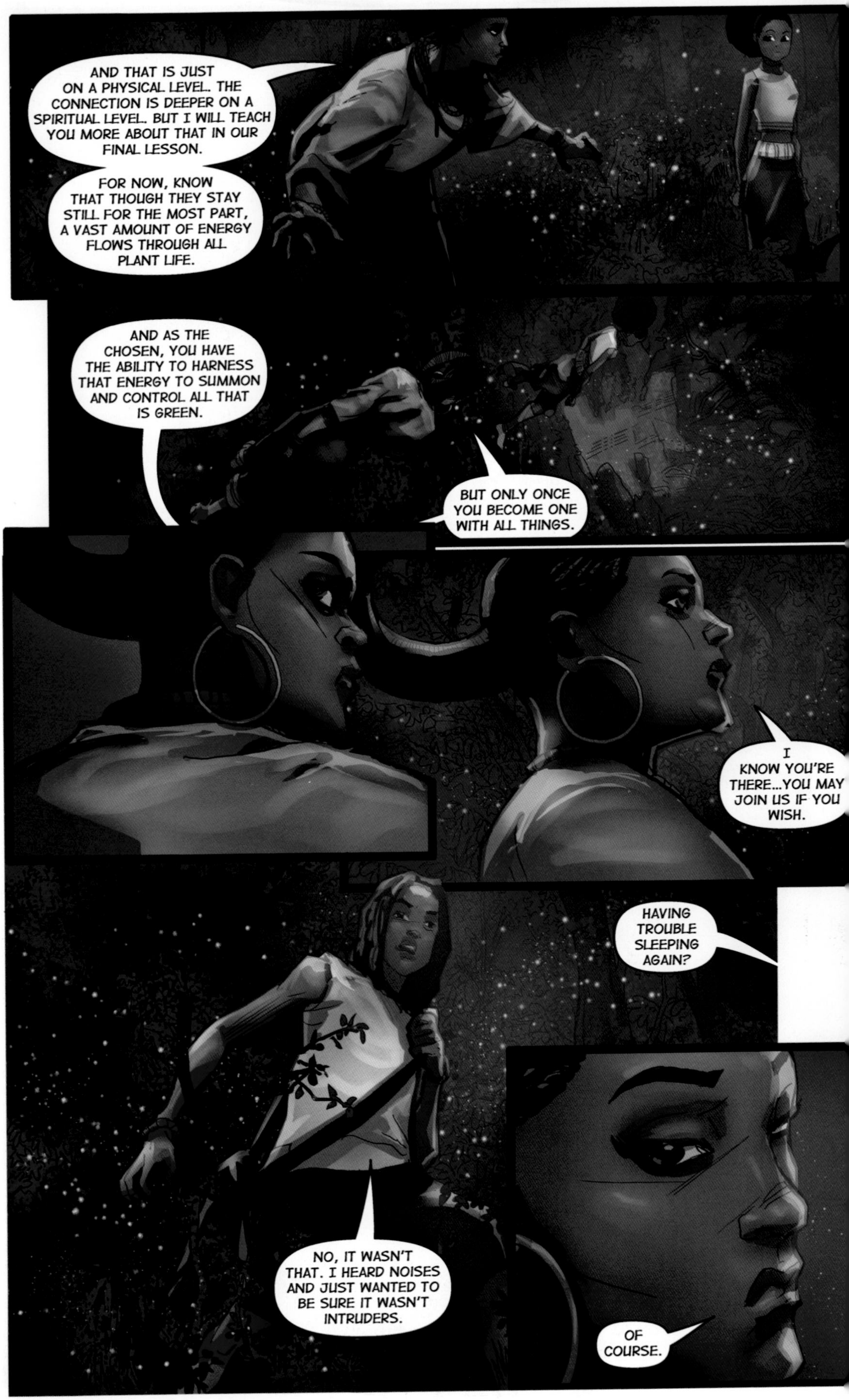
AND THAT IS JUST ON A PHYSICAL LEVEL. THE CONNECTION IS DEEPER ON A SPIRITUAL LEVEL. BUT I WILL TEACH YOU MORE ABOUT THAT IN OUR FINAL LESSON.
FOR NOW, KNOW THAT THOUGH THEY STAY STILL FOR THE MOST PART, A VAST AMOUNT OF ENERGY FLOWS THROUGH ALL PLANT LIFE.
AND AS THE CHOSEN, YOU HAVE THE ABILITY TO HARNESS THAT ENERGY TO SUMMON AND CONTROL ALL THAT IS GREEN.
BUT ONLY ONCE YOU BECOME ONE WITH ALL THINGS.
I KNOW YOU'RE THERE...YOU MAY JOIN US IF YOU WISH.
HAVING TROUBLE SLEEPING AGAIN?
NO, IT WASN'T THAT. I HEARD NOISES AND JUST WANTED TO BE SURE IT WASN'T INTRUDERS.
OF COURSE.

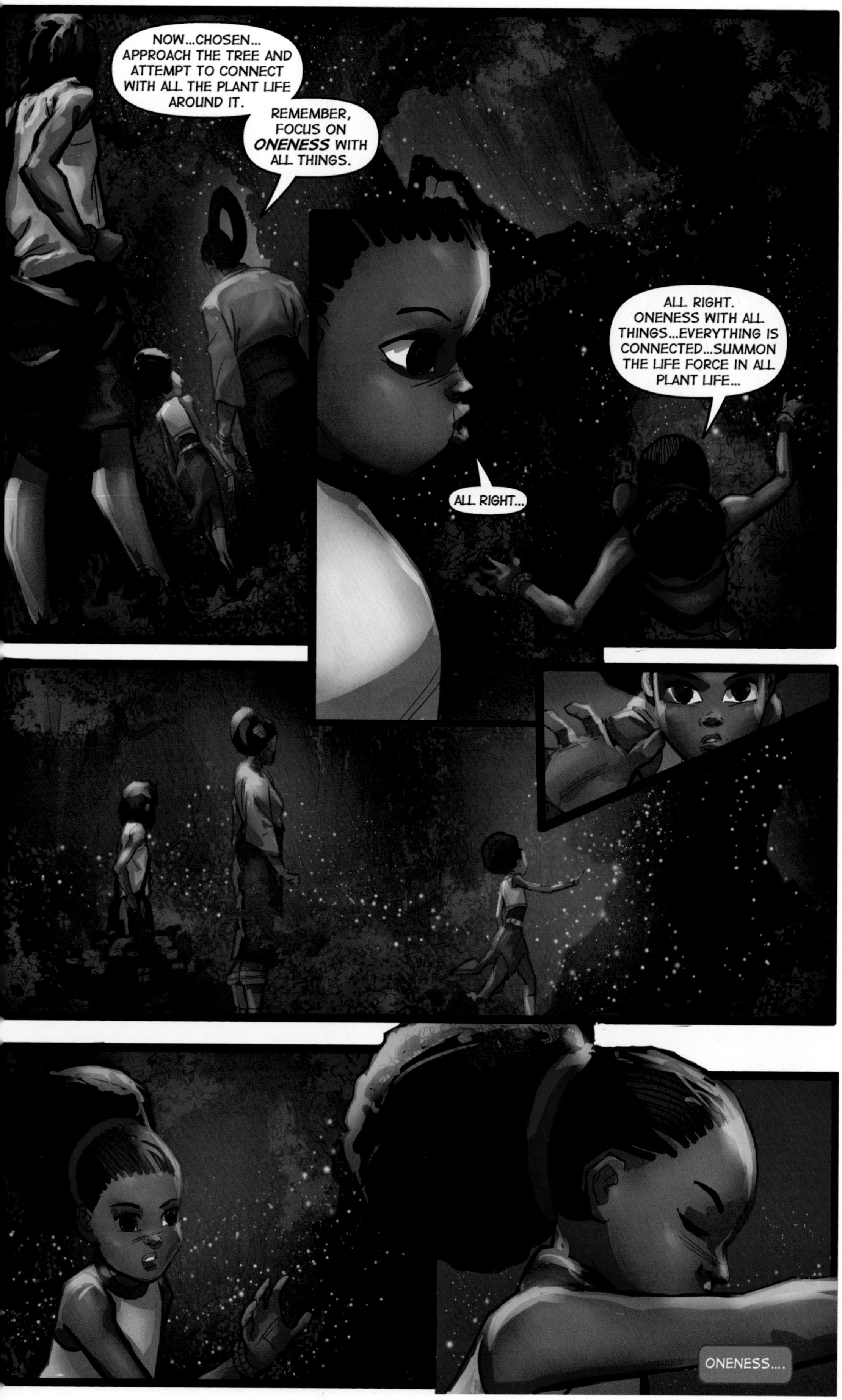
NOW...CHOSEN... APPROACH THE TREE AND ATTEMPT TO CONNECT WITH ALL THE PLANT LIFE AROUND IT.
REMEMBER, FOCUS ON *ONENESS* WITH ALL THINGS.
ALL RIGHT...
ALL RIGHT. ONENESS WITH ALL THINGS...EVERYTHING IS CONNECTED...SUMMON THE LIFE FORCE IN ALL PLANT LIFE...
ONENESS....

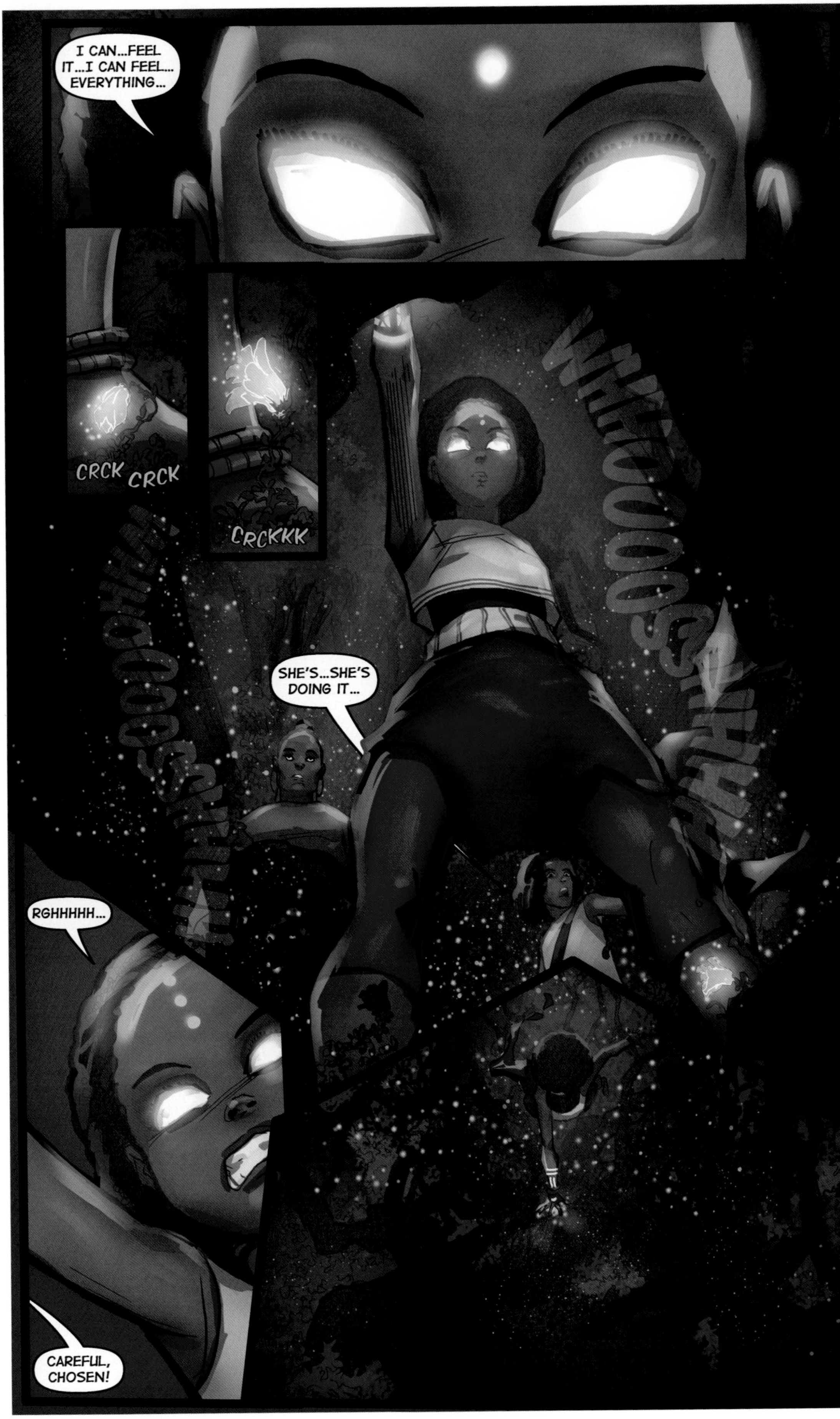
I CAN...FEEL IT...I CAN FEEL... EVERYTHING...
CRCK CRCK
CRCKKK
SHE'S...SHE'S DOING IT...
RGHHHHH...
CAREFUL, CHOSEN!

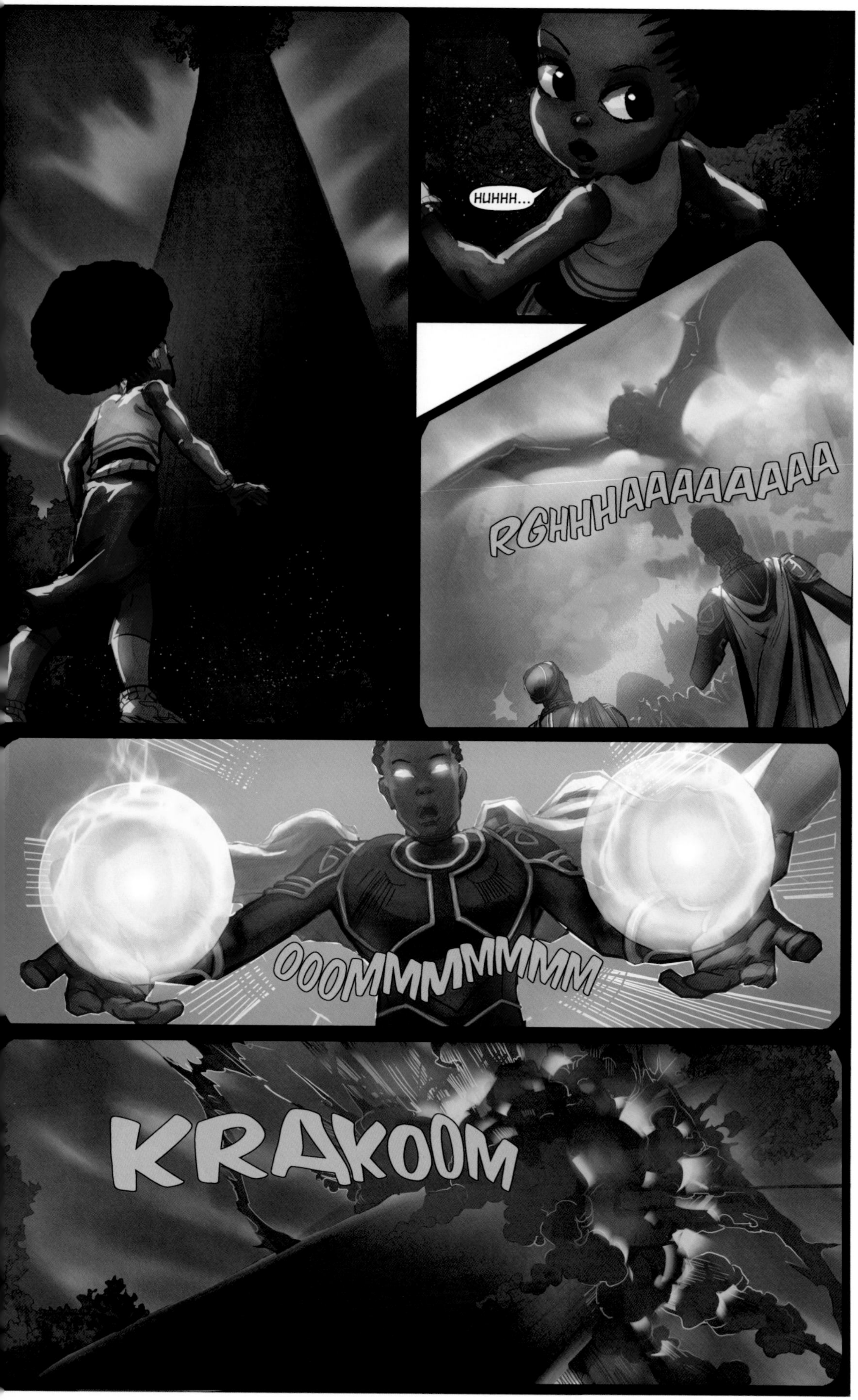
HUHHH...
RGHHHAAAAAAAAA
OOOMMMMMMMM
KRAKOOM

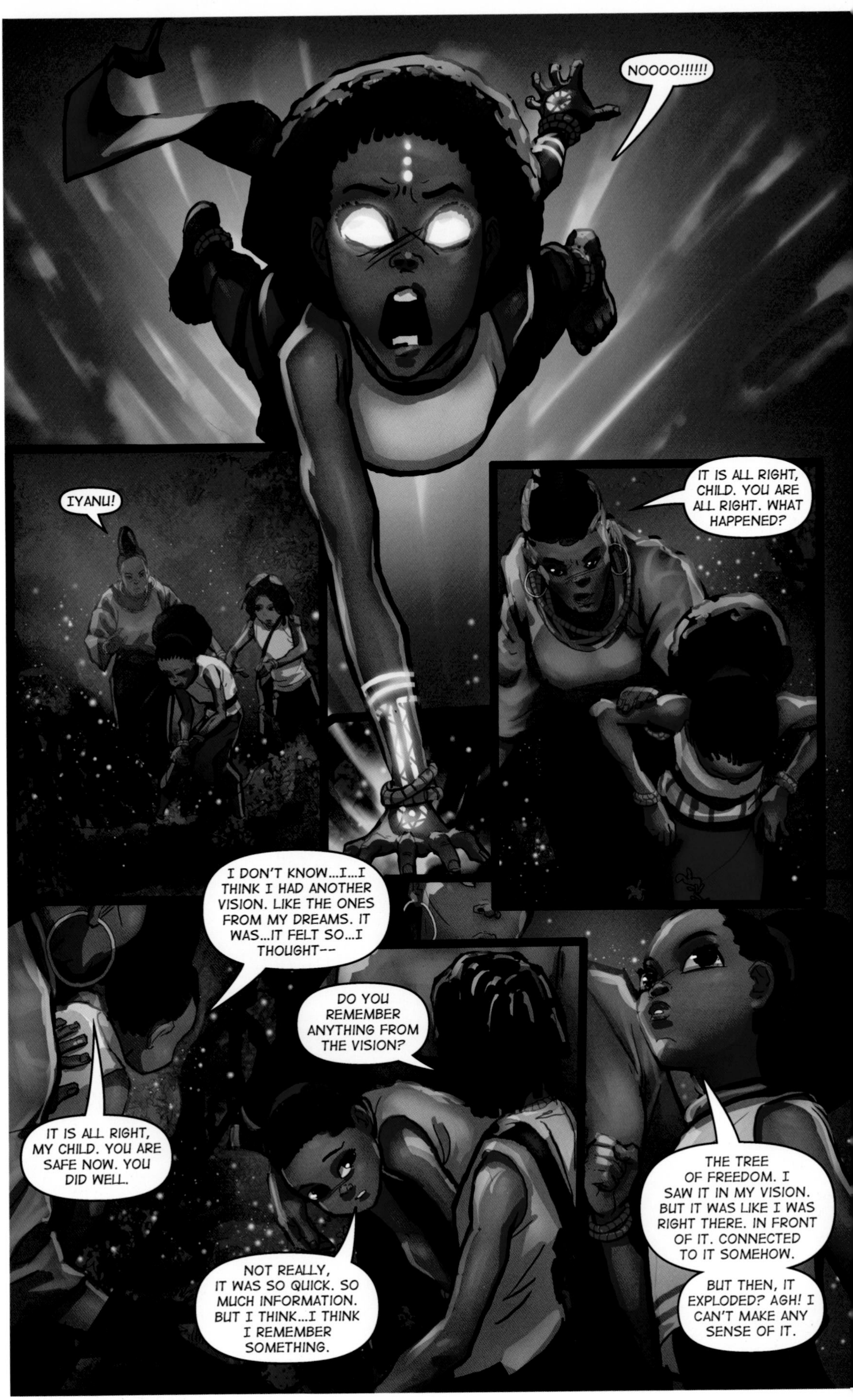
NOOOO!!!!!!
IYANU!
IT IS ALL RIGHT, CHILD. YOU ARE ALL RIGHT. WHAT HAPPENED?
I DON'T KNOW...I...I THINK I HAD ANOTHER VISION. LIKE THE ONES FROM MY DREAMS. IT WAS...IT FELT SO...I THOUGHT--
IT IS ALL RIGHT, MY CHILD. YOU ARE SAFE NOW. YOU DID WELL.
DO YOU REMEMBER ANYTHING FROM THE VISION?
NOT REALLY, IT WAS SO QUICK. SO MUCH INFORMATION. BUT I THINK...I THINK I REMEMBER SOMETHING.
THE TREE OF FREEDOM. I SAW IT IN MY VISION. BUT IT WAS LIKE I WAS RIGHT THERE. IN FRONT OF IT. CONNECTED TO IT SOMEHOW.
BUT THEN, IT EXPLODED? AGH! I CAN'T MAKE ANY SENSE OF IT.

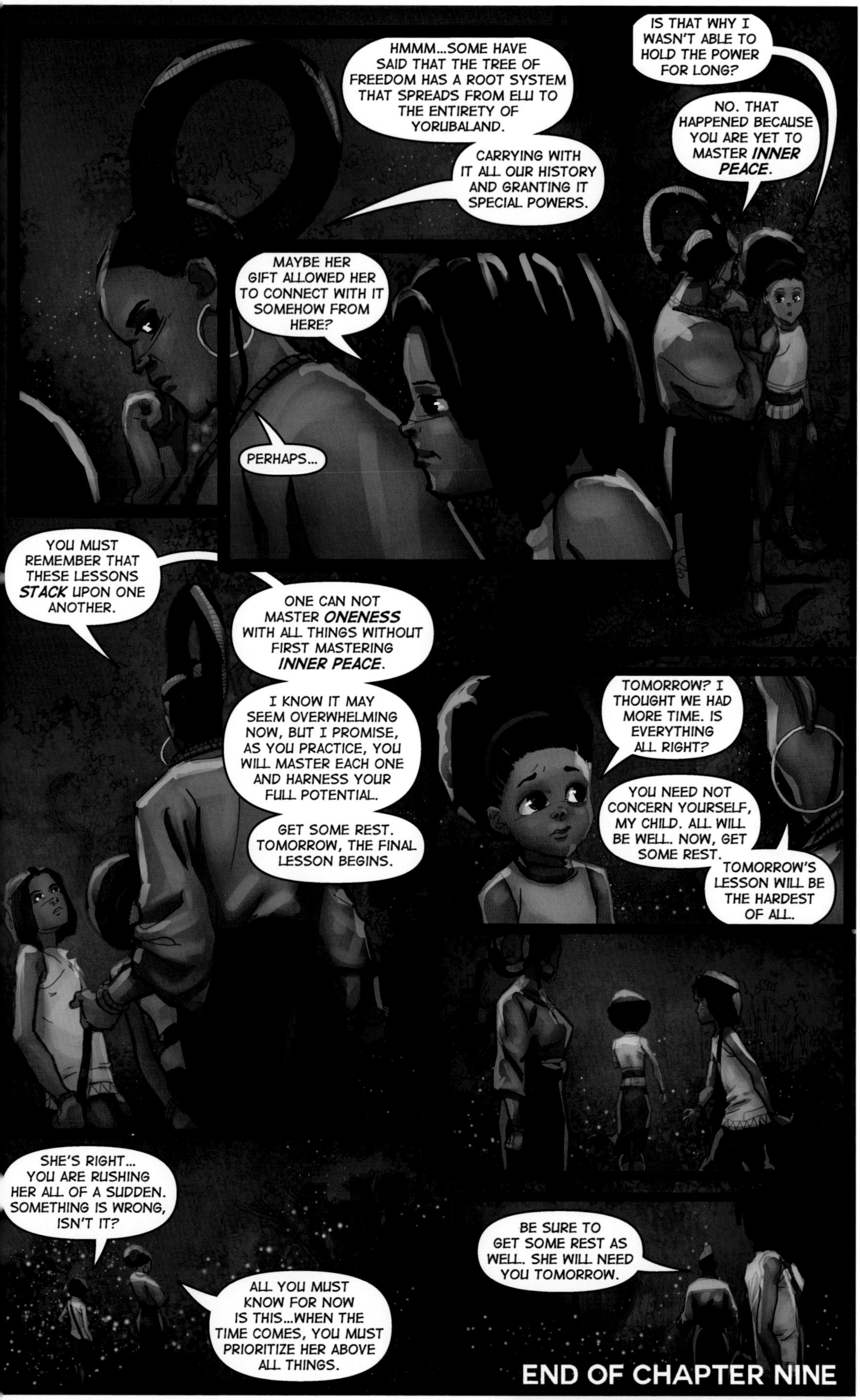
HMMM...SOME HAVE SAID THAT THE TREE OF FREEDOM HAS A ROOT SYSTEM THAT SPREADS FROM ELU TO THE ENTIRETY OF YORUBALAND.
CARRYING WITH IT ALL OUR HISTORY AND GRANTING IT SPECIAL POWERS.
IS THAT WHY I WASN'T ABLE TO HOLD THE POWER FOR LONG?
NO. THAT HAPPENED BECAUSE YOU ARE YET TO MASTER INNER PEACE.
MAYBE HER GIFT ALLOWED HER TO CONNECT WITH IT SOMEHOW FROM HERE?
PERHAPS...
YOU MUST REMEMBER THAT THESE LESSONS STACK UPON ONE ANOTHER.
ONE CAN NOT MASTER ONENESS WITH ALL THINGS WITHOUT FIRST MASTERING INNER PEACE.
I KNOW IT MAY SEEM OVERWHELMING NOW, BUT I PROMISE, AS YOU PRACTICE, YOU WILL MASTER EACH ONE AND HARNESS YOUR FULL POTENTIAL.
GET SOME REST. TOMORROW, THE FINAL LESSON BEGINS.
TOMORROW? I THOUGHT WE HAD MORE TIME. IS EVERYTHING ALL RIGHT?
YOU NEED NOT CONCERN YOURSELF, MY CHILD. ALL WILL BE WELL. NOW, GET SOME REST.
TOMORROW'S LESSON WILL BE THE HARDEST OF ALL.
SHE'S RIGHT... YOU ARE RUSHING HER ALL OF A SUDDEN. SOMETHING IS WRONG, ISN'T IT?
ALL YOU MUST KNOW FOR NOW IS THIS...WHEN THE TIME COMES, YOU MUST PRIORITIZE HER ABOVE ALL THINGS.
BE SURE TO GET SOME REST AS WELL. SHE WILL NEED YOU TOMORROW.
END OF CHAPTER NINE

CHAPTER TEN

The Agoni

Self-proclaimed "Keepers of the History of Yorubaland," the Agoni are a group of female-only priestesses that have existed in Elu since the New Beginning. While everyone else turned their backs on the Divine Ones and history following the end of the Divine Wars, the Agoni instead chose to salvage what they could and preserve the old ways and some of its teachings. This led to the break-through of Abo Dust. A concoction that lifts the curse over the corrupt (individually).

For centuries, the Agoni kept the secret of this concoction to themselves. This act has always caused some form of strife between the Agoni and the leaders of multiple regimes in Elu. But it was under the rule of Oba Adeniyi and Nuro, Chancellor of the Elu Mesi (the Council of Elu), that things took a turn for the worse during the Agoni rebellion. An event that led to the eradication of all the members of the Agoni, except one.

It was also common practice for the Agoni to take an apprentice from the community at large. Ones they deemed holy and fit to join the cause. But they selected from a pool of orphans exclusively. This was the Agoni's way of breeding the most loyal of people. Children who had no families to run back to. For once you're inducted into the order, you are sworn to ultimate secrecy and you pledge to live your life for the betterment of Elu and Yorubaland.

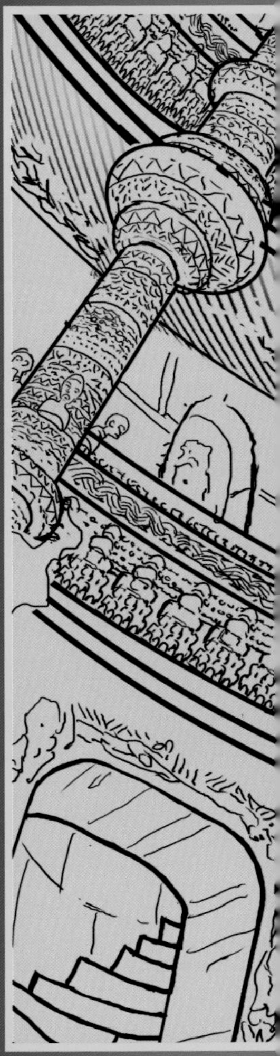

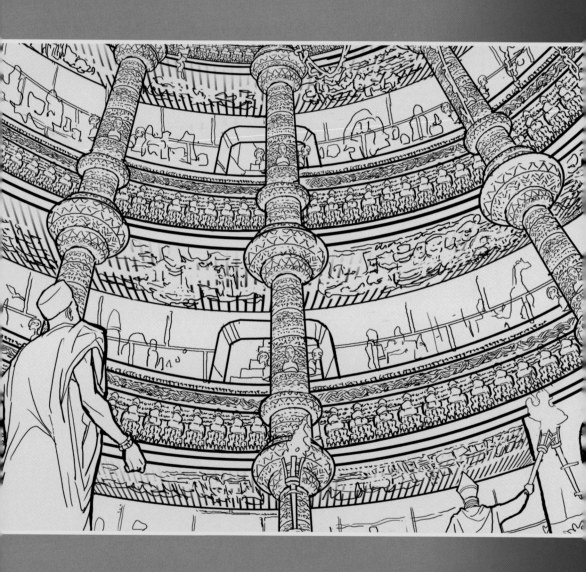

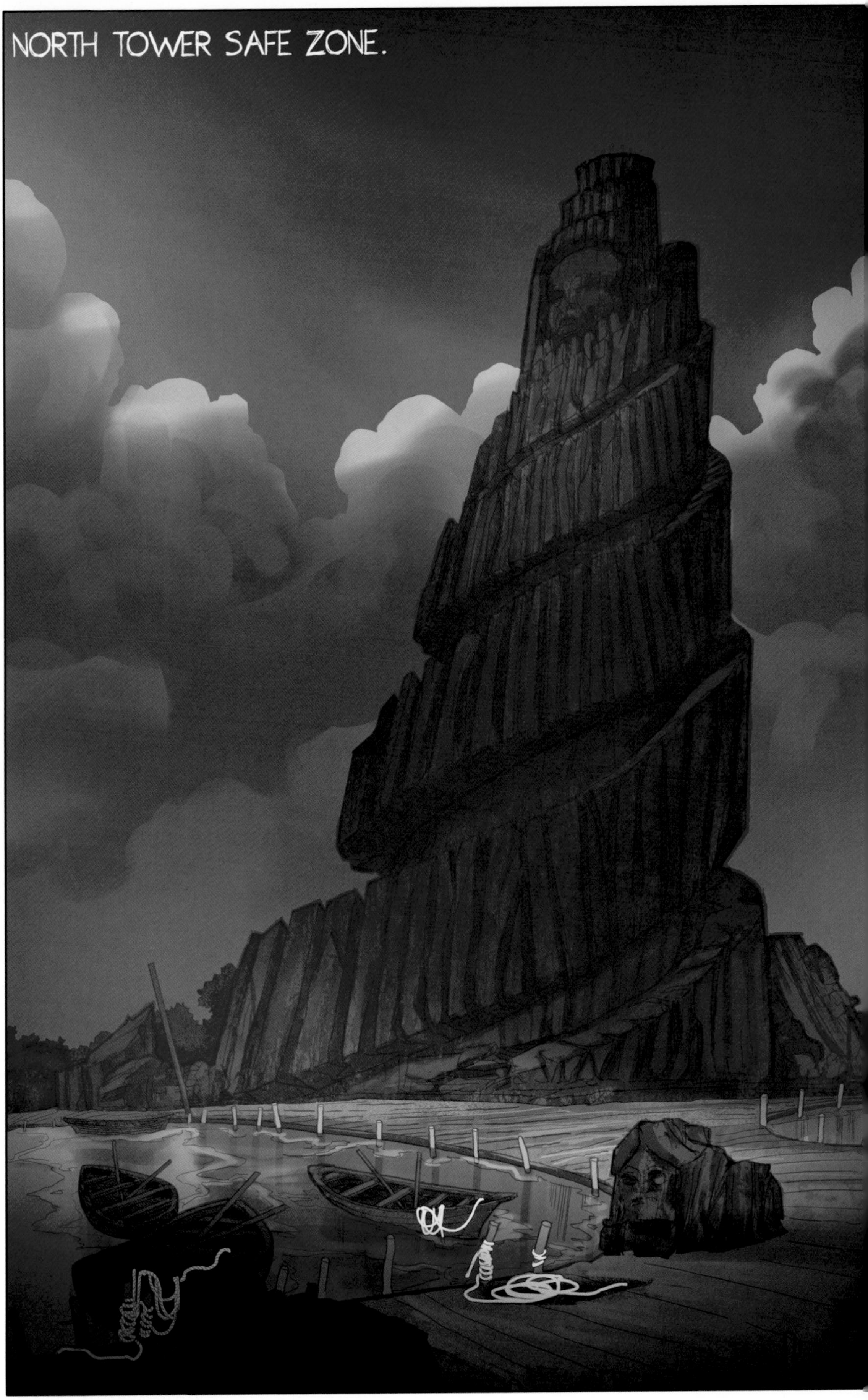
NORTH TOWER SAFE ZONE.

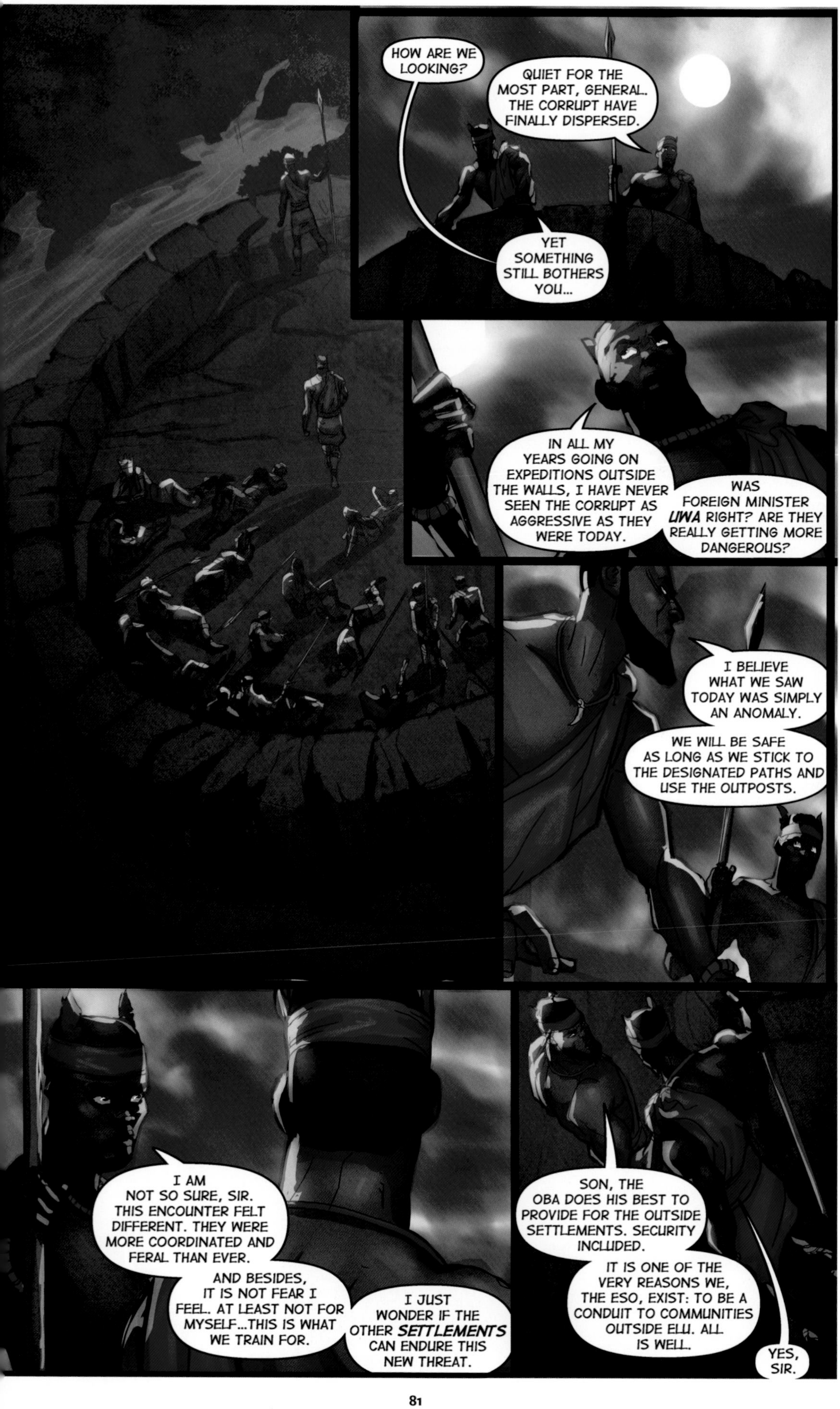
HOW ARE WE LOOKING?
QUIET FOR THE MOST PART, GENERAL. THE CORRUPT HAVE FINALLY DISPERSED.
YET SOMETHING STILL BOTHERS YOU...
IN ALL MY YEARS GOING ON EXPEDITIONS OUTSIDE THE WALLS, I HAVE NEVER SEEN THE CORRUPT AS AGGRESSIVE AS THEY WERE TODAY.
WAS FOREIGN MINISTER UWA RIGHT? ARE THEY REALLY GETTING MORE DANGEROUS?
I BELIEVE WHAT WE SAW TODAY WAS SIMPLY AN ANOMALY.
WE WILL BE SAFE AS LONG AS WE STICK TO THE DESIGNATED PATHS AND USE THE OUTPOSTS.
I AM NOT SO SURE, SIR. THIS ENCOUNTER FELT DIFFERENT. THEY WERE MORE COORDINATED AND FERAL THAN EVER.
AND BESIDES, IT IS NOT FEAR I FEEL. AT LEAST NOT FOR MYSELF...THIS IS WHAT WE TRAIN FOR.
I JUST WONDER IF THE OTHER SETTLEMENTS CAN ENDURE THIS NEW THREAT.
SON, THE OBA DOES HIS BEST TO PROVIDE FOR THE OUTSIDE SETTLEMENTS. SECURITY INCLUDED.
IT IS ONE OF THE VERY REASONS WE, THE ESO, EXIST: TO BE A CONDUIT TO COMMUNITIES OUTSIDE ELU. ALL IS WELL.
YES, SIR.

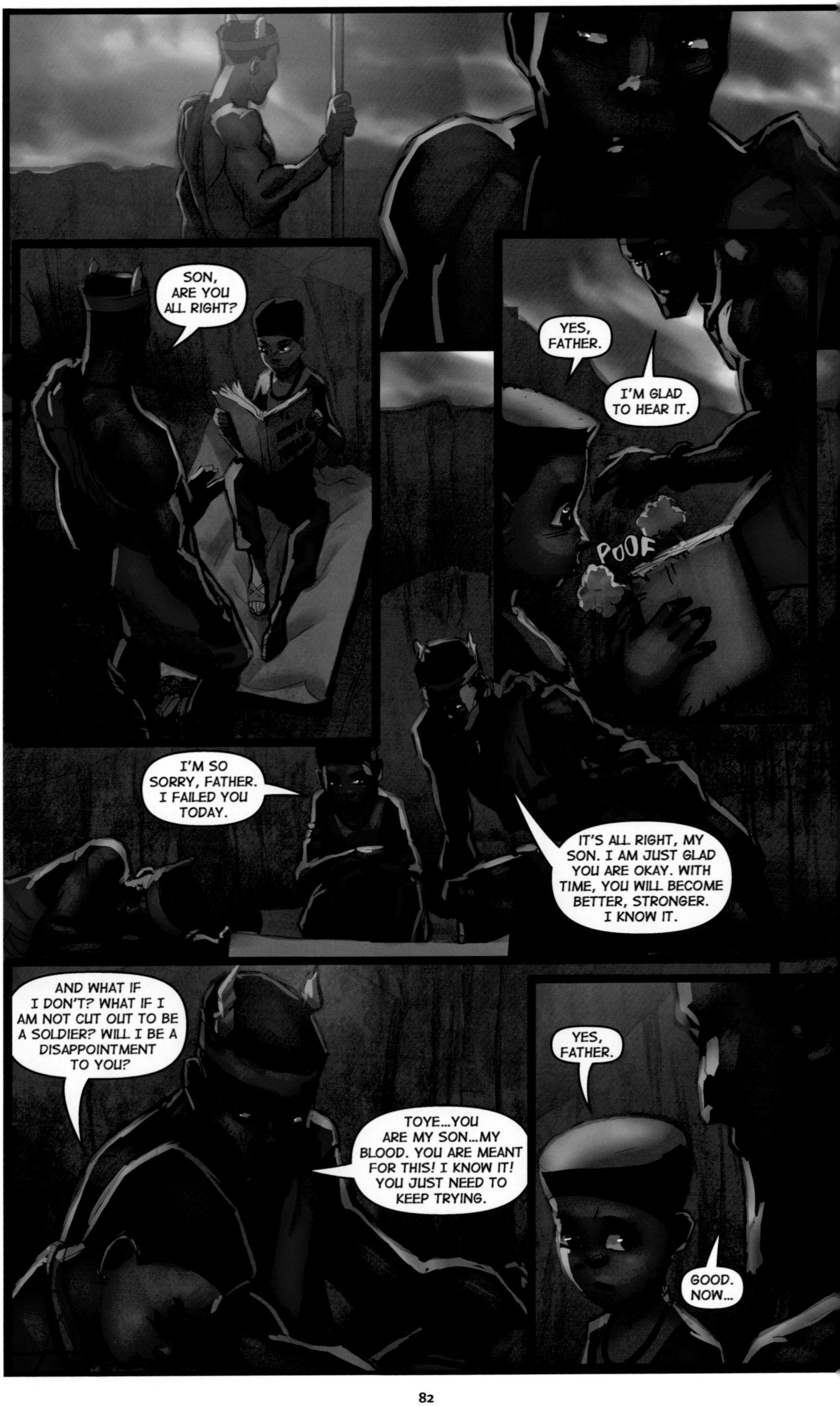
SON, ARE YOU ALL RIGHT?
YES, FATHER.
I'M GLAD TO HEAR IT.
POOF
I'M SO SORRY, FATHER. I FAILED YOU TODAY.
IT'S ALL RIGHT, MY SON. I AM JUST GLAD YOU ARE OKAY. WITH TIME, YOU WILL BECOME BETTER, STRONGER. I KNOW IT.
AND WHAT IF I DON'T? WHAT IF I AM NOT CUT OUT TO BE A SOLDIER? WILL I BE A DISAPPOINTMENT TO YOU?
TOYE...YOU ARE MY SON...MY BLOOD. YOU ARE MEANT FOR THIS! I KNOW IT! YOU JUST NEED TO KEEP TRYING.
YES, FATHER.
GOOD. NOW...

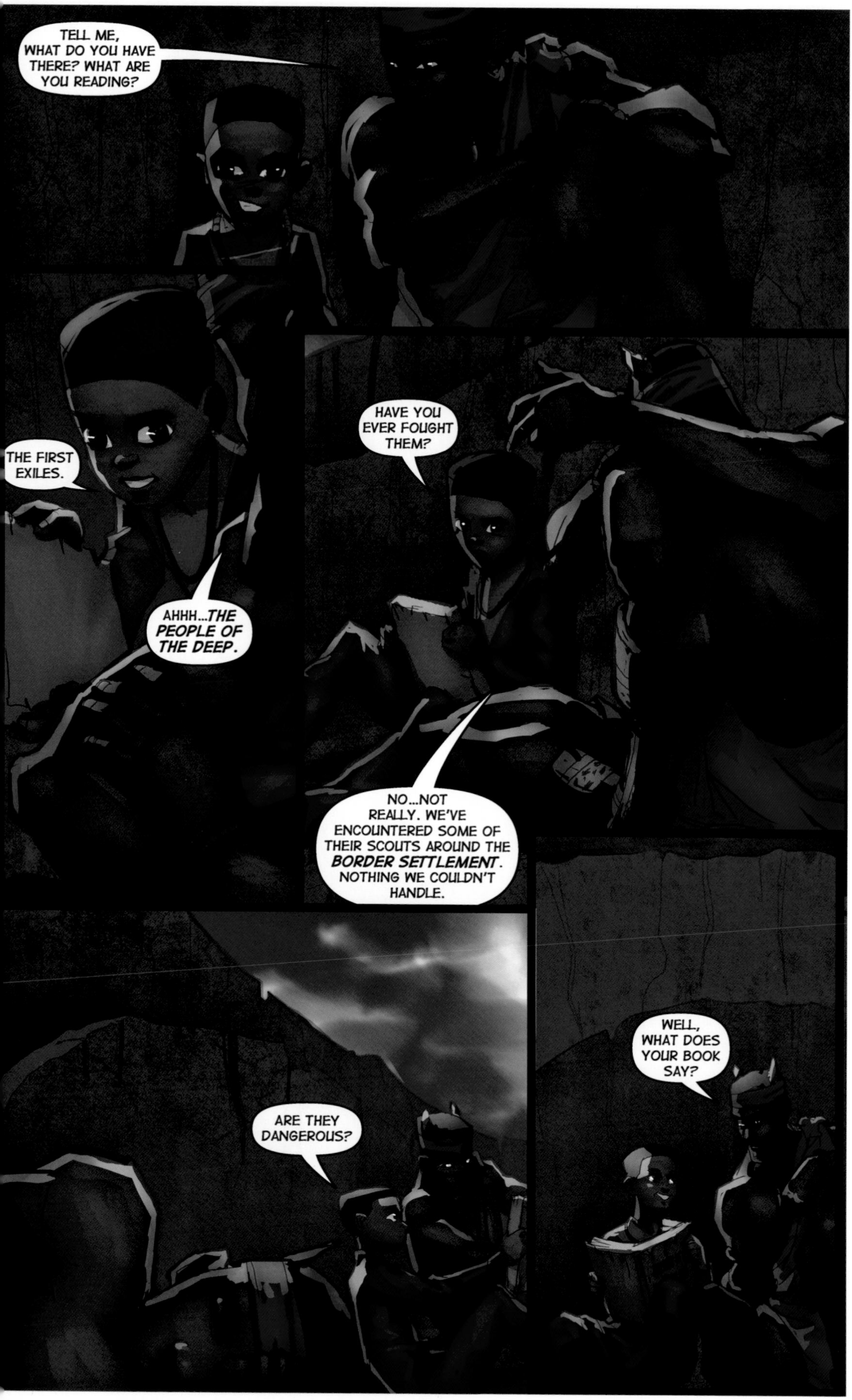
TELL ME, WHAT DO YOU HAVE THERE? WHAT ARE YOU READING?
THE FIRST EXILES.
AHHH...*THE PEOPLE OF THE DEEP*.
HAVE YOU EVER FOUGHT THEM?
NO...NOT REALLY. WE'VE ENCOUNTERED SOME OF THEIR SCOUTS AROUND THE ***BORDER SETTLEMENT***. NOTHING WE COULDN'T HANDLE.
ARE THEY DANGEROUS?
WELL, WHAT DOES YOUR BOOK SAY?

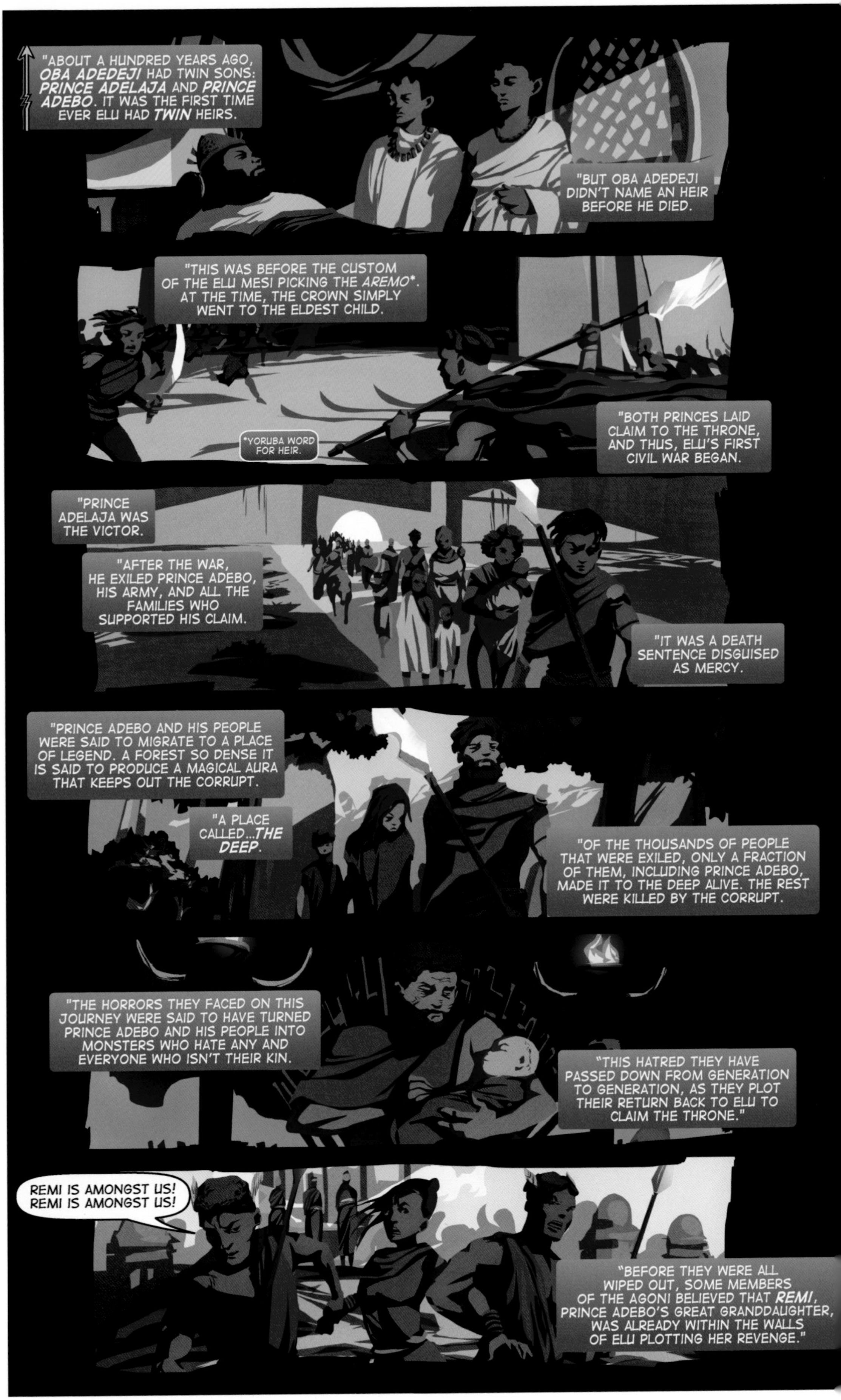
"ABOUT A HUNDRED YEARS AGO, OBA ADEDEJI HAD TWIN SONS: PRINCE ADELAJA AND PRINCE ADEBO. IT WAS THE FIRST TIME EVER ELU HAD TWIN HEIRS.
"BUT OBA ADEDEJI DIDN'T NAME AN HEIR BEFORE HE DIED.
"THIS WAS BEFORE THE CUSTOM OF THE ELU MESI PICKING THE AREMO*. AT THE TIME, THE CROWN SIMPLY WENT TO THE ELDEST CHILD.
*YORUBA WORD FOR HEIR.
"BOTH PRINCES LAID CLAIM TO THE THRONE, AND THUS, ELU'S FIRST CIVIL WAR BEGAN.
"PRINCE ADELAJA WAS THE VICTOR.
"AFTER THE WAR, HE EXILED PRINCE ADEBO, HIS ARMY, AND ALL THE FAMILIES WHO SUPPORTED HIS CLAIM.
"IT WAS A DEATH SENTENCE DISGUISED AS MERCY.
"PRINCE ADEBO AND HIS PEOPLE WERE SAID TO MIGRATE TO A PLACE OF LEGEND. A FOREST SO DENSE IT IS SAID TO PRODUCE A MAGICAL AURA THAT KEEPS OUT THE CORRUPT.
"A PLACE CALLED...THE DEEP.
"OF THE THOUSANDS OF PEOPLE THAT WERE EXILED, ONLY A FRACTION OF THEM, INCLUDING PRINCE ADEBO, MADE IT TO THE DEEP ALIVE. THE REST WERE KILLED BY THE CORRUPT.
"THE HORRORS THEY FACED ON THIS JOURNEY WERE SAID TO HAVE TURNED PRINCE ADEBO AND HIS PEOPLE INTO MONSTERS WHO HATE ANY AND EVERYONE WHO ISN'T THEIR KIN.
"THIS HATRED THEY HAVE PASSED DOWN FROM GENERATION TO GENERATION, AS THEY PLOT THEIR RETURN BACK TO ELU TO CLAIM THE THRONE."
REMI IS AMONGST US! REMI IS AMONGST US!
"BEFORE THEY WERE ALL WIPED OUT, SOME MEMBERS OF THE AGONI BELIEVED THAT REMI, PRINCE ADEBO'S GREAT GRANDDAUGHTER, WAS ALREADY WITHIN THE WALLS OF ELU PLOTTING HER REVENGE."

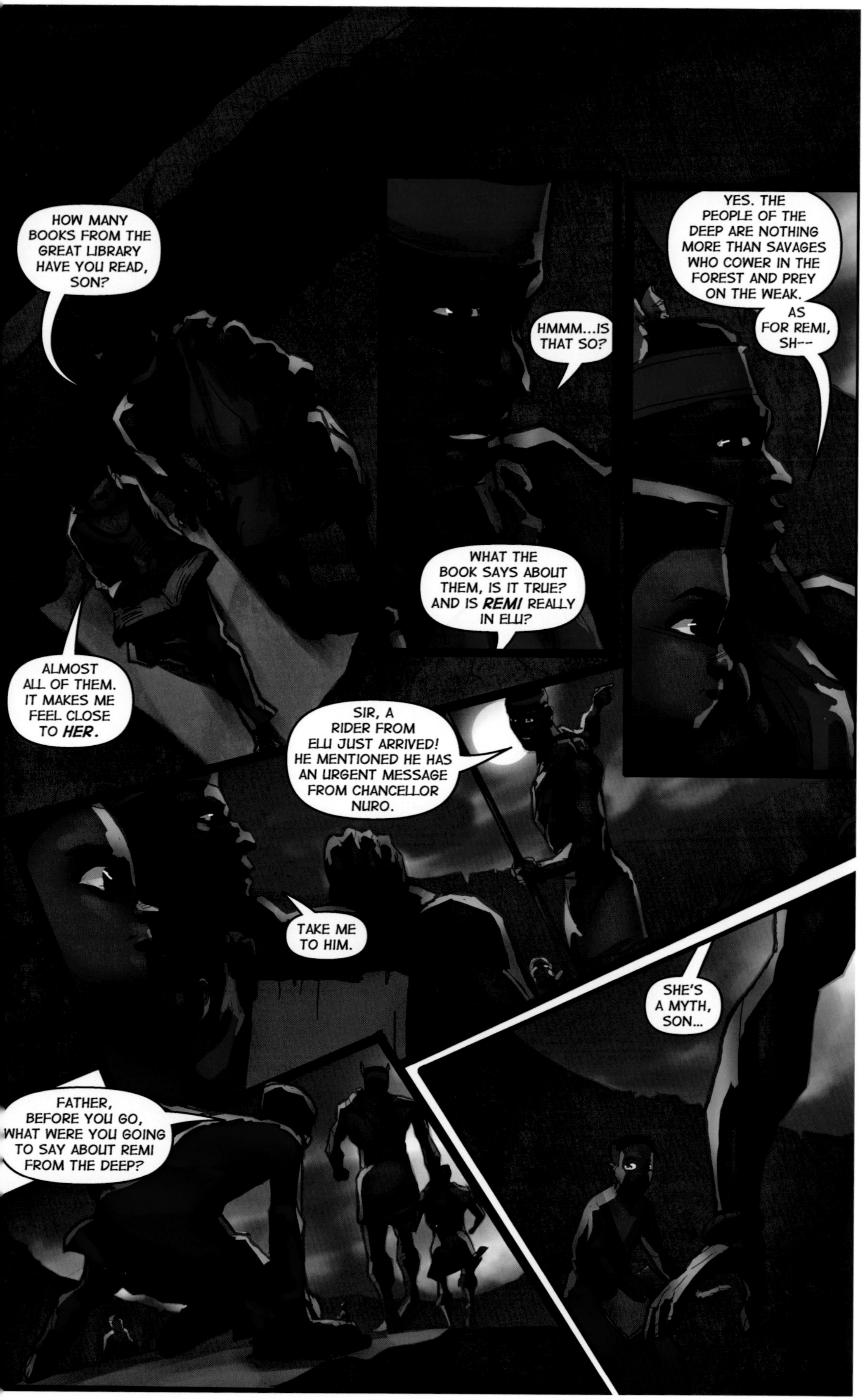
HOW MANY BOOKS FROM THE GREAT LIBRARY HAVE YOU READ, SON?
HMMM...IS THAT SO?
YES. THE PEOPLE OF THE DEEP ARE NOTHING MORE THAN SAVAGES WHO COWER IN THE FOREST AND PREY ON THE WEAK.
AS FOR REMI, SH--
WHAT THE BOOK SAYS ABOUT THEM, IS IT TRUE? AND IS REMI REALLY IN ELU?
ALMOST ALL OF THEM. IT MAKES ME FEEL CLOSE TO HER.
SIR, A RIDER FROM ELU JUST ARRIVED! HE MENTIONED HE HAS AN URGENT MESSAGE FROM CHANCELLOR NURO.
TAKE ME TO HIM.
SHE'S A MYTH, SON...
FATHER, BEFORE YOU GO, WHAT WERE YOU GOING TO SAY ABOUT REMI FROM THE DEEP?

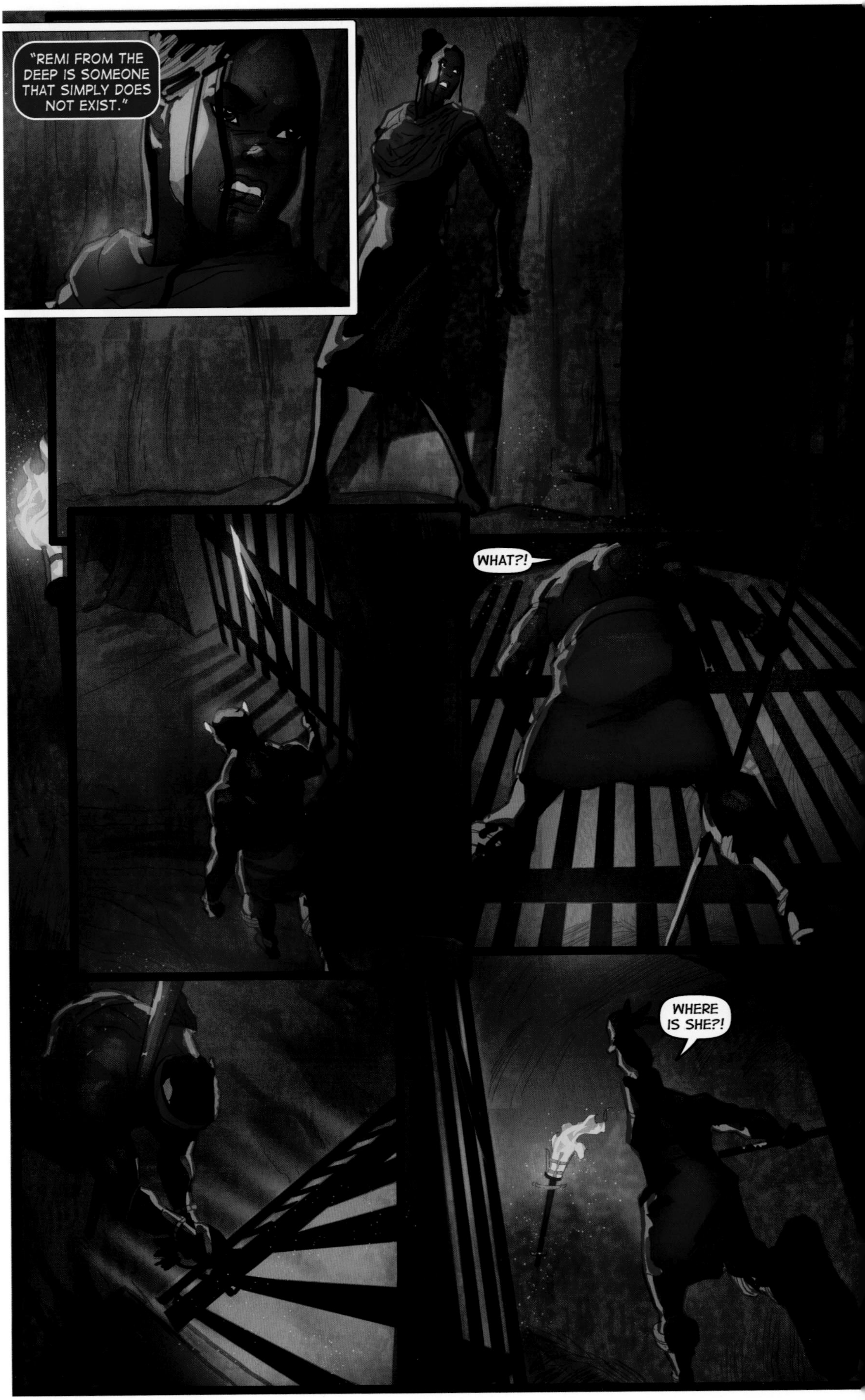
"REMI FROM THE DEEP IS SOMEONE THAT SIMPLY DOES NOT EXIST."
WHAT?!
WHERE IS SHE?!

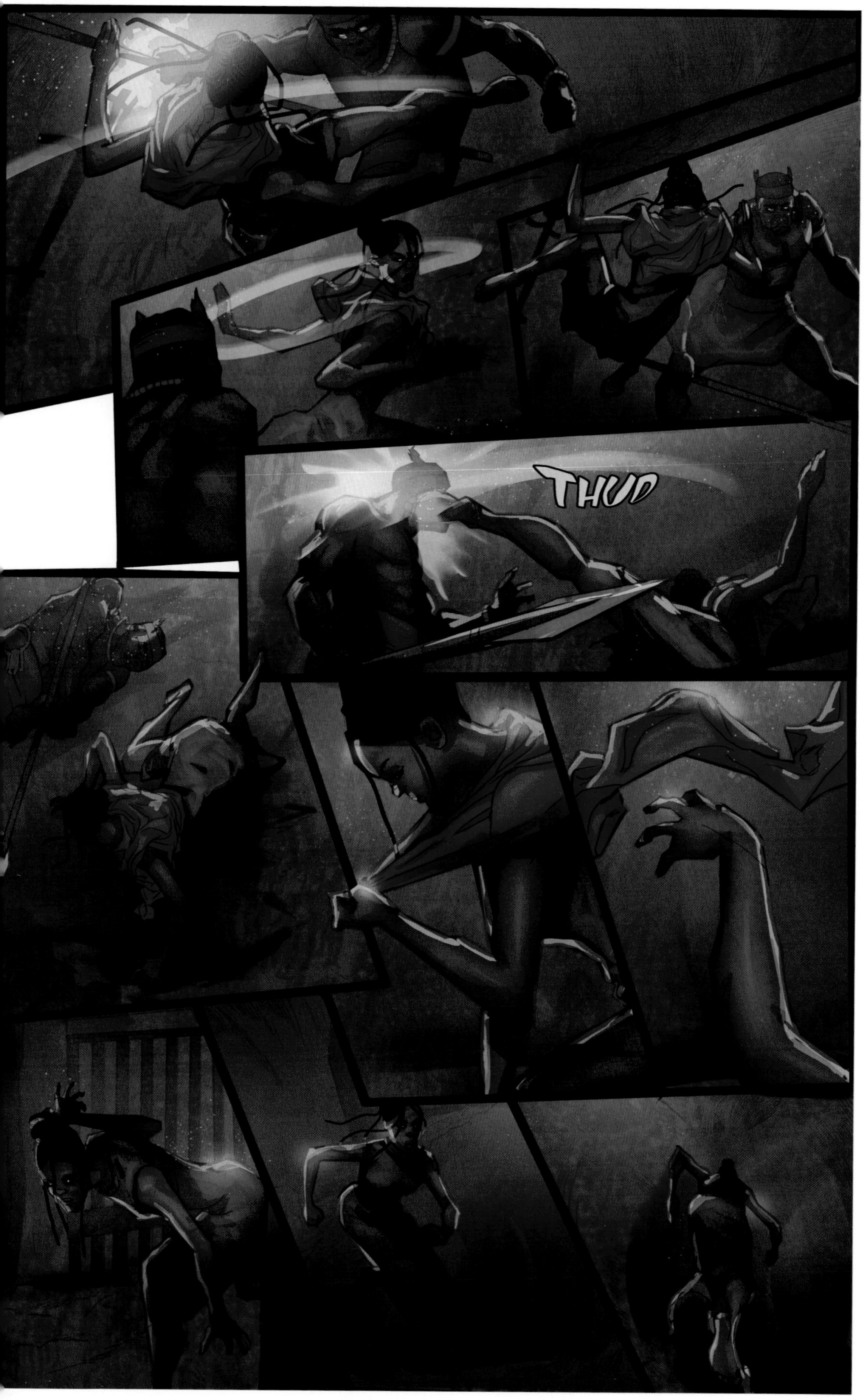
THUD

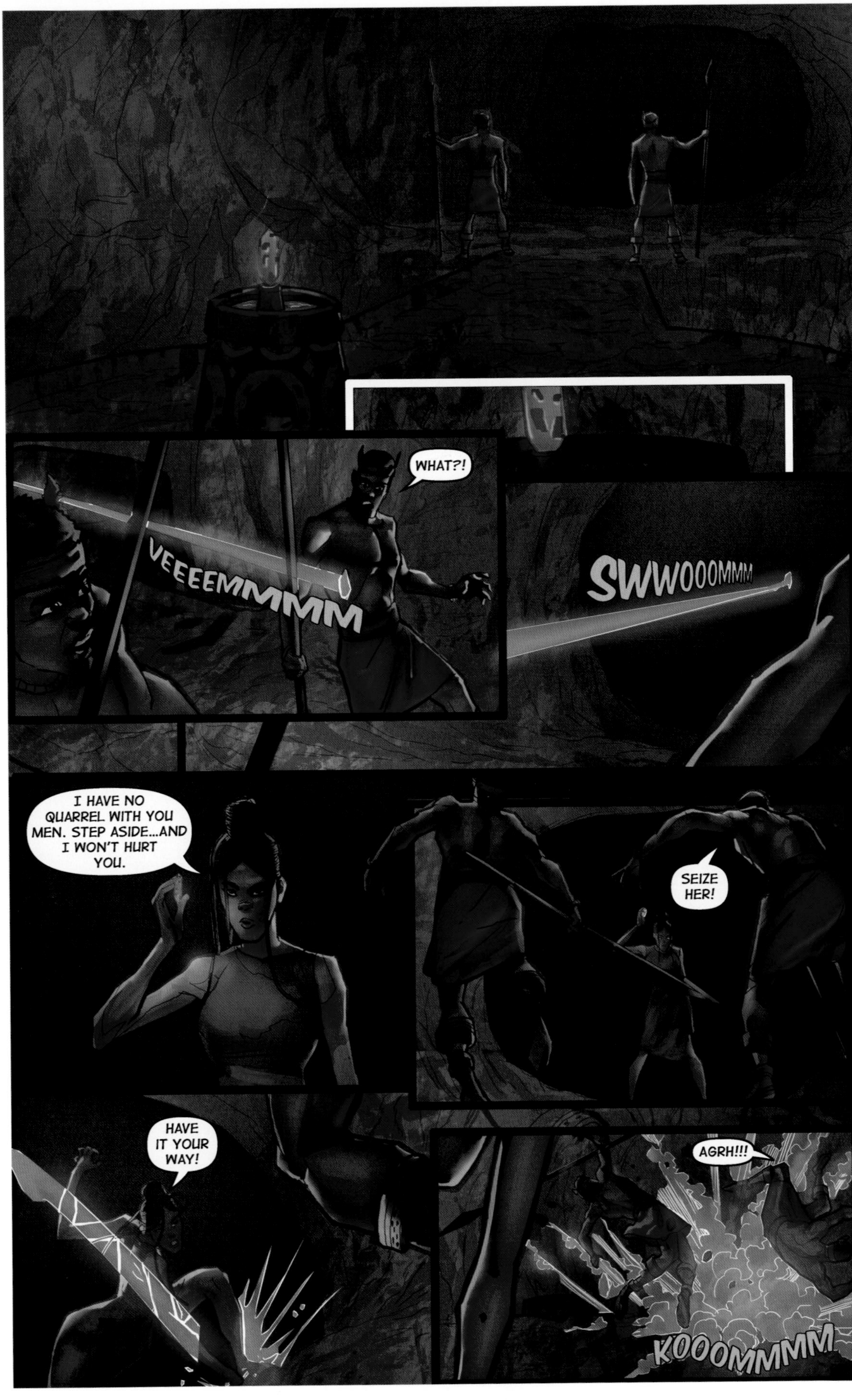
WHAT?!
VEEEEMMMMM
SWWOOOMMM
I HAVE NO QUARREL WITH YOU MEN. STEP ASIDE...AND I WON'T HURT YOU.
SEIZE HER!
HAVE IT YOUR WAY!
AGRH!!!
KOOOMMMM

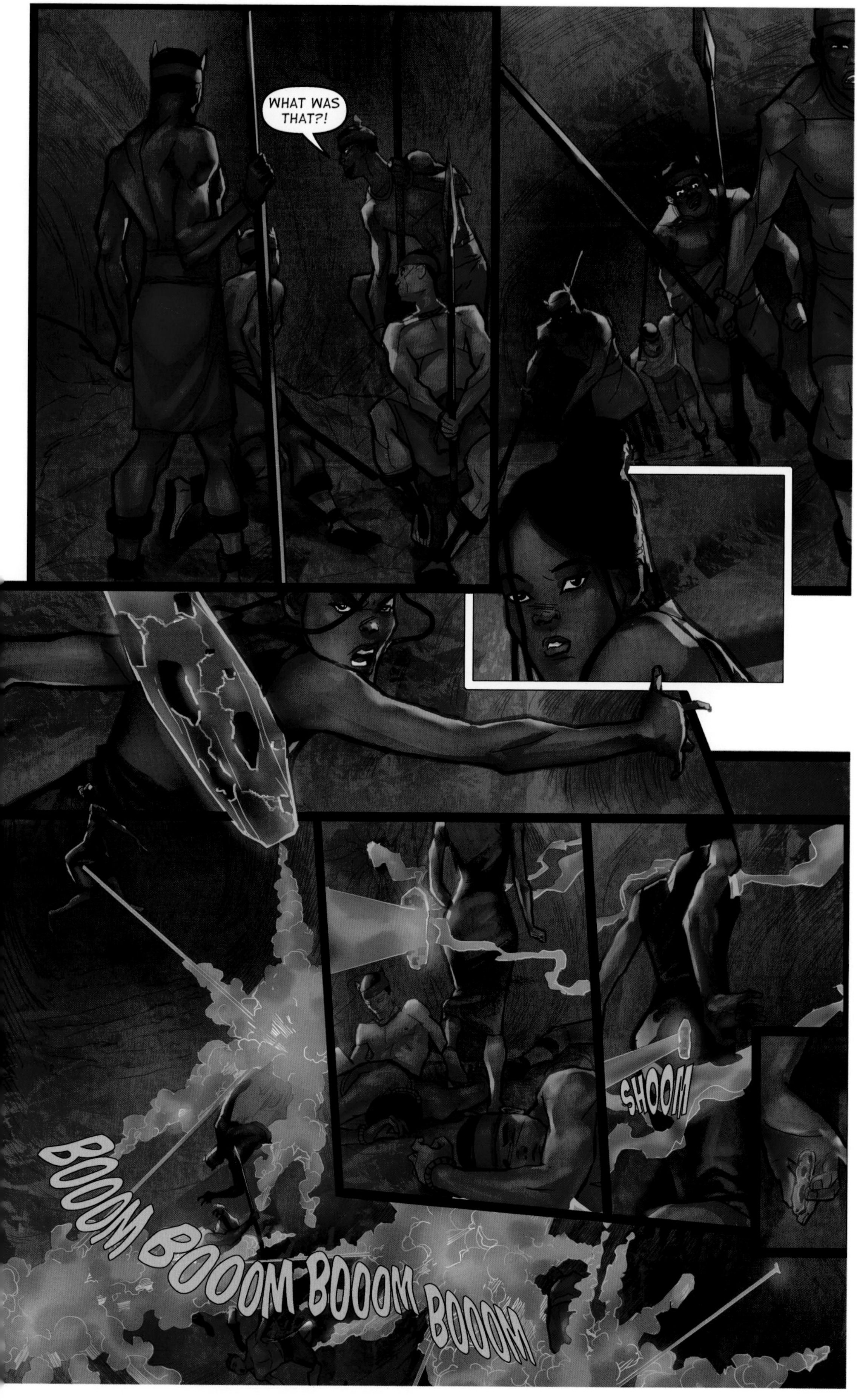
WHAT WAS THAT?!
SHOOM
BOOOM BOOOM BOOOM BOOOM

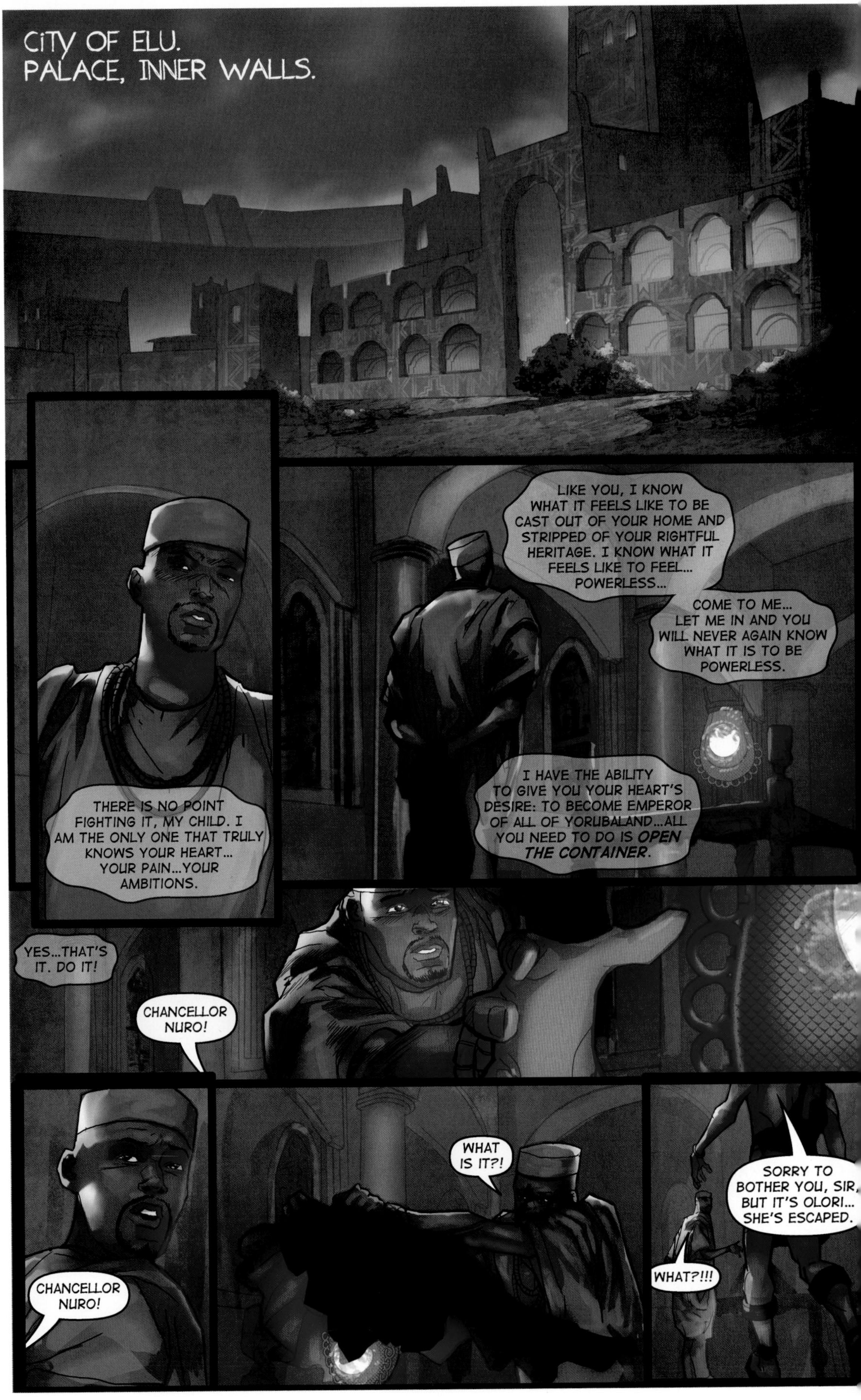

CITY OF ELU.
PALACE, INNER WALLS.
LIKE YOU, I KNOW WHAT IT FEELS LIKE TO BE CAST OUT OF YOUR HOME AND STRIPPED OF YOUR RIGHTFUL HERITAGE. I KNOW WHAT IT FEELS LIKE TO FEEL... POWERLESS...
COME TO ME... LET ME IN AND YOU WILL NEVER AGAIN KNOW WHAT IT IS TO BE POWERLESS.
I HAVE THE ABILITY TO GIVE YOU YOUR HEART'S DESIRE: TO BECOME EMPEROR OF ALL OF YORUBALAND...ALL YOU NEED TO DO IS OPEN THE CONTAINER.
THERE IS NO POINT FIGHTING IT, MY CHILD. I AM THE ONLY ONE THAT TRULY KNOWS YOUR HEART... YOUR PAIN...YOUR AMBITIONS.
YES...THAT'S IT. DO IT!
CHANCELLOR NURO!
CHANCELLOR NURO!
WHAT IS IT?!
SORRY TO BOTHER YOU, SIR, BUT IT'S OLORI... SHE'S ESCAPED.
WHAT?!!!

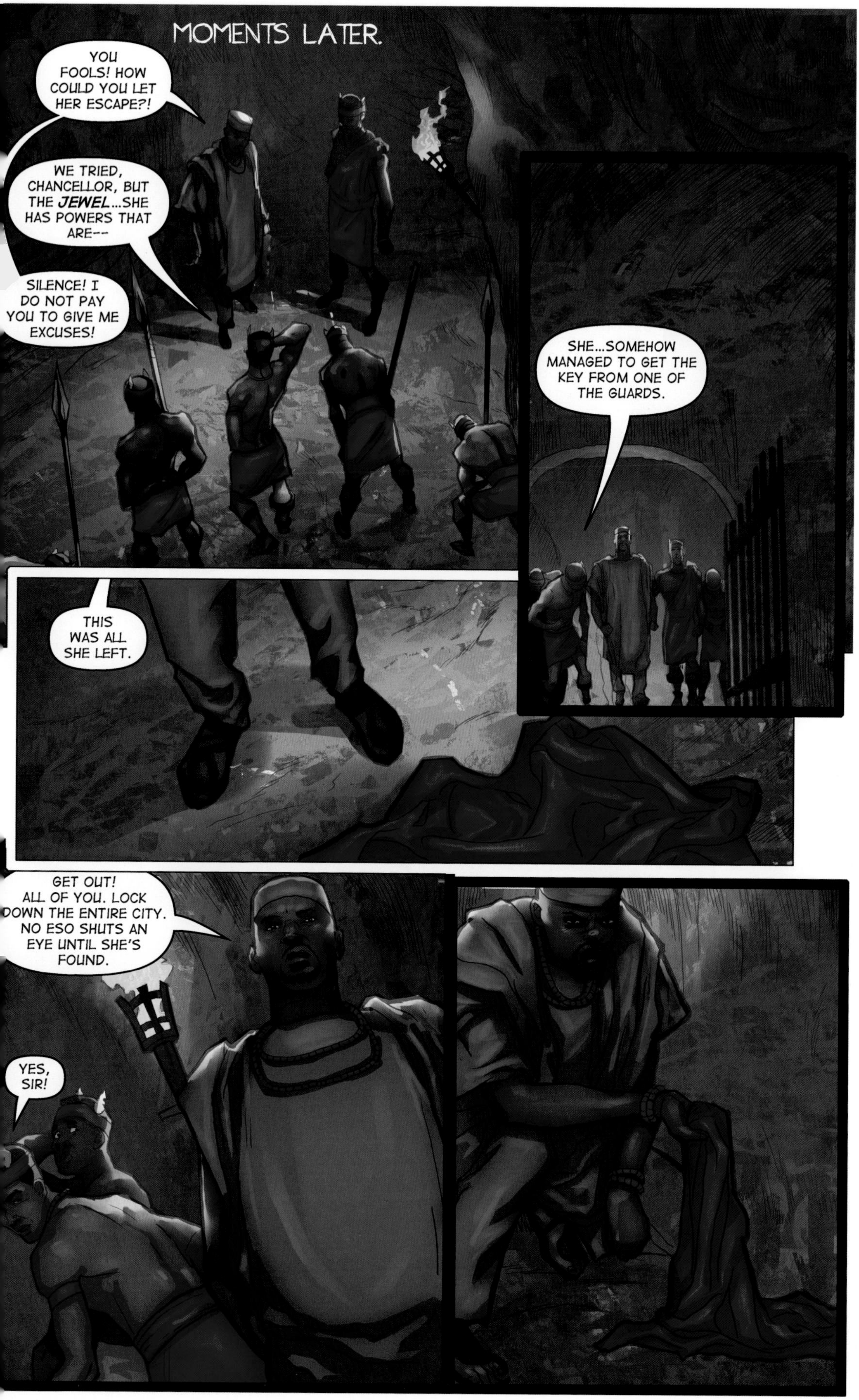
MOMENTS LATER.
YOU FOOLS! HOW COULD YOU LET HER ESCAPE?!
WE TRIED, CHANCELLOR, BUT THE *JEWEL*...SHE HAS POWERS THAT ARE--
SILENCE! I DO NOT PAY YOU TO GIVE ME EXCUSES!
SHE...SOMEHOW MANAGED TO GET THE KEY FROM ONE OF THE GUARDS.
THIS WAS ALL SHE LEFT.
GET OUT! ALL OF YOU. LOCK DOWN THE ENTIRE CITY. NO ESO SHUTS AN EYE UNTIL SHE'S FOUND.
YES, SIR!

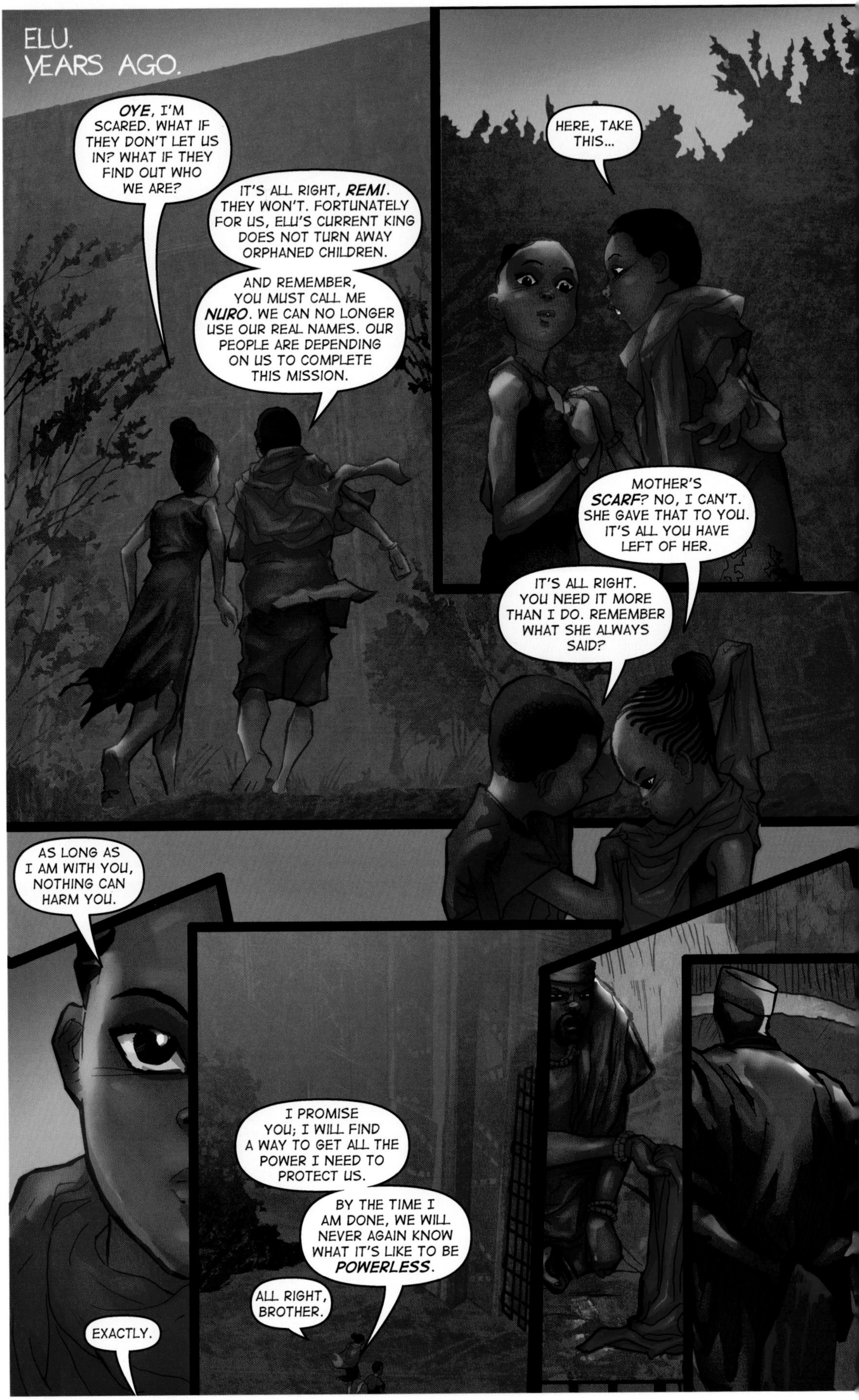
ELU.
YEARS AGO.
OYE, I'M SCARED. WHAT IF THEY DON'T LET US IN? WHAT IF THEY FIND OUT WHO WE ARE?
IT'S ALL RIGHT, REMI. THEY WON'T. FORTUNATELY FOR US, ELU'S CURRENT KING DOES NOT TURN AWAY ORPHANED CHILDREN.
AND REMEMBER, YOU MUST CALL ME NURO. WE CAN NO LONGER USE OUR REAL NAMES. OUR PEOPLE ARE DEPENDING ON US TO COMPLETE THIS MISSION.
HERE, TAKE THIS...
MOTHER'S SCARF? NO, I CAN'T. SHE GAVE THAT TO YOU. IT'S ALL YOU HAVE LEFT OF HER.
IT'S ALL RIGHT. YOU NEED IT MORE THAN I DO. REMEMBER WHAT SHE ALWAYS SAID?
AS LONG AS I AM WITH YOU, NOTHING CAN HARM YOU.
EXACTLY.
I PROMISE YOU; I WILL FIND A WAY TO GET ALL THE POWER I NEED TO PROTECT US.
BY THE TIME I AM DONE, WE WILL NEVER AGAIN KNOW WHAT IT'S LIKE TO BE POWERLESS.
ALL RIGHT, BROTHER.

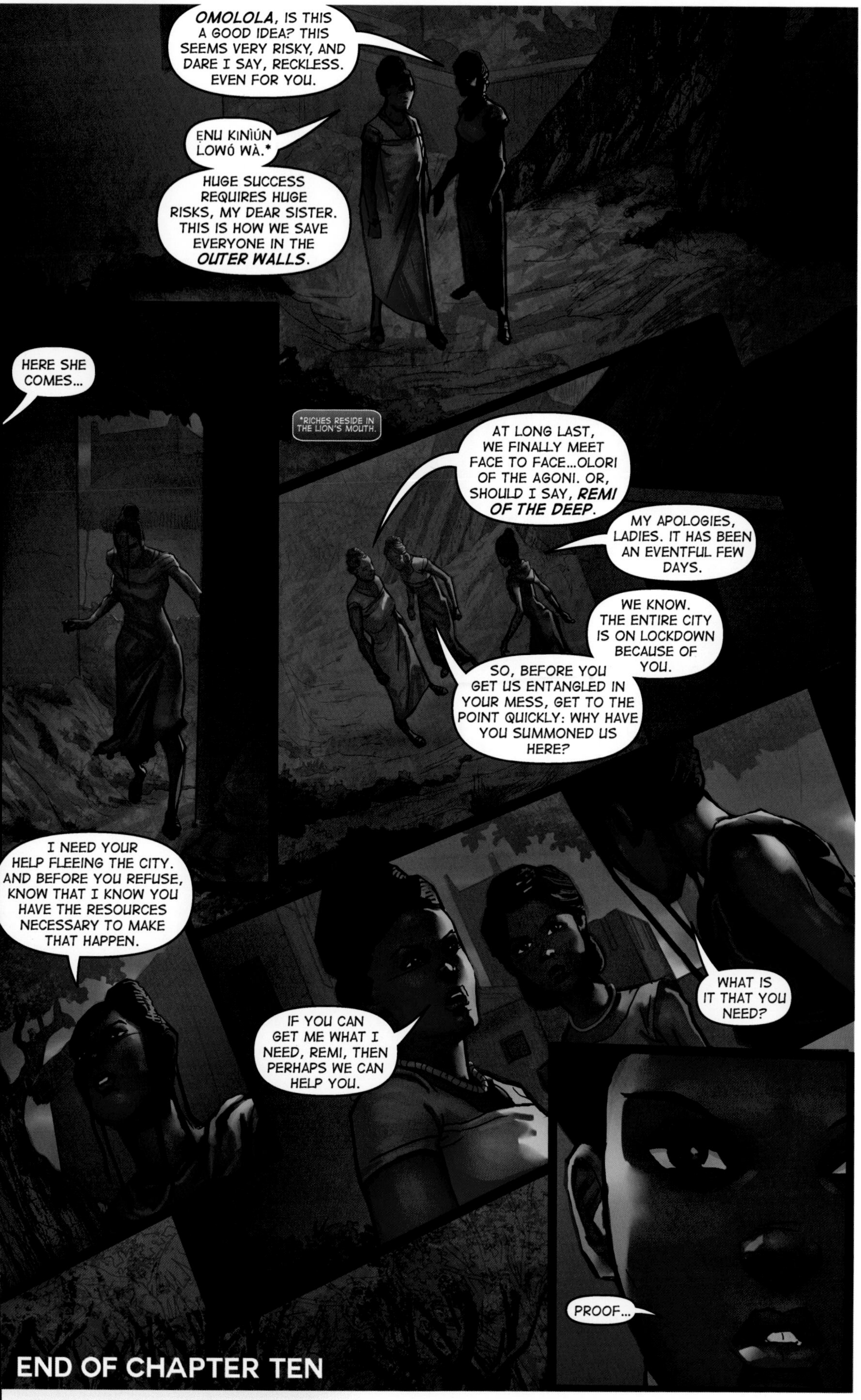
OMOLOLA, IS THIS A GOOD IDEA? THIS SEEMS VERY RISKY, AND DARE I SAY, RECKLESS. EVEN FOR YOU.
ẸNU KINÌÚN LOWÓ WÀ.*
HUGE SUCCESS REQUIRES HUGE RISKS, MY DEAR SISTER. THIS IS HOW WE SAVE EVERYONE IN THE OUTER WALLS.
*RICHES RESIDE IN THE LION'S MOUTH.
HERE SHE COMES...
AT LONG LAST, WE FINALLY MEET FACE TO FACE...OLORI OF THE AGONI. OR, SHOULD I SAY, REMI OF THE DEEP.
MY APOLOGIES, LADIES. IT HAS BEEN AN EVENTFUL FEW DAYS.
WE KNOW. THE ENTIRE CITY IS ON LOCKDOWN BECAUSE OF YOU.
SO, BEFORE YOU GET US ENTANGLED IN YOUR MESS, GET TO THE POINT QUICKLY: WHY HAVE YOU SUMMONED US HERE?
I NEED YOUR HELP FLEEING THE CITY. AND BEFORE YOU REFUSE, KNOW THAT I KNOW YOU HAVE THE RESOURCES NECESSARY TO MAKE THAT HAPPEN.
WHAT IS IT THAT YOU NEED?
IF YOU CAN GET ME WHAT I NEED, REMI, THEN PERHAPS WE CAN HELP YOU.
PROOF...
END OF CHAPTER TEN

CHAPTER ELEVEN

The People of The Deep

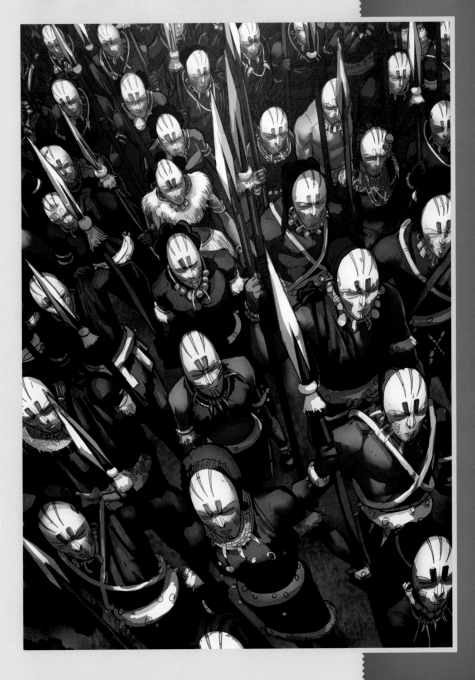

Descendants of exiled prince Debo, the People of the Deep are dangerous raiders who prey on defenseless settlements in Yorubaland.

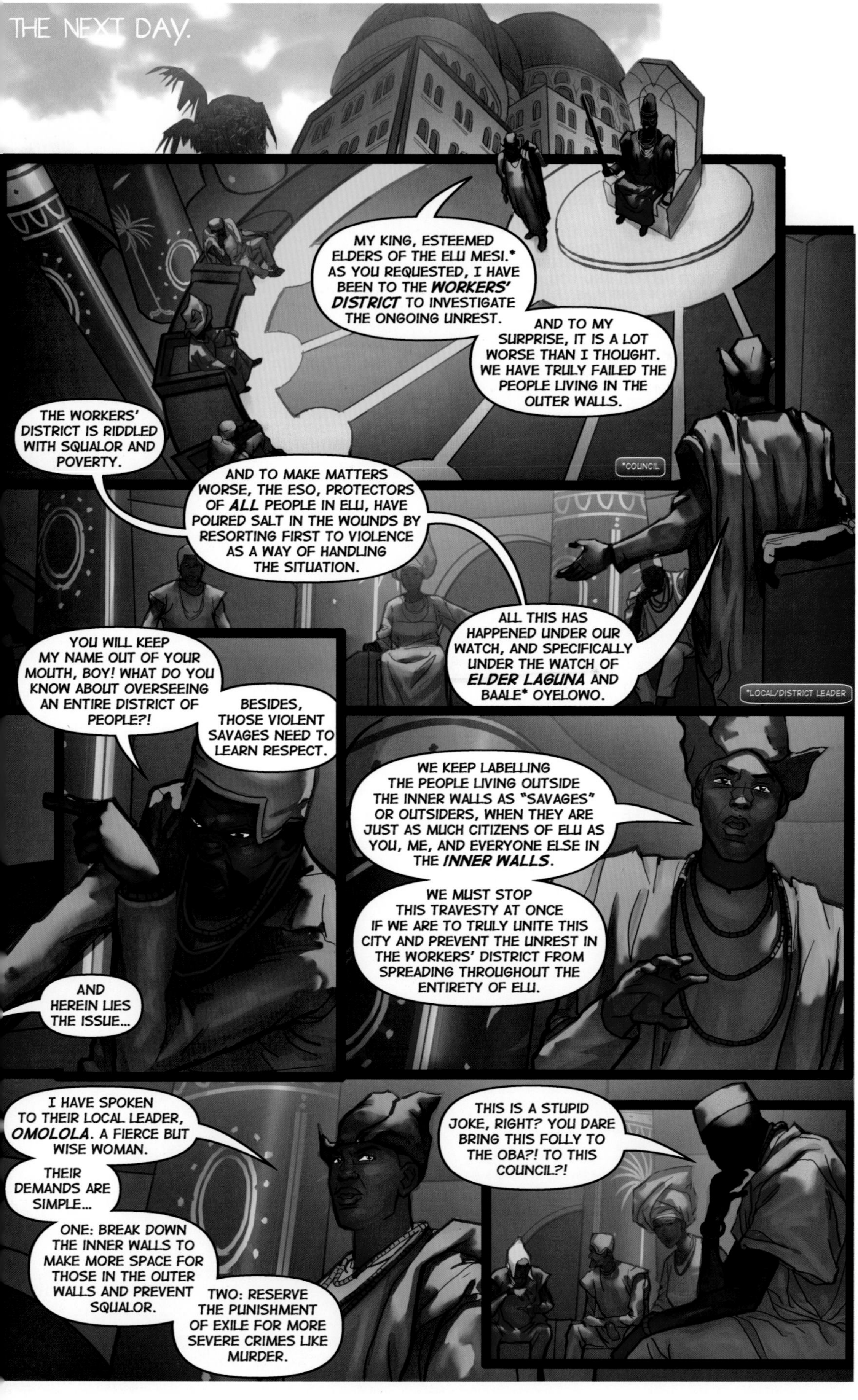
THE NEXT DAY.
MY KING, ESTEEMED ELDERS OF THE ELU MESI.* AS YOU REQUESTED, I HAVE BEEN TO THE WORKERS' DISTRICT TO INVESTIGATE THE ONGOING UNREST.
AND TO MY SURPRISE, IT IS A LOT WORSE THAN I THOUGHT. WE HAVE TRULY FAILED THE PEOPLE LIVING IN THE OUTER WALLS.
THE WORKERS' DISTRICT IS RIDDLED WITH SQUALOR AND POVERTY.
*COUNCIL
AND TO MAKE MATTERS WORSE, THE ESO, PROTECTORS OF ALL PEOPLE IN ELU, HAVE POURED SALT IN THE WOUNDS BY RESORTING FIRST TO VIOLENCE AS A WAY OF HANDLING THE SITUATION.
ALL THIS HAS HAPPENED UNDER OUR WATCH, AND SPECIFICALLY UNDER THE WATCH OF ELDER LAGUNA AND BAALE* OYELOWO.
*LOCAL/DISTRICT LEADER
YOU WILL KEEP MY NAME OUT OF YOUR MOUTH, BOY! WHAT DO YOU KNOW ABOUT OVERSEEING AN ENTIRE DISTRICT OF PEOPLE?!
BESIDES, THOSE VIOLENT SAVAGES NEED TO LEARN RESPECT.
AND HEREIN LIES THE ISSUE...
WE KEEP LABELLING THE PEOPLE LIVING OUTSIDE THE INNER WALLS AS "SAVAGES" OR OUTSIDERS, WHEN THEY ARE JUST AS MUCH CITIZENS OF ELU AS YOU, ME, AND EVERYONE ELSE IN THE INNER WALLS.
WE MUST STOP THIS TRAVESTY AT ONCE IF WE ARE TO TRULY UNITE THIS CITY AND PREVENT THE UNREST IN THE WORKERS' DISTRICT FROM SPREADING THROUGHOUT THE ENTIRETY OF ELU.
I HAVE SPOKEN TO THEIR LOCAL LEADER, OMOLOLA. A FIERCE BUT WISE WOMAN.
THEIR DEMANDS ARE SIMPLE...
ONE: BREAK DOWN THE INNER WALLS TO MAKE MORE SPACE FOR THOSE IN THE OUTER WALLS AND PREVENT SQUALOR.
TWO: RESERVE THE PUNISHMENT OF EXILE FOR MORE SEVERE CRIMES LIKE MURDER.
THIS IS A STUPID JOKE, RIGHT? YOU DARE BRING THIS FOLLY TO THE OBA?! TO THIS COUNCIL?!

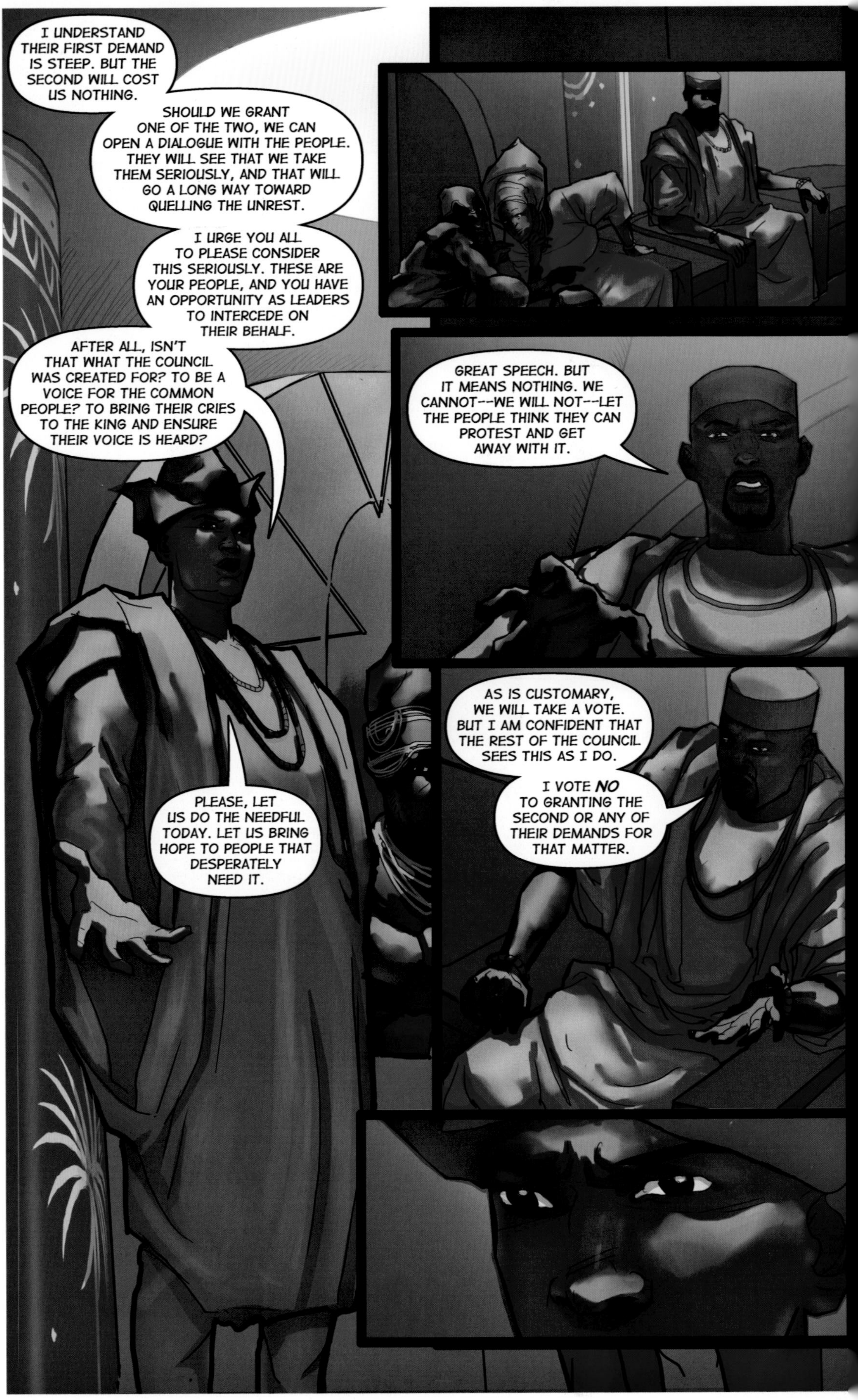
I UNDERSTAND THEIR FIRST DEMAND IS STEEP. BUT THE SECOND WILL COST US NOTHING.
SHOULD WE GRANT ONE OF THE TWO, WE CAN OPEN A DIALOGUE WITH THE PEOPLE. THEY WILL SEE THAT WE TAKE THEM SERIOUSLY, AND THAT WILL GO A LONG WAY TOWARD QUELLING THE UNREST.
I URGE YOU ALL TO PLEASE CONSIDER THIS SERIOUSLY. THESE ARE YOUR PEOPLE, AND YOU HAVE AN OPPORTUNITY AS LEADERS TO INTERCEDE ON THEIR BEHALF.
AFTER ALL, ISN'T THAT WHAT THE COUNCIL WAS CREATED FOR? TO BE A VOICE FOR THE COMMON PEOPLE? TO BRING THEIR CRIES TO THE KING AND ENSURE THEIR VOICE IS HEARD?
PLEASE, LET US DO THE NEEDFUL TODAY. LET US BRING HOPE TO PEOPLE THAT DESPERATELY NEED IT.
GREAT SPEECH. BUT IT MEANS NOTHING. WE CANNOT--WE WILL NOT--LET THE PEOPLE THINK THEY CAN PROTEST AND GET AWAY WITH IT.
AS IS CUSTOMARY, WE WILL TAKE A VOTE. BUT I AM CONFIDENT THAT THE REST OF THE COUNCIL SEES THIS AS I DO.
I VOTE ***NO*** TO GRANTING THE SECOND OR ANY OF THEIR DEMANDS FOR THAT MATTER.

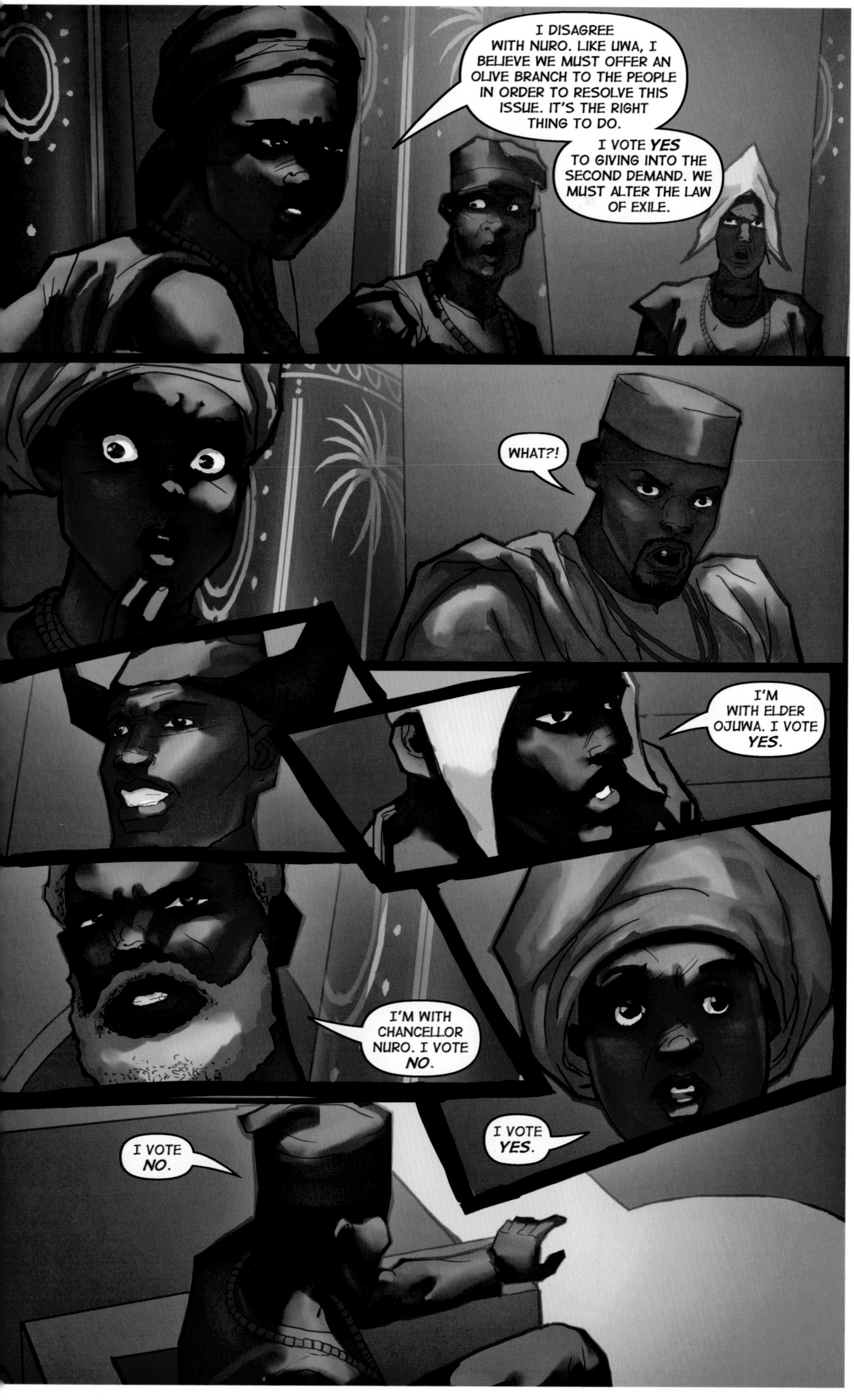
I DISAGREE WITH NURO. LIKE UWA, I BELIEVE WE MUST OFFER AN OLIVE BRANCH TO THE PEOPLE IN ORDER TO RESOLVE THIS ISSUE. IT'S THE RIGHT THING TO DO.
I VOTE *YES* TO GIVING INTO THE SECOND DEMAND. WE MUST ALTER THE LAW OF EXILE.
WHAT?!
I'M WITH ELDER OJUWA. I VOTE *YES*.
I'M WITH CHANCELLOR NURO. I VOTE *NO*.
I VOTE *YES*.
I VOTE *NO*.

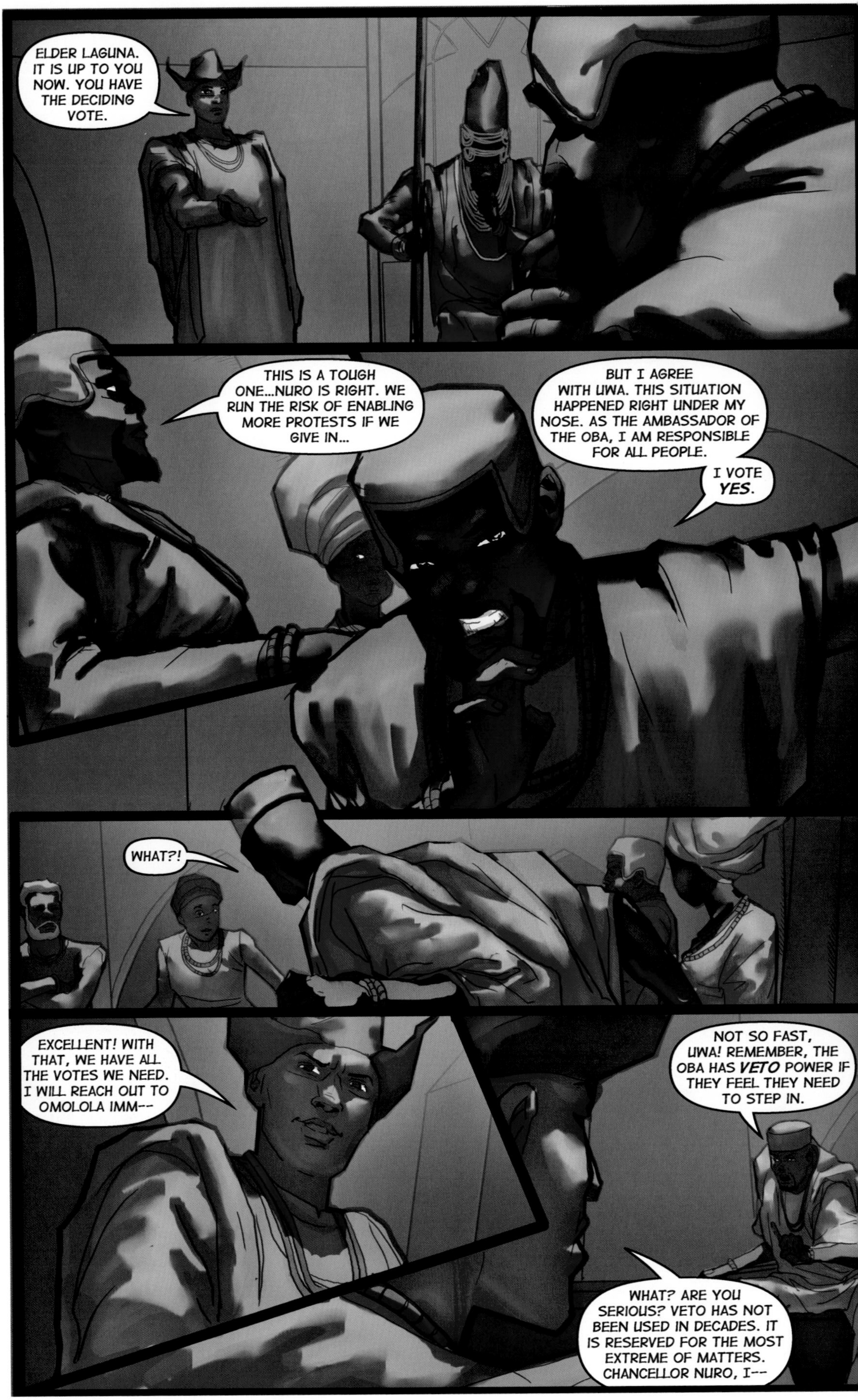
ELDER LAGUNA. IT IS UP TO YOU NOW. YOU HAVE THE DECIDING VOTE.
THIS IS A TOUGH ONE...NURO IS RIGHT. WE RUN THE RISK OF ENABLING MORE PROTESTS IF WE GIVE IN...
BUT I AGREE WITH UWA. THIS SITUATION HAPPENED RIGHT UNDER MY NOSE. AS THE AMBASSADOR OF THE OBA, I AM RESPONSIBLE FOR ALL PEOPLE.
I VOTE ***YES***.
WHAT?!
EXCELLENT! WITH THAT, WE HAVE ALL THE VOTES WE NEED. I WILL REACH OUT TO OMOLOLA IMM--
NOT SO FAST, UWA! REMEMBER, THE OBA HAS ***VETO*** POWER IF THEY FEEL THEY NEED TO STEP IN.
WHAT? ARE YOU SERIOUS? VETO HAS NOT BEEN USED IN DECADES. IT IS RESERVED FOR THE MOST EXTREME OF MATTERS. CHANCELLOR NURO, I--

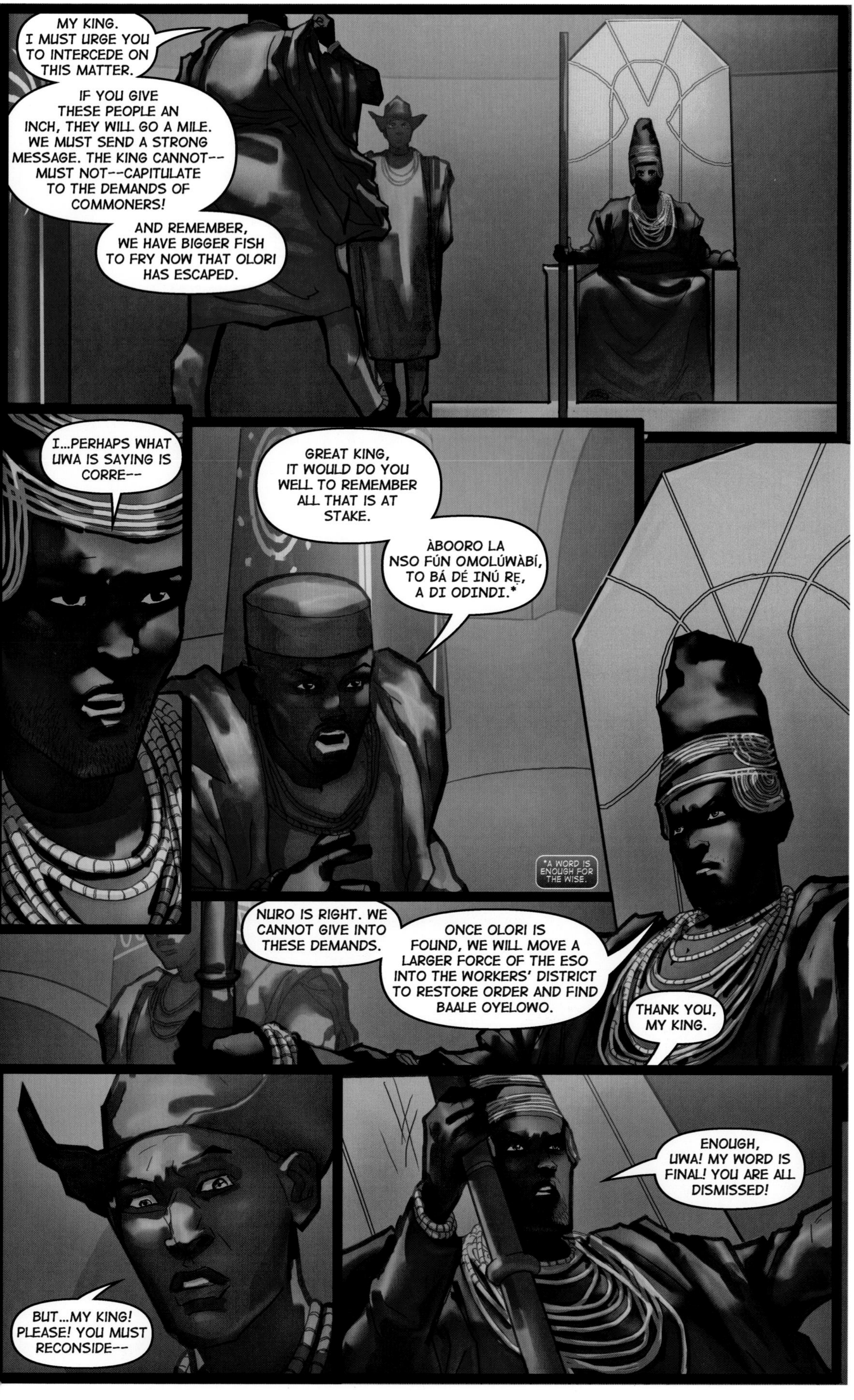
MY KING. I MUST URGE YOU TO INTERCEDE ON THIS MATTER.
IF YOU GIVE THESE PEOPLE AN INCH, THEY WILL GO A MILE. WE MUST SEND A STRONG MESSAGE. THE KING CANNOT--MUST NOT--CAPITULATE TO THE DEMANDS OF COMMONERS!
AND REMEMBER, WE HAVE BIGGER FISH TO FRY NOW THAT OLORI HAS ESCAPED.
I...PERHAPS WHAT UWA IS SAYING IS CORRE--
GREAT KING, IT WOULD DO YOU WELL TO REMEMBER ALL THAT IS AT STAKE.
ÀBOORO LA NSO FÚN OMOLÚWÀBÍ, TO BÁ DÉ INÚ RẸ, A DI ODINDI.*
*A WORD IS ENOUGH FOR THE WISE.
NURO IS RIGHT. WE CANNOT GIVE INTO THESE DEMANDS.
ONCE OLORI IS FOUND, WE WILL MOVE A LARGER FORCE OF THE ESO INTO THE WORKERS' DISTRICT TO RESTORE ORDER AND FIND BAALE OYELOWO.
THANK YOU, MY KING.
BUT...MY KING! PLEASE! YOU MUST RECONSIDE--
ENOUGH, UWA! MY WORD IS FINAL! YOU ARE ALL DISMISSED!

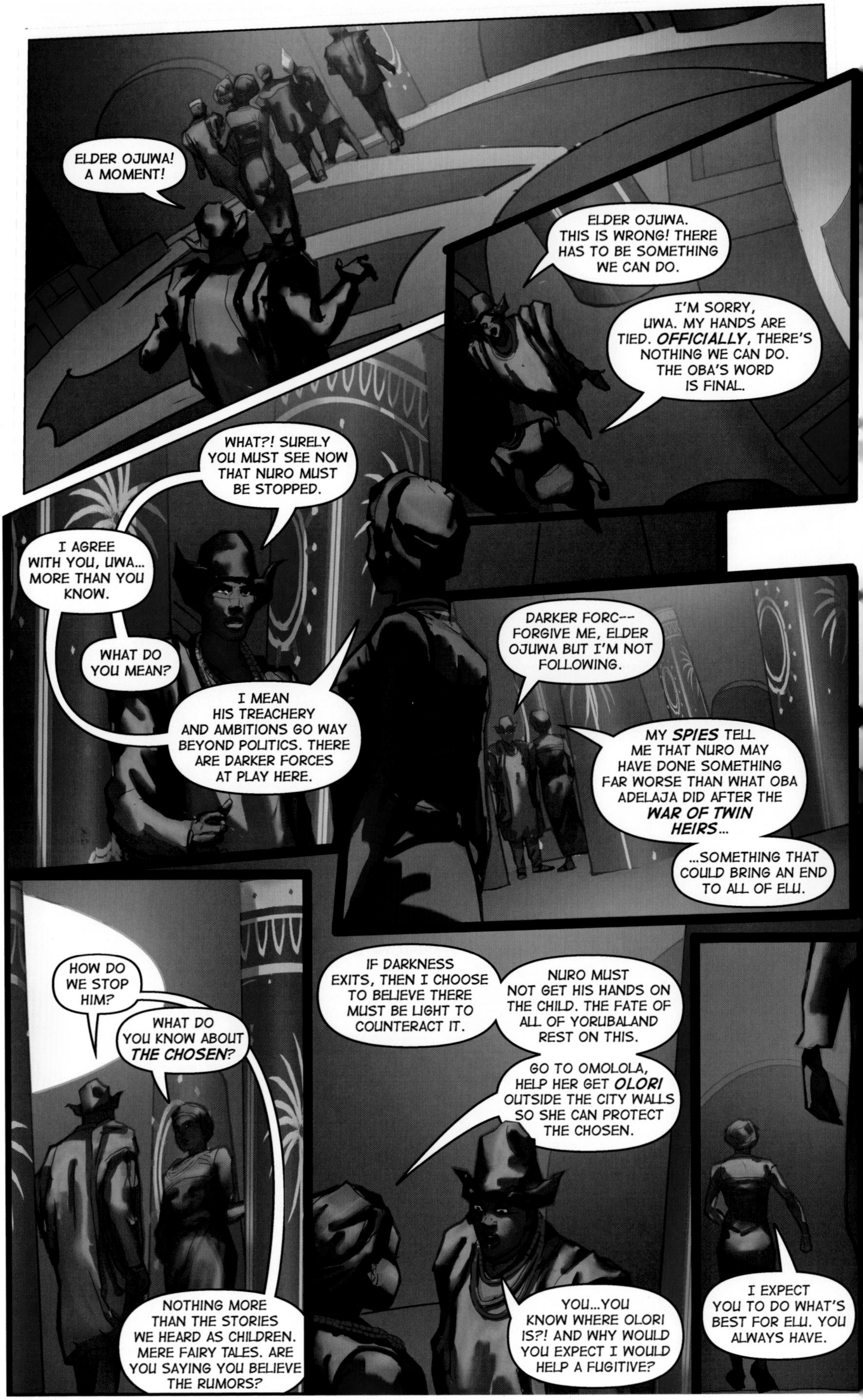
ELDER OJUWA! A MOMENT!
ELDER OJUWA. THIS IS WRONG! THERE HAS TO BE SOMETHING WE CAN DO.
I'M SORRY, UWA. MY HANDS ARE TIED. OFFICIALLY, THERE'S NOTHING WE CAN DO. THE OBA'S WORD IS FINAL.
WHAT?! SURELY YOU MUST SEE NOW THAT NURO MUST BE STOPPED.
I AGREE WITH YOU, UWA... MORE THAN YOU KNOW.
WHAT DO YOU MEAN?
I MEAN HIS TREACHERY AND AMBITIONS GO WAY BEYOND POLITICS. THERE ARE DARKER FORCES AT PLAY HERE.
DARKER FORC-- FORGIVE ME, ELDER OJUWA BUT I'M NOT FOLLOWING.
MY SPIES TELL ME THAT NURO MAY HAVE DONE SOMETHING FAR WORSE THAN WHAT OBA ADELAJA DID AFTER THE WAR OF TWIN HEIRS...
...SOMETHING THAT COULD BRING AN END TO ALL OF ELU.
HOW DO WE STOP HIM?
WHAT DO YOU KNOW ABOUT THE CHOSEN?
NOTHING MORE THAN THE STORIES WE HEARD AS CHILDREN. MERE FAIRY TALES. ARE YOU SAYING YOU BELIEVE THE RUMORS?
IF DARKNESS EXITS, THEN I CHOOSE TO BELIEVE THERE MUST BE LIGHT TO COUNTERACT IT.
NURO MUST NOT GET HIS HANDS ON THE CHILD. THE FATE OF ALL OF YORUBALAND REST ON THIS.
GO TO OMOLOLA, HELP HER GET OLORI OUTSIDE THE CITY WALLS SO SHE CAN PROTECT THE CHOSEN.
YOU...YOU KNOW WHERE OLORI IS?! AND WHY WOULD YOU EXPECT I WOULD HELP A FUGITIVE?
I EXPECT YOU TO DO WHAT'S BEST FOR ELU. YOU ALWAYS HAVE.

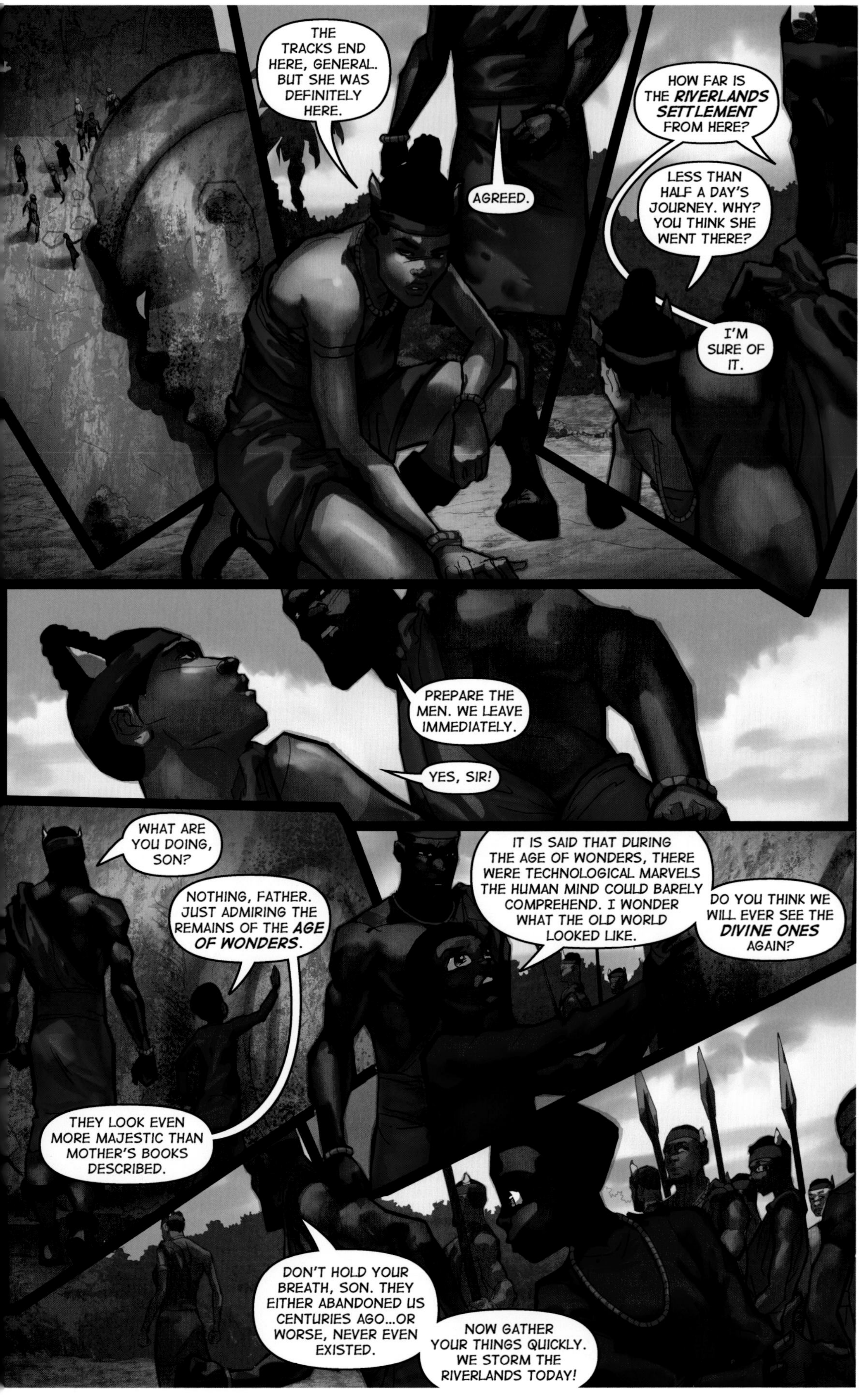
THE TRACKS END HERE, GENERAL. BUT SHE WAS DEFINITELY HERE.
AGREED.
HOW FAR IS THE RIVERLANDS SETTLEMENT FROM HERE?
LESS THAN HALF A DAY'S JOURNEY. WHY? YOU THINK SHE WENT THERE?
I'M SURE OF IT.
PREPARE THE MEN. WE LEAVE IMMEDIATELY.
YES, SIR!
WHAT ARE YOU DOING, SON?
NOTHING, FATHER. JUST ADMIRING THE REMAINS OF THE AGE OF WONDERS.
THEY LOOK EVEN MORE MAJESTIC THAN MOTHER'S BOOKS DESCRIBED.
IT IS SAID THAT DURING THE AGE OF WONDERS, THERE WERE TECHNOLOGICAL MARVELS THE HUMAN MIND COULD BARELY COMPREHEND. I WONDER WHAT THE OLD WORLD LOOKED LIKE.
DO YOU THINK WE WILL EVER SEE THE DIVINE ONES AGAIN?
DON'T HOLD YOUR BREATH, SON. THEY EITHER ABANDONED US CENTURIES AGO...OR WORSE, NEVER EVEN EXISTED.
NOW GATHER YOUR THINGS QUICKLY. WE STORM THE RIVERLANDS TODAY!

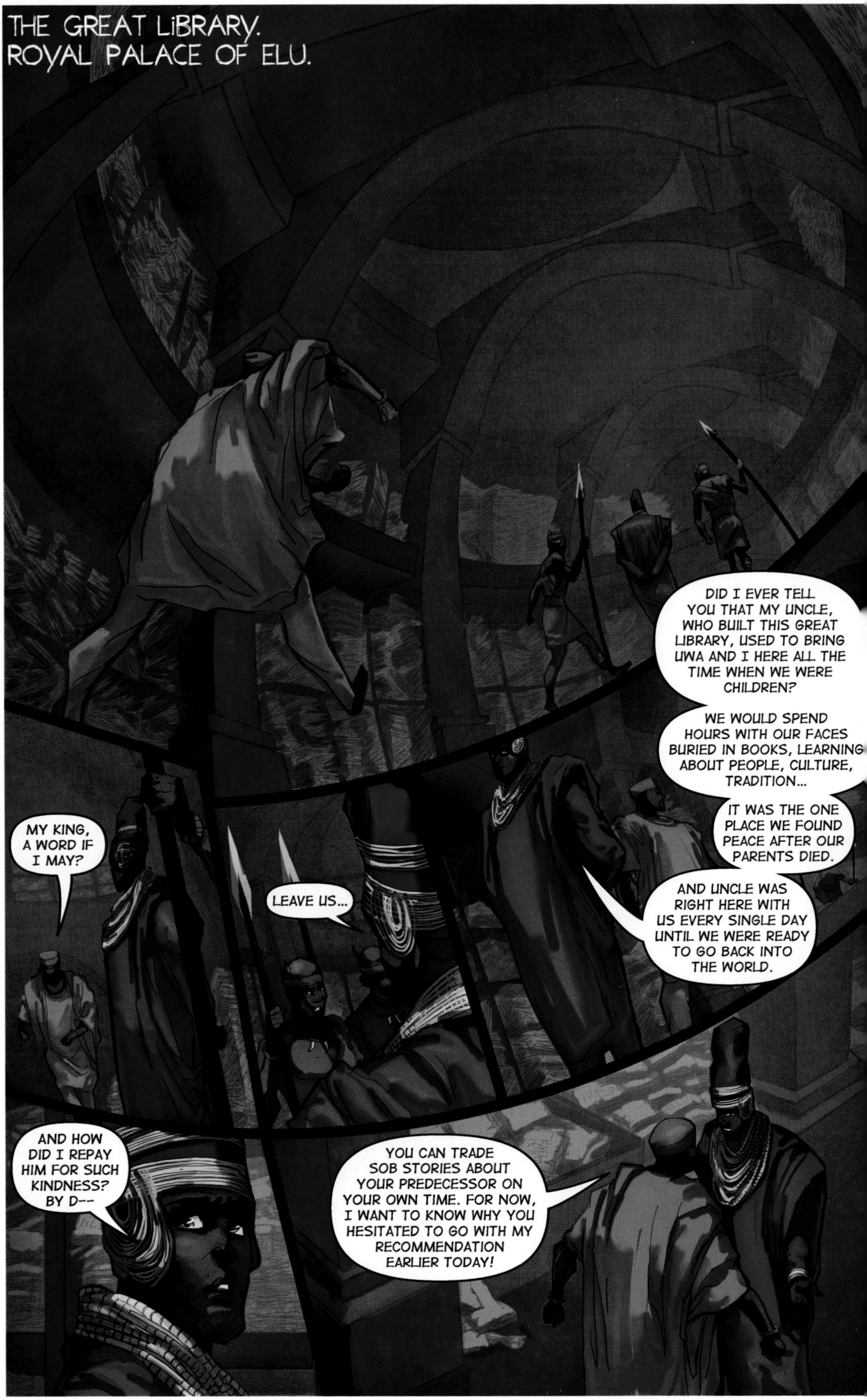
THE GREAT LIBRARY.
ROYAL PALACE OF ELU.
DID I EVER TELL YOU THAT MY UNCLE, WHO BUILT THIS GREAT LIBRARY, USED TO BRING UWA AND I HERE ALL THE TIME WHEN WE WERE CHILDREN?
WE WOULD SPEND HOURS WITH OUR FACES BURIED IN BOOKS, LEARNING ABOUT PEOPLE, CULTURE, TRADITION...
IT WAS THE ONE PLACE WE FOUND PEACE AFTER OUR PARENTS DIED.
MY KING, A WORD IF I MAY?
LEAVE US...
AND UNCLE WAS RIGHT HERE WITH US EVERY SINGLE DAY UNTIL WE WERE READY TO GO BACK INTO THE WORLD.
AND HOW DID I REPAY HIM FOR SUCH KINDNESS? BY D--
YOU CAN TRADE SOB STORIES ABOUT YOUR PREDECESSOR ON YOUR OWN TIME. FOR NOW, I WANT TO KNOW WHY YOU HESITATED TO GO WITH MY RECOMMENDATION EARLIER TODAY!

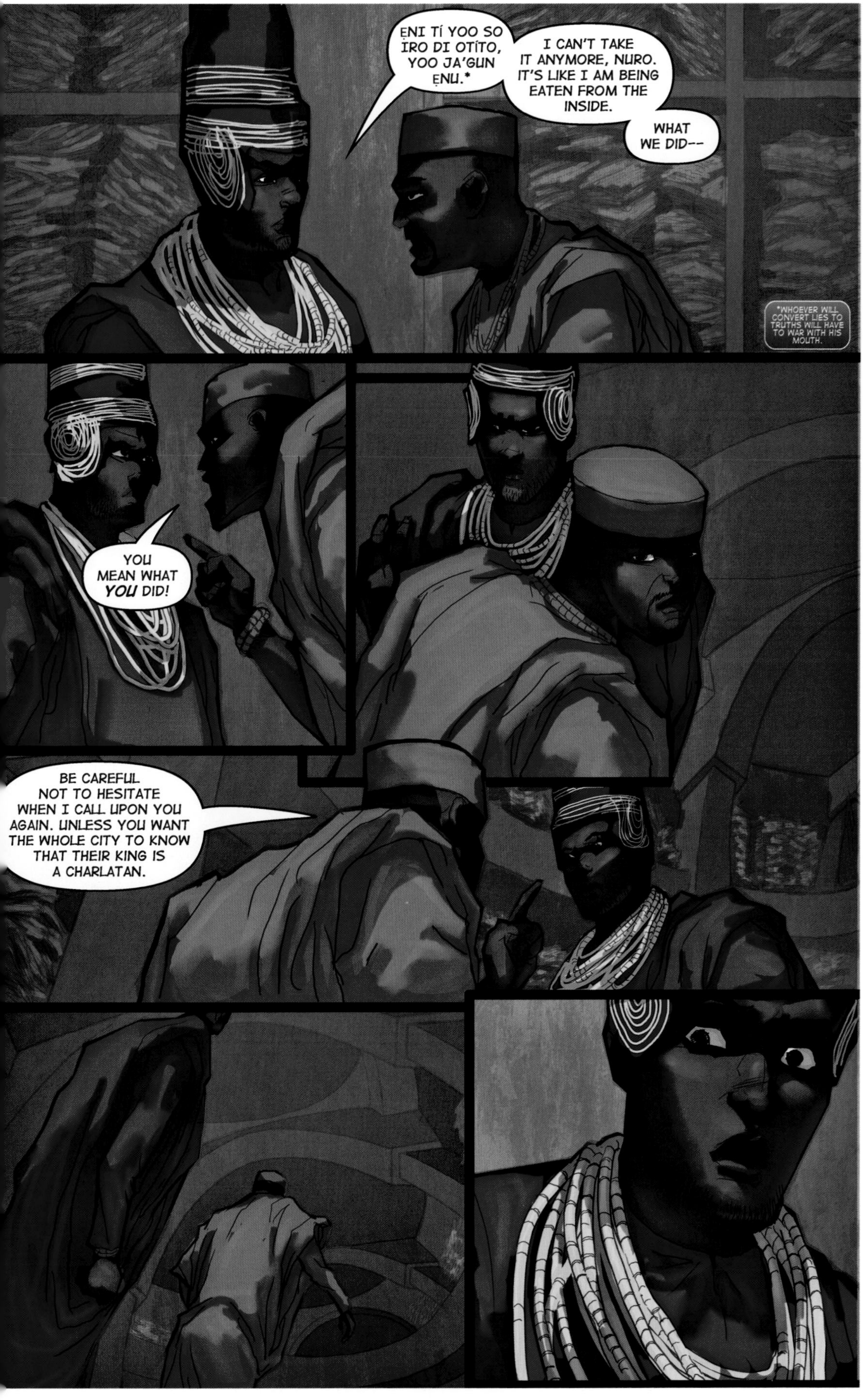
ẸNI TÍ YOO SO ÌRO DI OTÍTO, YOO JA'GUN ẸNU.*
I CAN'T TAKE IT ANYMORE, NURO. IT'S LIKE I AM BEING EATEN FROM THE INSIDE.
WHAT WE DID--
*WHOEVER WILL CONVERT LIES TO TRUTHS WILL HAVE TO WAR WITH HIS MOUTH.
YOU MEAN WHAT *YOU* DID!
BE CAREFUL NOT TO HESITATE WHEN I CALL UPON YOU AGAIN. UNLESS YOU WANT THE WHOLE CITY TO KNOW THAT THEIR KING IS A CHARLATAN.

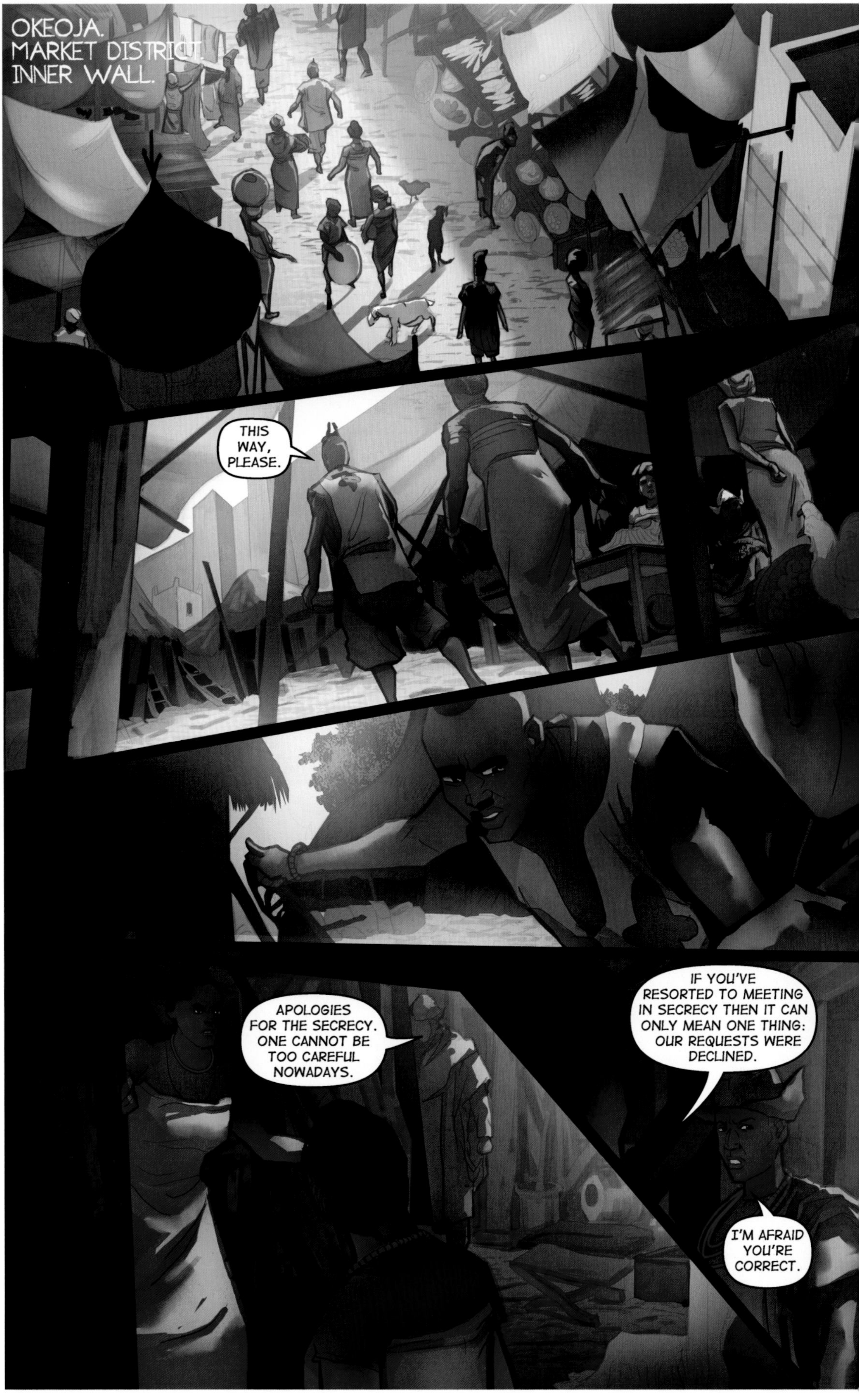
OKEOJA.
MARKET DISTRICT.
INNER WALL.
THIS WAY, PLEASE.
APOLOGIES FOR THE SECRECY. ONE CANNOT BE TOO CAREFUL NOWADAYS.
IF YOU'VE RESORTED TO MEETING IN SECRECY THEN IT CAN ONLY MEAN ONE THING: OUR REQUESTS WERE DECLINED.
I'M AFRAID YOU'RE CORRECT.

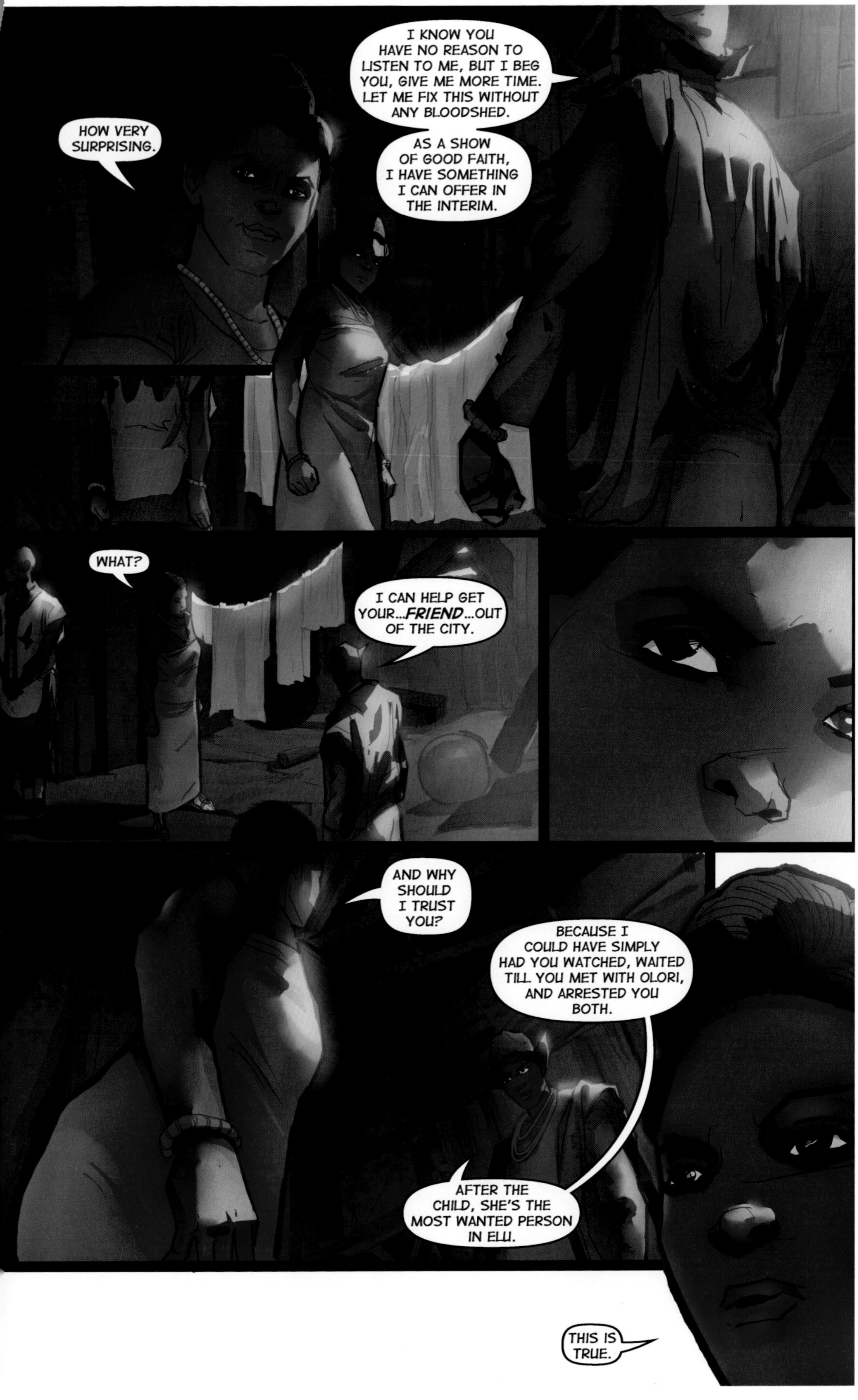
HOW VERY SURPRISING.
I KNOW YOU HAVE NO REASON TO LISTEN TO ME, BUT I BEG YOU, GIVE ME MORE TIME. LET ME FIX THIS WITHOUT ANY BLOODSHED.
AS A SHOW OF GOOD FAITH, I HAVE SOMETHING I CAN OFFER IN THE INTERIM.
WHAT?
I CAN HELP GET YOUR...**FRIEND**...OUT OF THE CITY.
AND WHY SHOULD I TRUST YOU?
BECAUSE I COULD HAVE SIMPLY HAD YOU WATCHED, WAITED TILL YOU MET WITH OLORI, AND ARRESTED YOU BOTH.
AFTER THE CHILD, SHE'S THE MOST WANTED PERSON IN ELU.
THIS IS TRUE.

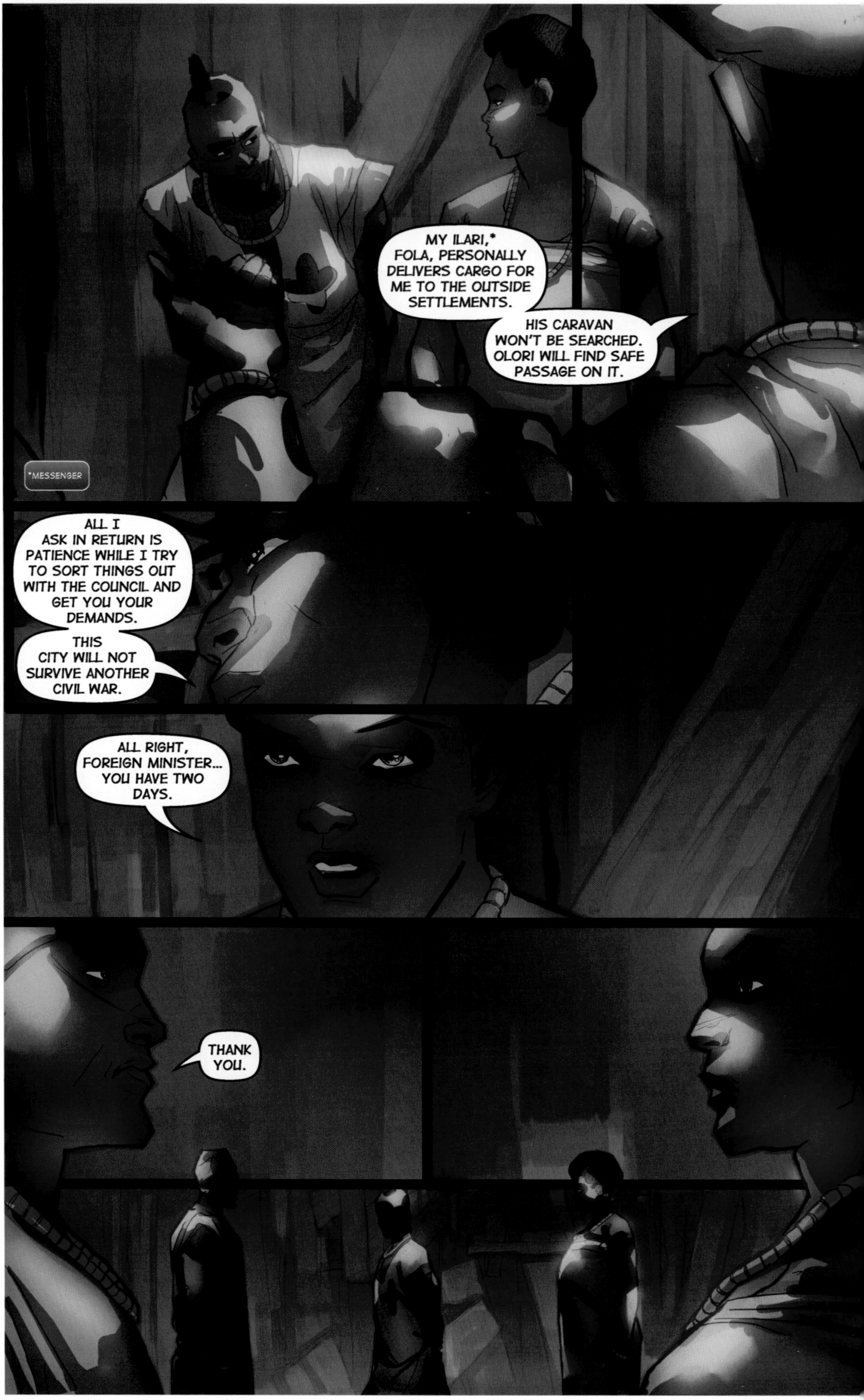
MY ILARI,* FOLA, PERSONALLY DELIVERS CARGO FOR ME TO THE OUTSIDE SETTLEMENTS.
HIS CARAVAN WON'T BE SEARCHED. OLORI WILL FIND SAFE PASSAGE ON IT.
*MESSENGER
ALL I ASK IN RETURN IS PATIENCE WHILE I TRY TO SORT THINGS OUT WITH THE COUNCIL AND GET YOU YOUR DEMANDS.
THIS CITY WILL NOT SURVIVE ANOTHER CIVIL WAR.
ALL RIGHT, FOREIGN MINISTER... YOU HAVE TWO DAYS.
THANK YOU.

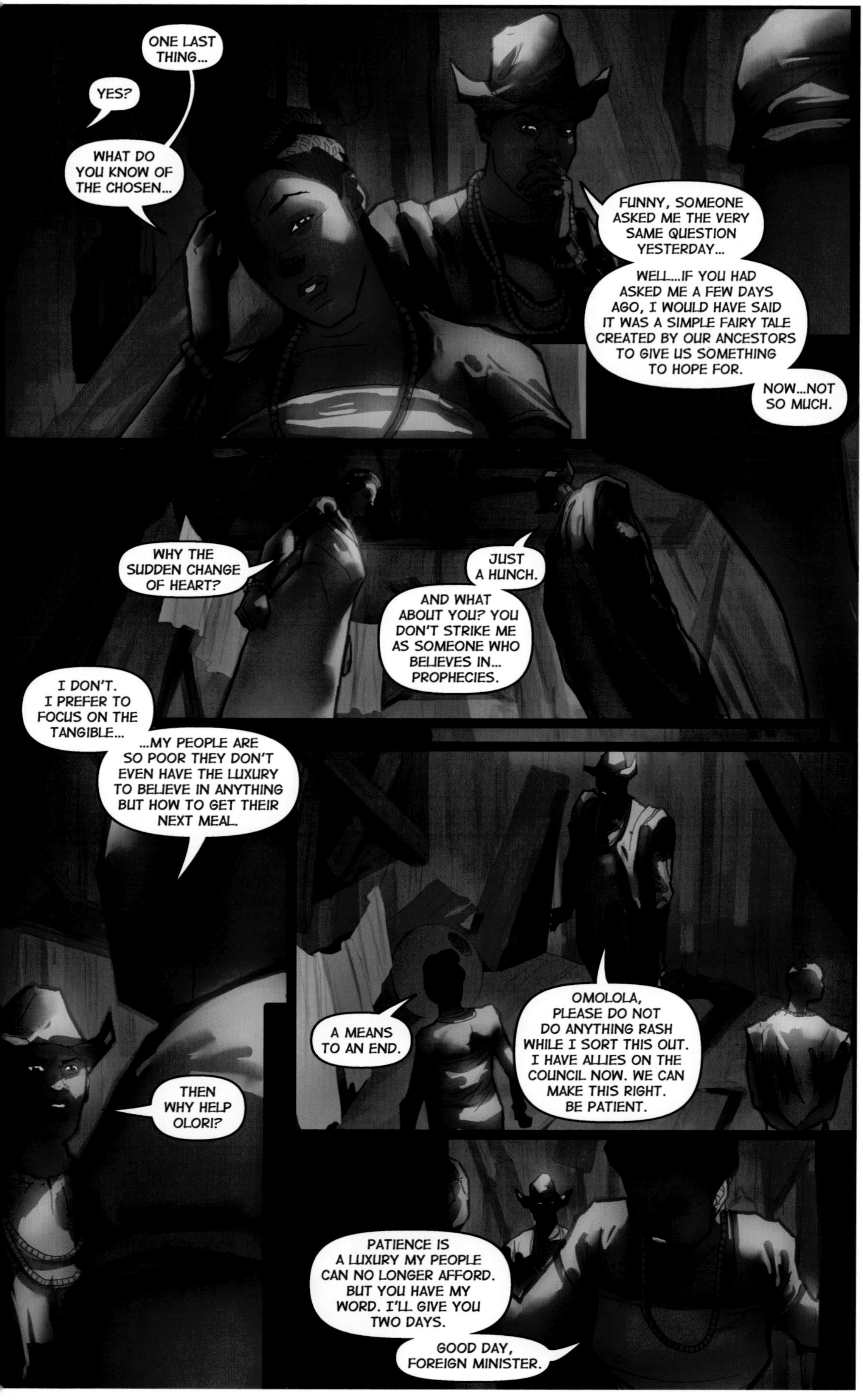
ONE LAST THING...
YES?
WHAT DO YOU KNOW OF THE CHOSEN...
FUNNY, SOMEONE ASKED ME THE VERY SAME QUESTION YESTERDAY...
WELL...IF YOU HAD ASKED ME A FEW DAYS AGO, I WOULD HAVE SAID IT WAS A SIMPLE FAIRY TALE CREATED BY OUR ANCESTORS TO GIVE US SOMETHING TO HOPE FOR.
NOW...NOT SO MUCH.
WHY THE SUDDEN CHANGE OF HEART?
JUST A HUNCH.
AND WHAT ABOUT YOU? YOU DON'T STRIKE ME AS SOMEONE WHO BELIEVES IN... PROPHECIES.
I DON'T. I PREFER TO FOCUS ON THE TANGIBLE...
...MY PEOPLE ARE SO POOR THEY DON'T EVEN HAVE THE LUXURY TO BELIEVE IN ANYTHING BUT HOW TO GET THEIR NEXT MEAL.
THEN WHY HELP OLORI?
A MEANS TO AN END.
OMOLOLA, PLEASE DO NOT DO ANYTHING RASH WHILE I SORT THIS OUT. I HAVE ALLIES ON THE COUNCIL NOW. WE CAN MAKE THIS RIGHT. BE PATIENT.
PATIENCE IS A LUXURY MY PEOPLE CAN NO LONGER AFFORD. BUT YOU HAVE MY WORD. I'LL GIVE YOU TWO DAYS.
GOOD DAY, FOREIGN MINISTER.

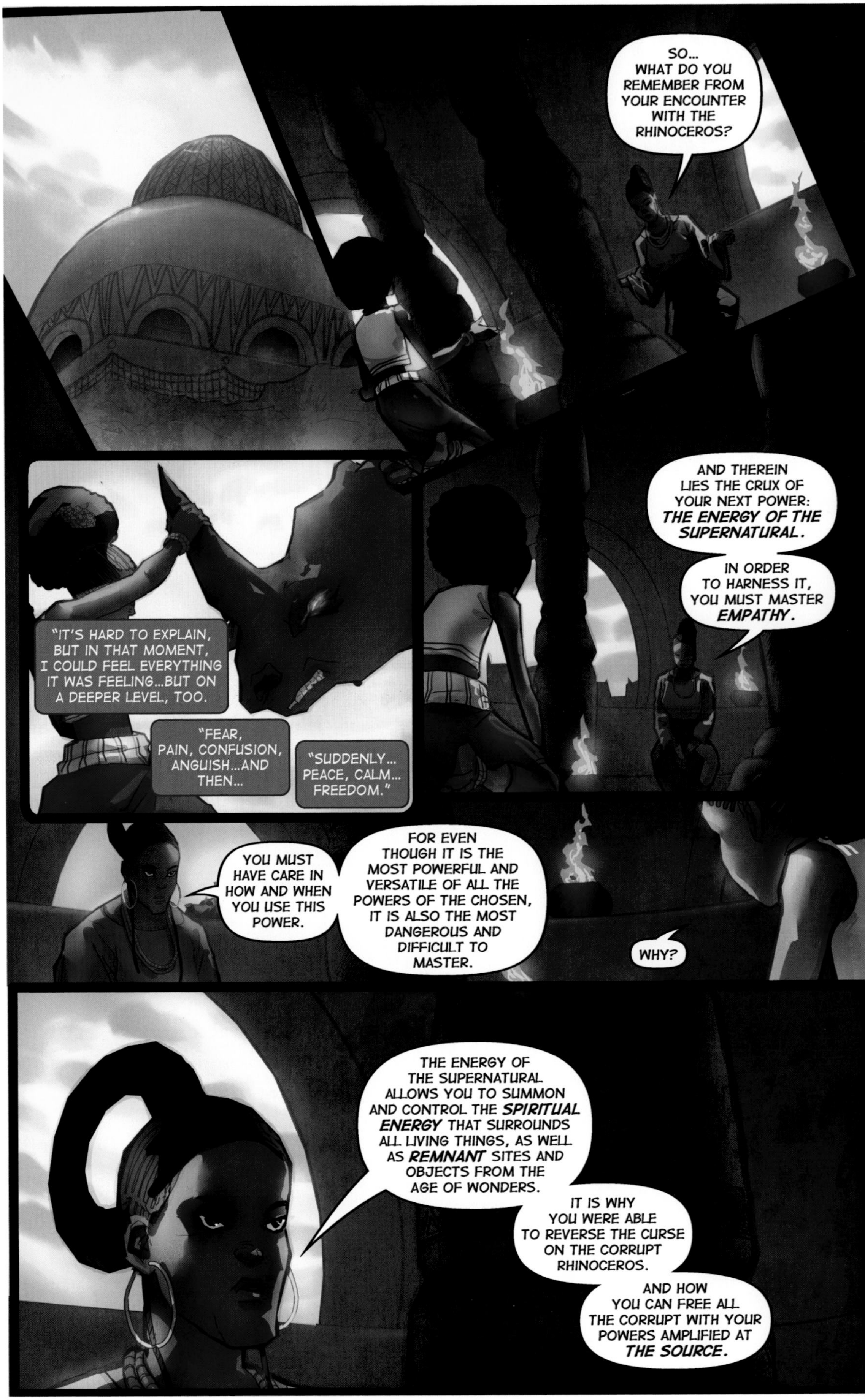
SO... WHAT DO YOU REMEMBER FROM YOUR ENCOUNTER WITH THE RHINOCEROS?
"IT'S HARD TO EXPLAIN, BUT IN THAT MOMENT, I COULD FEEL EVERYTHING IT WAS FEELING...BUT ON A DEEPER LEVEL, TOO.
"FEAR, PAIN, CONFUSION, ANGUISH...AND THEN...
"SUDDENLY... PEACE, CALM... FREEDOM."
AND THEREIN LIES THE CRUX OF YOUR NEXT POWER: ***THE ENERGY OF THE SUPERNATURAL.***
IN ORDER TO HARNESS IT, YOU MUST MASTER ***EMPATHY.***
YOU MUST HAVE CARE IN HOW AND WHEN YOU USE THIS POWER.
FOR EVEN THOUGH IT IS THE MOST POWERFUL AND VERSATILE OF ALL THE POWERS OF THE CHOSEN, IT IS ALSO THE MOST DANGEROUS AND DIFFICULT TO MASTER.
WHY?
THE ENERGY OF THE SUPERNATURAL ALLOWS YOU TO SUMMON AND CONTROL THE ***SPIRITUAL ENERGY*** THAT SURROUNDS ALL LIVING THINGS, AS WELL AS ***REMNANT*** SITES AND OBJECTS FROM THE AGE OF WONDERS.
IT IS WHY YOU WERE ABLE TO REVERSE THE CURSE ON THE CORRUPT RHINOCEROS.
AND HOW YOU CAN FREE ALL THE CORRUPT WITH YOUR POWERS AMPLIFIED AT ***THE SOURCE.***

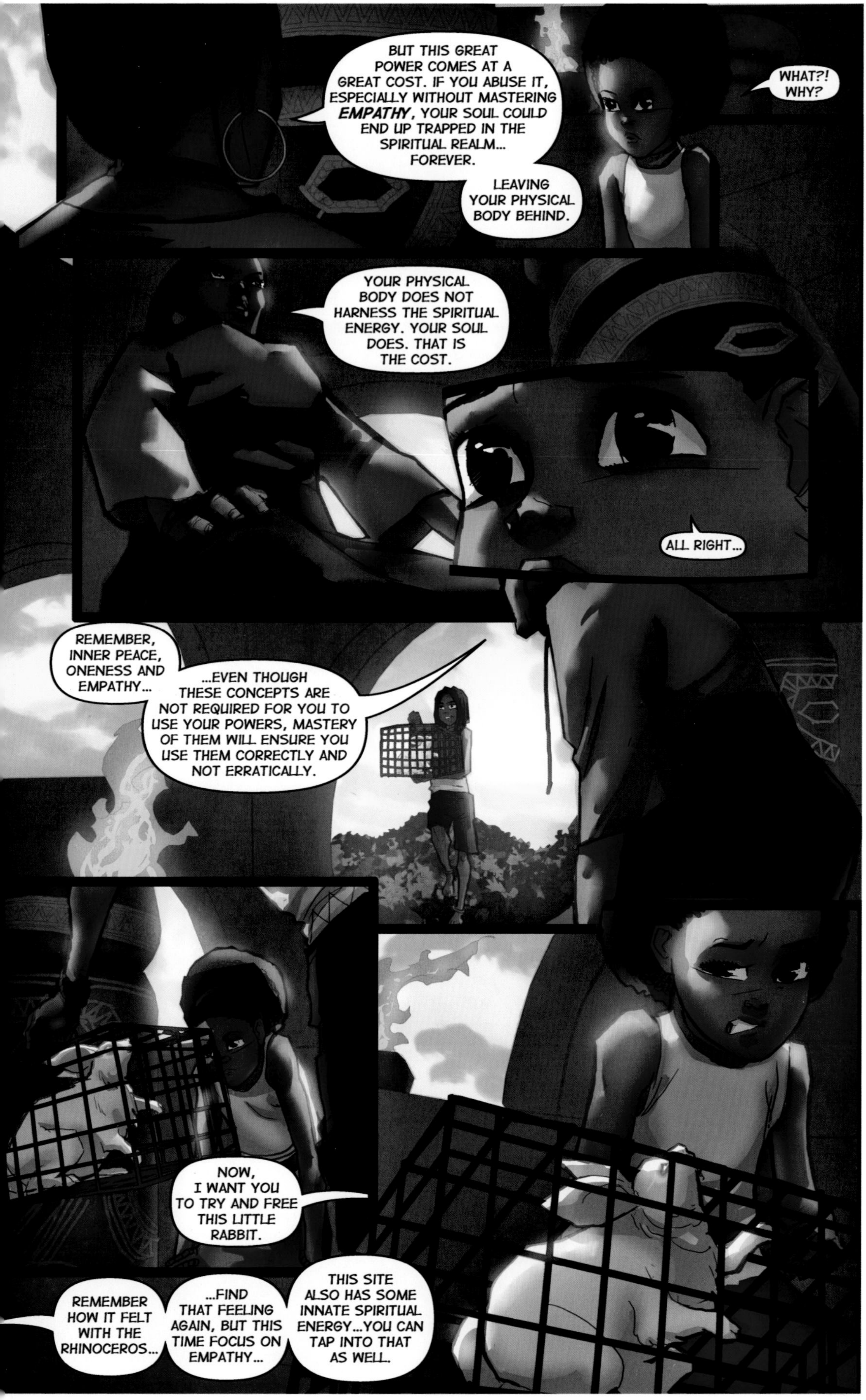
BUT THIS GREAT POWER COMES AT A GREAT COST. IF YOU ABUSE IT, ESPECIALLY WITHOUT MASTERING *EMPATHY*, YOUR SOUL COULD END UP TRAPPED IN THE SPIRITUAL REALM... FOREVER.
WHAT?! WHY?
LEAVING YOUR PHYSICAL BODY BEHIND.
YOUR PHYSICAL BODY DOES NOT HARNESS THE SPIRITUAL ENERGY. YOUR SOUL DOES. THAT IS THE COST.
ALL RIGHT...
REMEMBER, INNER PEACE, ONENESS AND EMPATHY...
...EVEN THOUGH THESE CONCEPTS ARE NOT REQUIRED FOR YOU TO USE YOUR POWERS, MASTERY OF THEM WILL ENSURE YOU USE THEM CORRECTLY AND NOT ERRATICALLY.
NOW, I WANT YOU TO TRY AND FREE THIS LITTLE RABBIT.
REMEMBER HOW IT FELT WITH THE RHINOCEROS...
...FIND THAT FEELING AGAIN, BUT THIS TIME FOCUS ON EMPATHY...
THIS SITE ALSO HAS SOME INNATE SPIRITUAL ENERGY... YOU CAN TAP INTO THAT AS WELL.

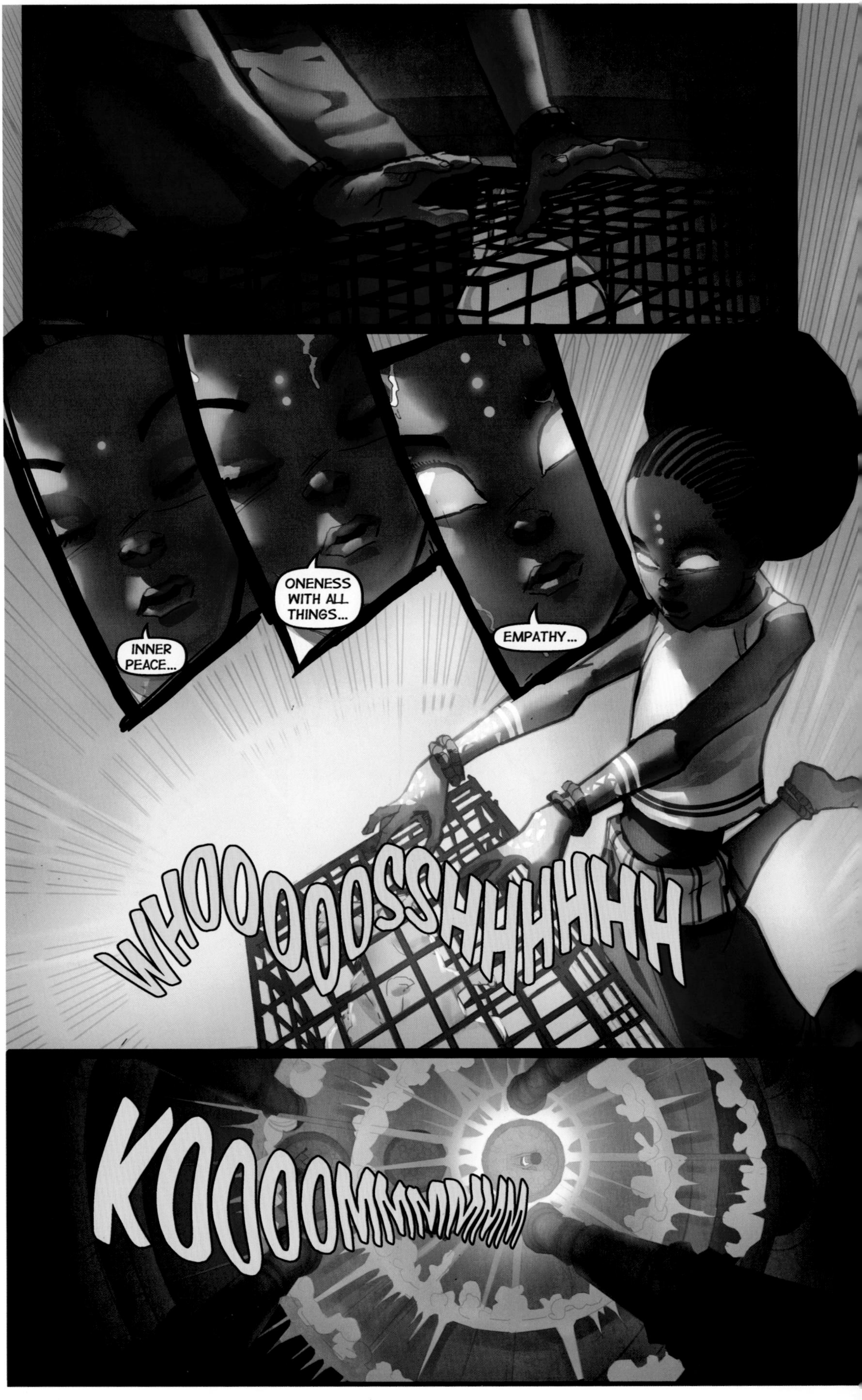
INNER PEACE...
ONENESS WITH ALL THINGS...
EMPATHY...
WHOOOOOOSSHHHHHH
KOOOOMMMMMMM

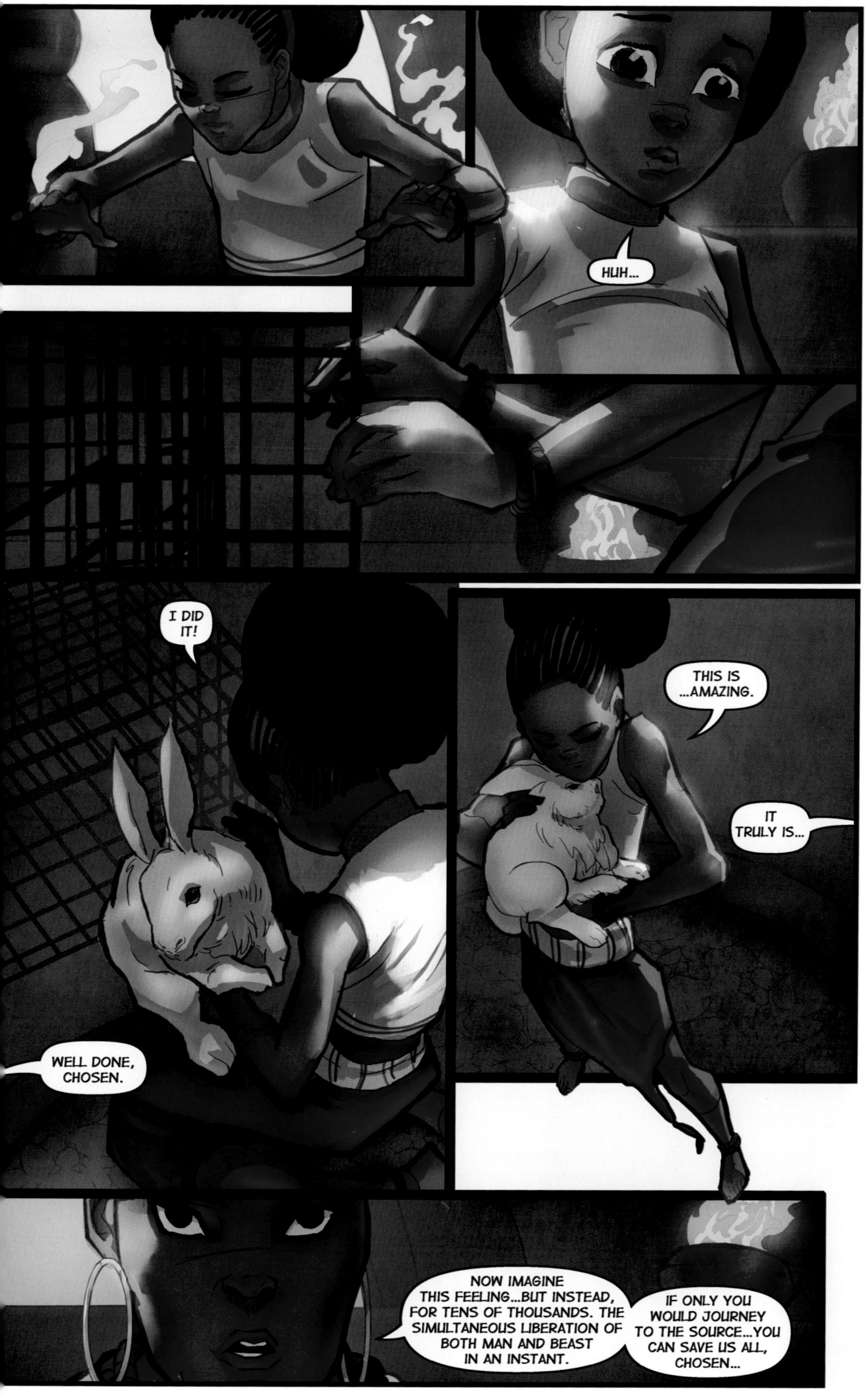
HUH...
I DID IT!
WELL DONE, CHOSEN.
THIS IS ...AMAZING.
IT TRULY IS...
NOW IMAGINE THIS FEELING...BUT INSTEAD, FOR TENS OF THOUSANDS. THE SIMULTANEOUS LIBERATION OF BOTH MAN AND BEAST IN AN INSTANT.
IF ONLY YOU WOULD JOURNEY TO THE SOURCE...YOU CAN SAVE US ALL, CHOSEN...

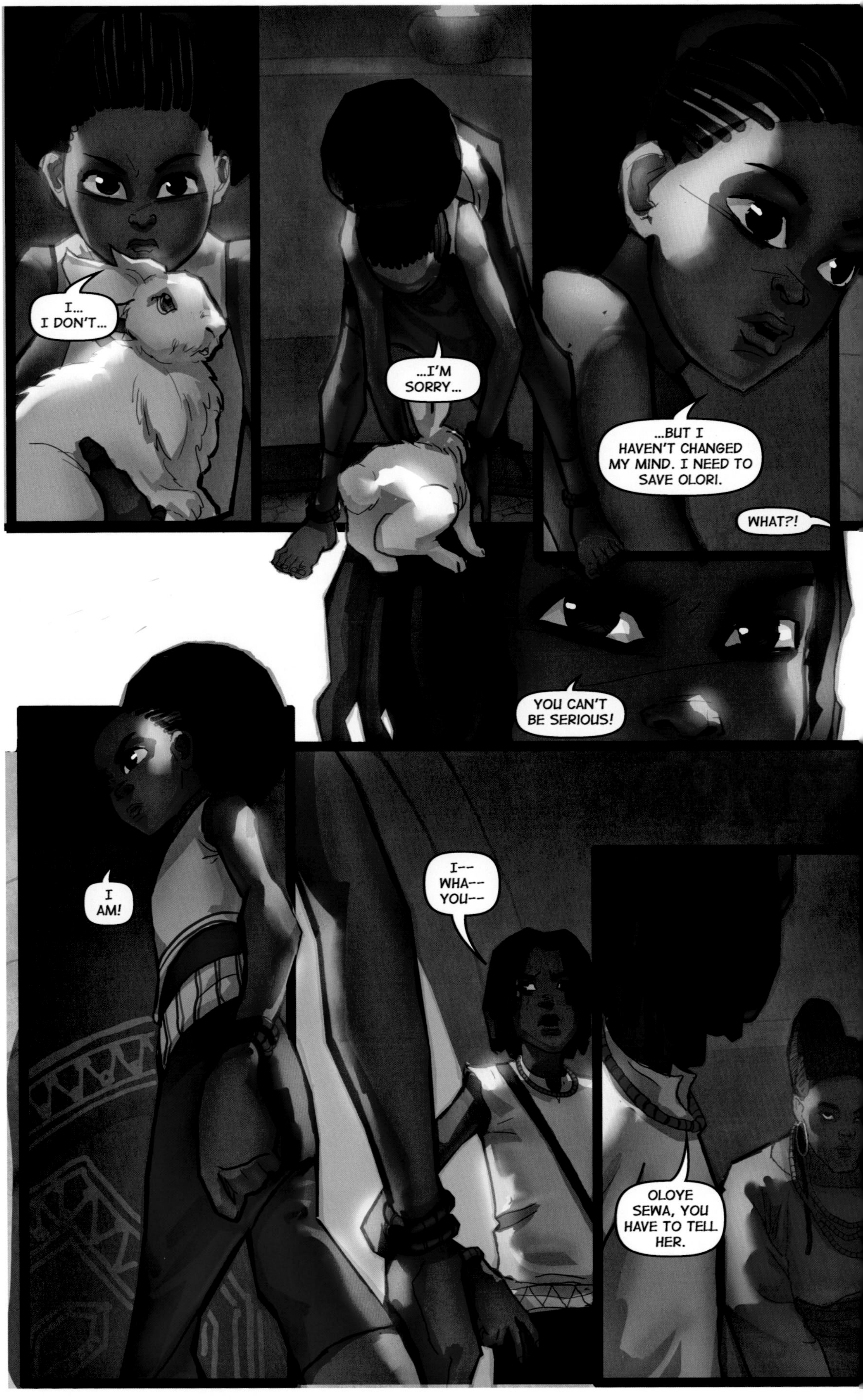

I... I DON'T...
...I'M SORRY...
...BUT I HAVEN'T CHANGED MY MIND. I NEED TO SAVE OLORI.
WHAT?!
YOU CAN'T BE SERIOUS!
I AM!
I-- WHA-- YOU--
OLOYE SEWA, YOU HAVE TO TELL HER.

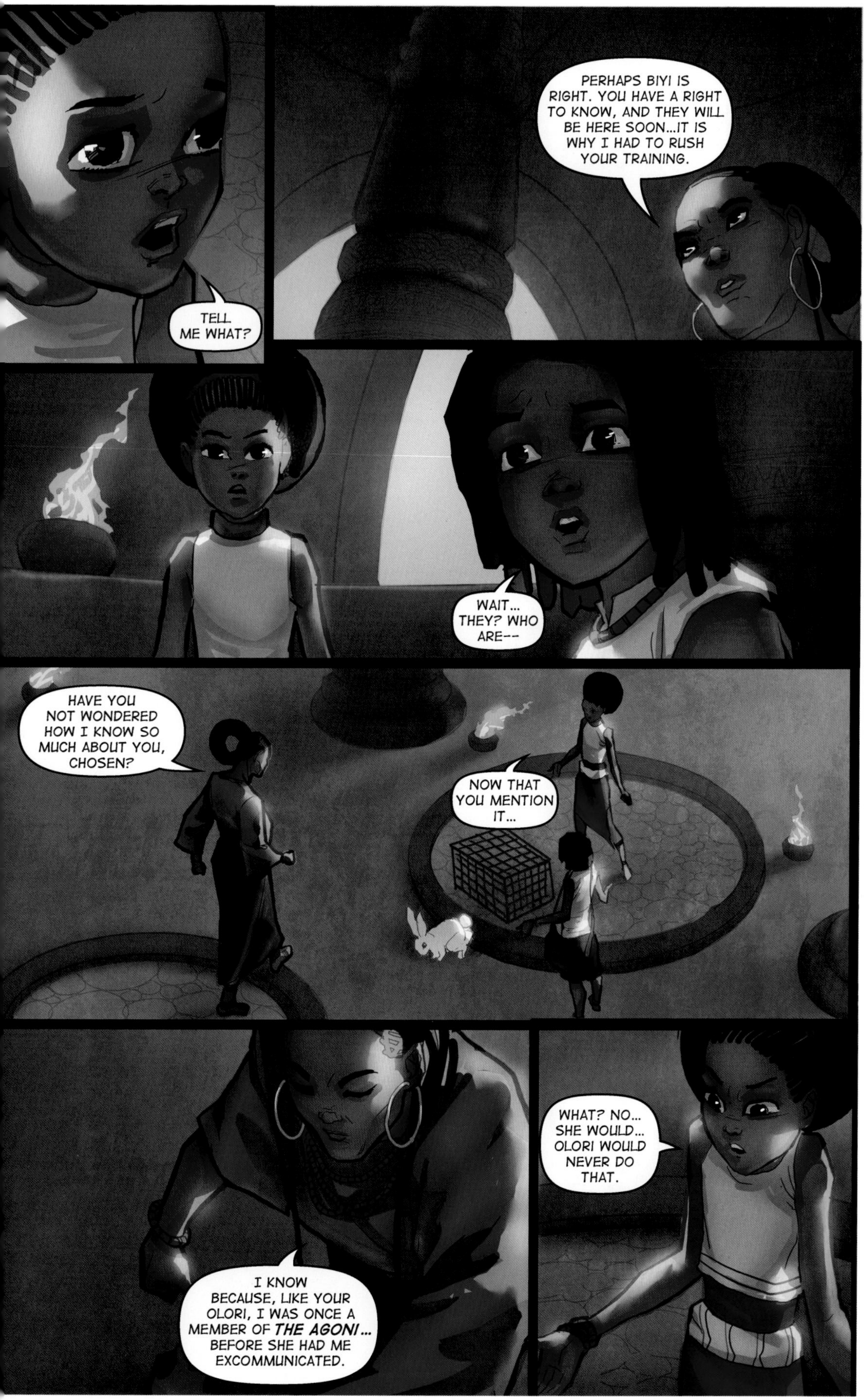
TELL ME WHAT?
PERHAPS BIYI IS RIGHT. YOU HAVE A RIGHT TO KNOW, AND THEY WILL BE HERE SOON...IT IS WHY I HAD TO RUSH YOUR TRAINING.
WAIT... THEY? WHO ARE--
HAVE YOU NOT WONDERED HOW I KNOW SO MUCH ABOUT YOU, CHOSEN?
NOW THAT YOU MENTION IT...
I KNOW BECAUSE, LIKE YOUR OLORI, I WAS ONCE A MEMBER OF ***THE AGONI***... BEFORE SHE HAD ME EXCOMMUNICATED.
WHAT? NO... SHE WOULD... OLORI WOULD NEVER DO THAT.

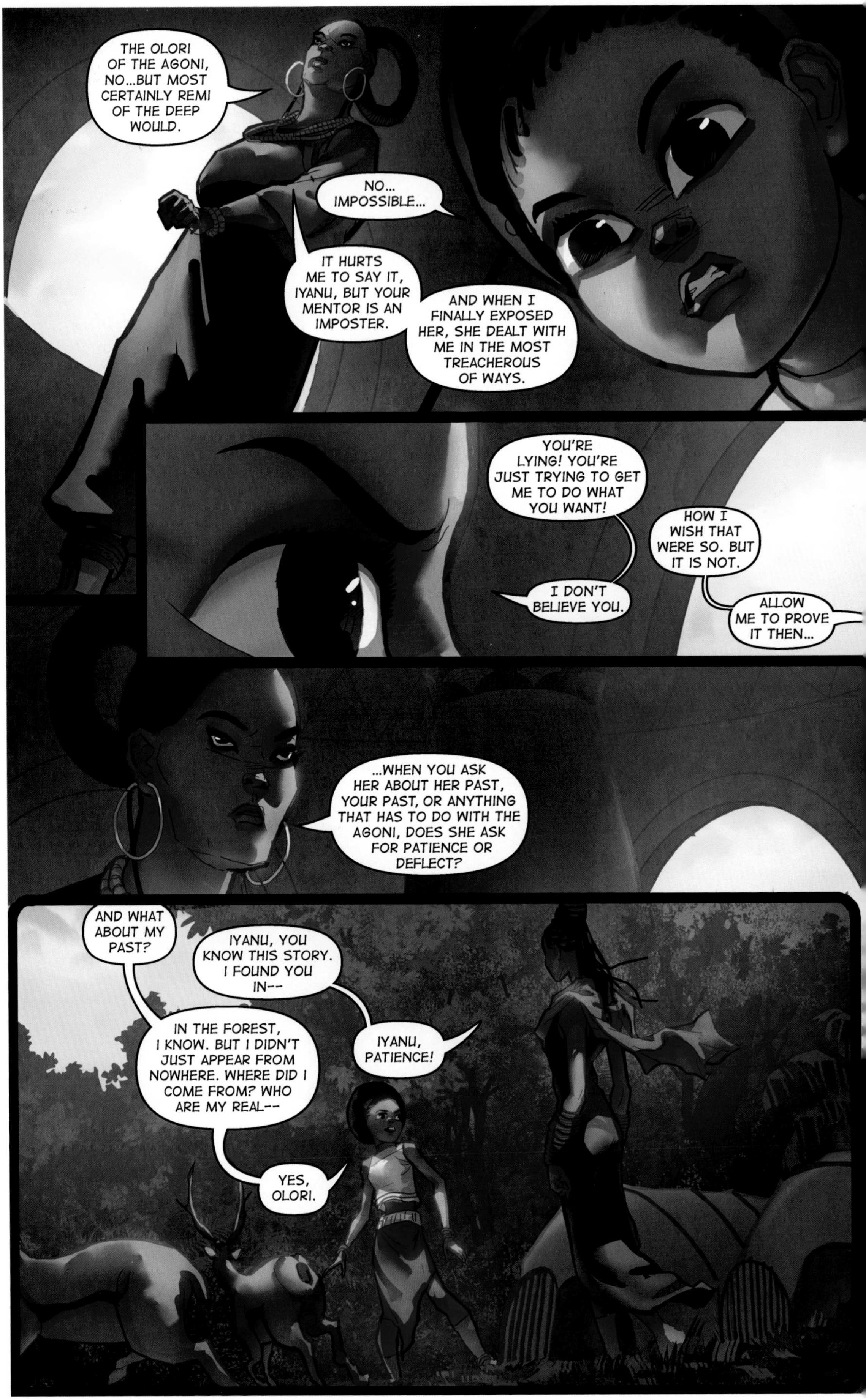
THE OLORI OF THE AGONI, NO...BUT MOST CERTAINLY REMI OF THE DEEP WOULD.
NO... IMPOSSIBLE...
IT HURTS ME TO SAY IT, IYANU, BUT YOUR MENTOR IS AN IMPOSTER.
AND WHEN I FINALLY EXPOSED HER, SHE DEALT WITH ME IN THE MOST TREACHEROUS OF WAYS.
YOU'RE LYING! YOU'RE JUST TRYING TO GET ME TO DO WHAT YOU WANT!
I DON'T BELIEVE YOU.
HOW I WISH THAT WERE SO. BUT IT IS NOT.
ALLOW ME TO PROVE IT THEN...
...WHEN YOU ASK HER ABOUT HER PAST, YOUR PAST, OR ANYTHING THAT HAS TO DO WITH THE AGONI, DOES SHE ASK FOR PATIENCE OR DEFLECT?
AND WHAT ABOUT MY PAST?
IYANU, YOU KNOW THIS STORY. I FOUND YOU IN--
IN THE FOREST, I KNOW. BUT I DIDN'T JUST APPEAR FROM NOWHERE. WHERE DID I COME FROM? WHO ARE MY REAL--
IYANU, PATIENCE!
YES, OLORI.

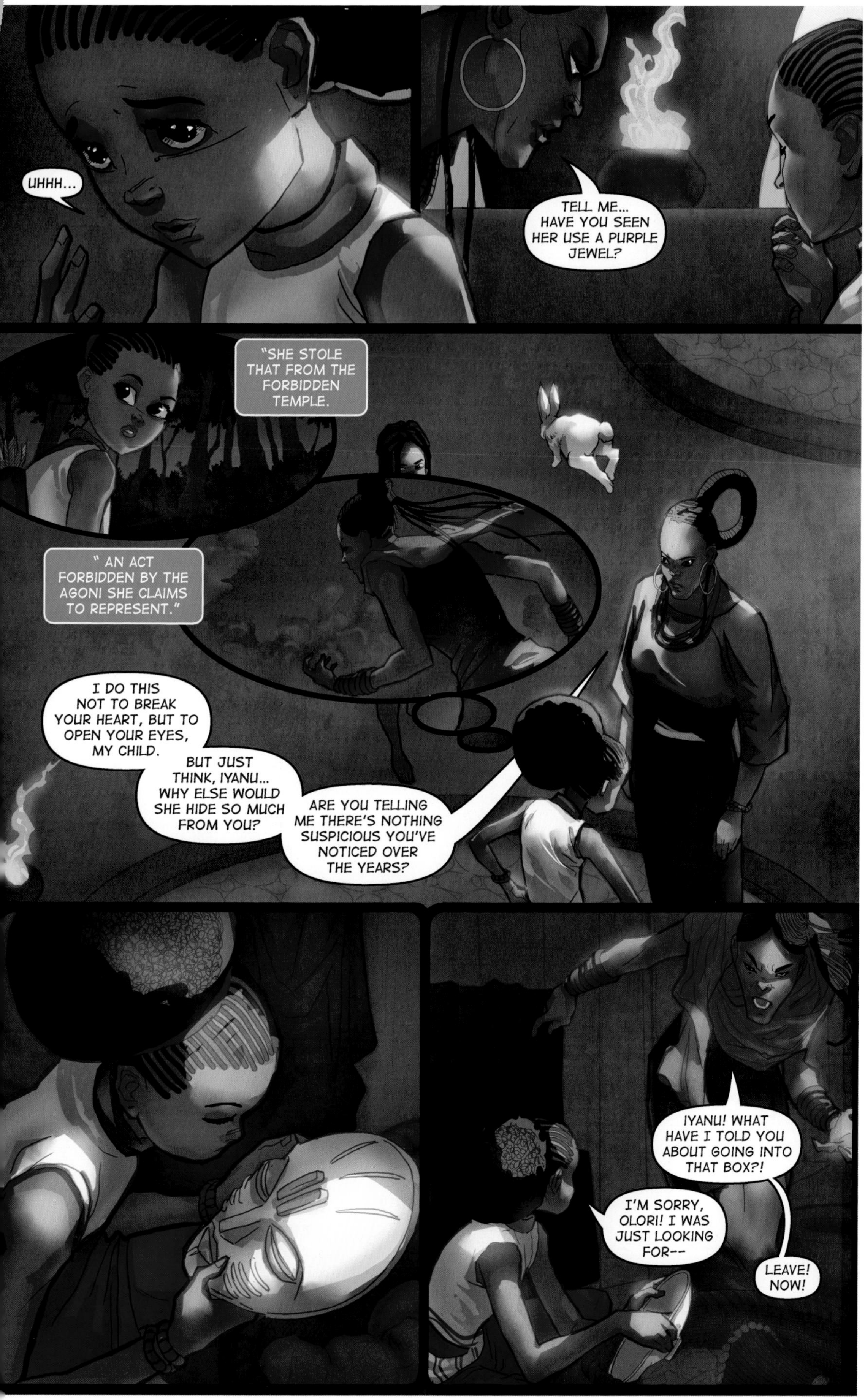
UHHH...
TELL ME... HAVE YOU SEEN HER USE A PURPLE JEWEL?
"SHE STOLE THAT FROM THE FORBIDDEN TEMPLE.
" AN ACT FORBIDDEN BY THE AGONI SHE CLAIMS TO REPRESENT."
I DO THIS NOT TO BREAK YOUR HEART, BUT TO OPEN YOUR EYES, MY CHILD.
BUT JUST THINK, IYANU... WHY ELSE WOULD SHE HIDE SO MUCH FROM YOU?
ARE YOU TELLING ME THERE'S NOTHING SUSPICIOUS YOU'VE NOTICED OVER THE YEARS?
IYANU! WHAT HAVE I TOLD YOU ABOUT GOING INTO THAT BOX?!
I'M SORRY, OLORI! I WAS JUST LOOKING FOR--
LEAVE! NOW!

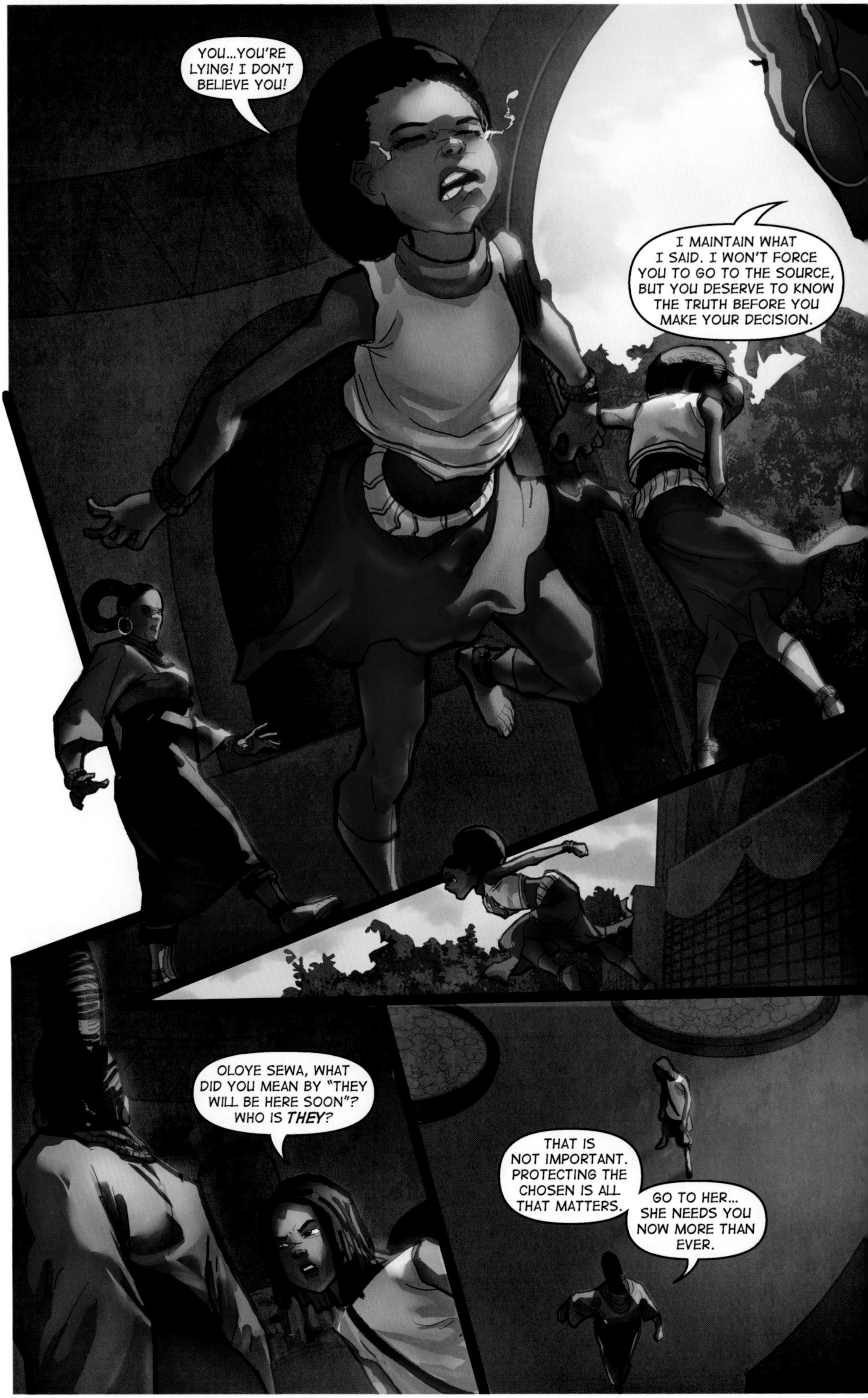
YOU...YOU'RE LYING! I DON'T BELIEVE YOU!
I MAINTAIN WHAT I SAID. I WON'T FORCE YOU TO GO TO THE SOURCE, BUT YOU DESERVE TO KNOW THE TRUTH BEFORE YOU MAKE YOUR DECISION.
OLOYE SEWA, WHAT DID YOU MEAN BY "THEY WILL BE HERE SOON"? WHO IS *THEY*?
THAT IS NOT IMPORTANT. PROTECTING THE CHOSEN IS ALL THAT MATTERS.
GO TO HER... SHE NEEDS YOU NOW MORE THAN EVER.

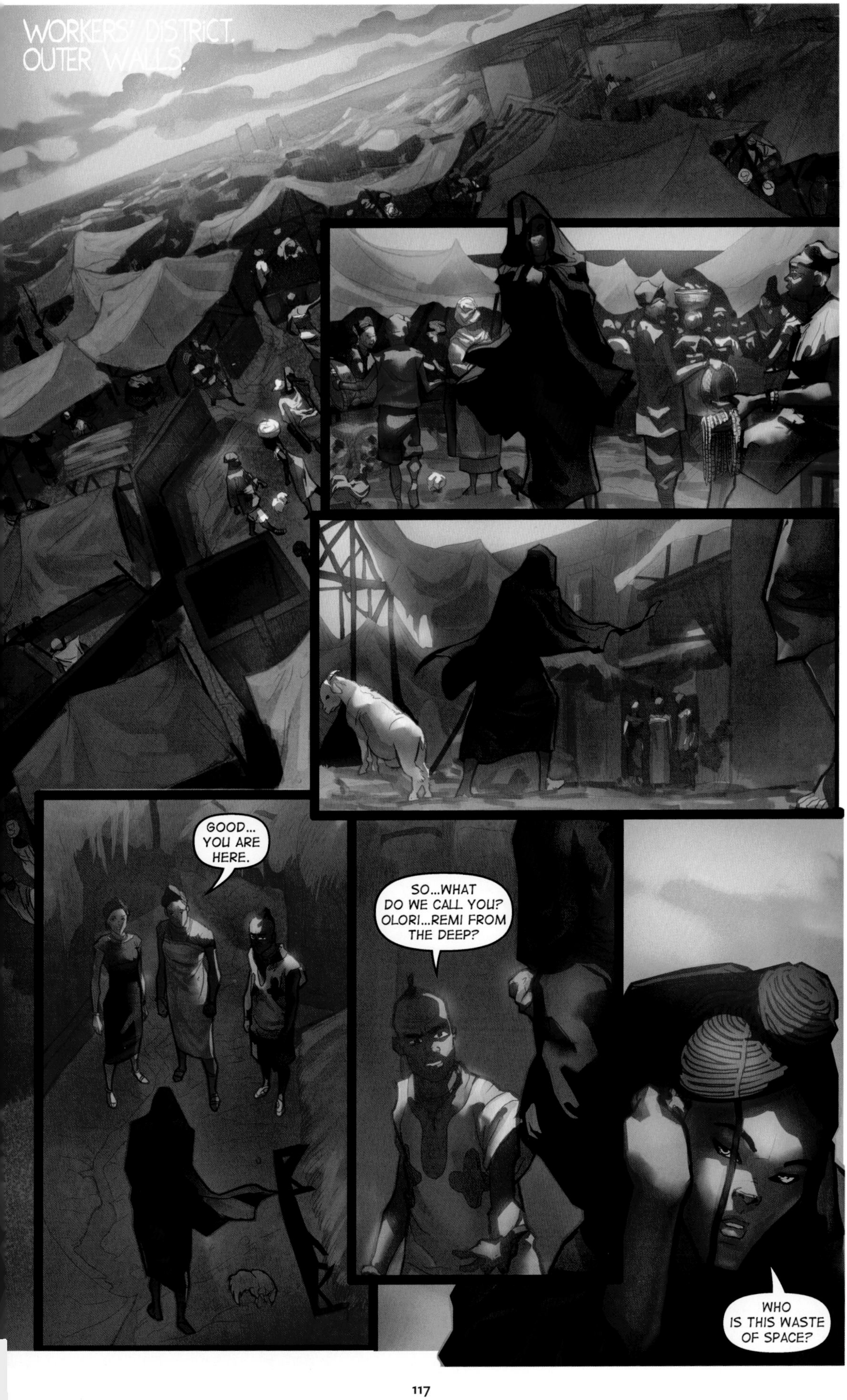
WORKERS' DISTRICT.
OUTER WALLS.
GOOD... YOU ARE HERE.
SO...WHAT DO WE CALL YOU? OLORI...REMI FROM THE DEEP?
WHO IS THIS WASTE OF SPACE?

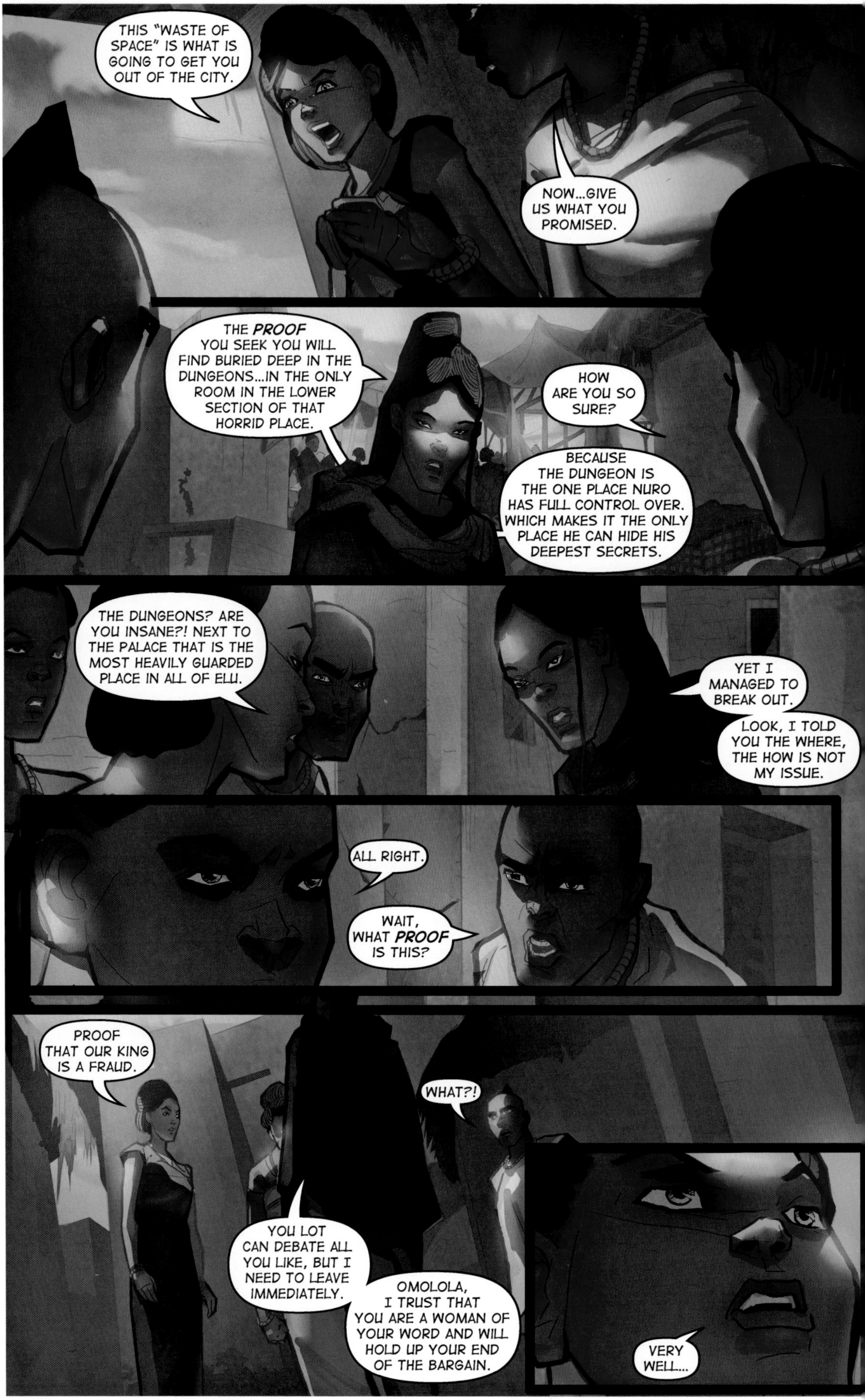
THIS "WASTE OF SPACE" IS WHAT IS GOING TO GET YOU OUT OF THE CITY.
NOW...GIVE US WHAT YOU PROMISED.
THE *PROOF* YOU SEEK YOU WILL FIND BURIED DEEP IN THE DUNGEONS...IN THE ONLY ROOM IN THE LOWER SECTION OF THAT HORRID PLACE.
HOW ARE YOU SO SURE?
BECAUSE THE DUNGEON IS THE ONE PLACE NURO HAS FULL CONTROL OVER. WHICH MAKES IT THE ONLY PLACE HE CAN HIDE HIS DEEPEST SECRETS.
THE DUNGEONS? ARE YOU INSANE?! NEXT TO THE PALACE THAT IS THE MOST HEAVILY GUARDED PLACE IN ALL OF ELU.
YET I MANAGED TO BREAK OUT.
LOOK, I TOLD YOU THE WHERE, THE HOW IS NOT MY ISSUE.
ALL RIGHT.
WAIT, WHAT *PROOF* IS THIS?
PROOF THAT OUR KING IS A FRAUD.
WHAT?!
YOU LOT CAN DEBATE ALL YOU LIKE, BUT I NEED TO LEAVE IMMEDIATELY.
OMOLOLA, I TRUST THAT YOU ARE A WOMAN OF YOUR WORD AND WILL HOLD UP YOUR END OF THE BARGAIN.
VERY WELL...

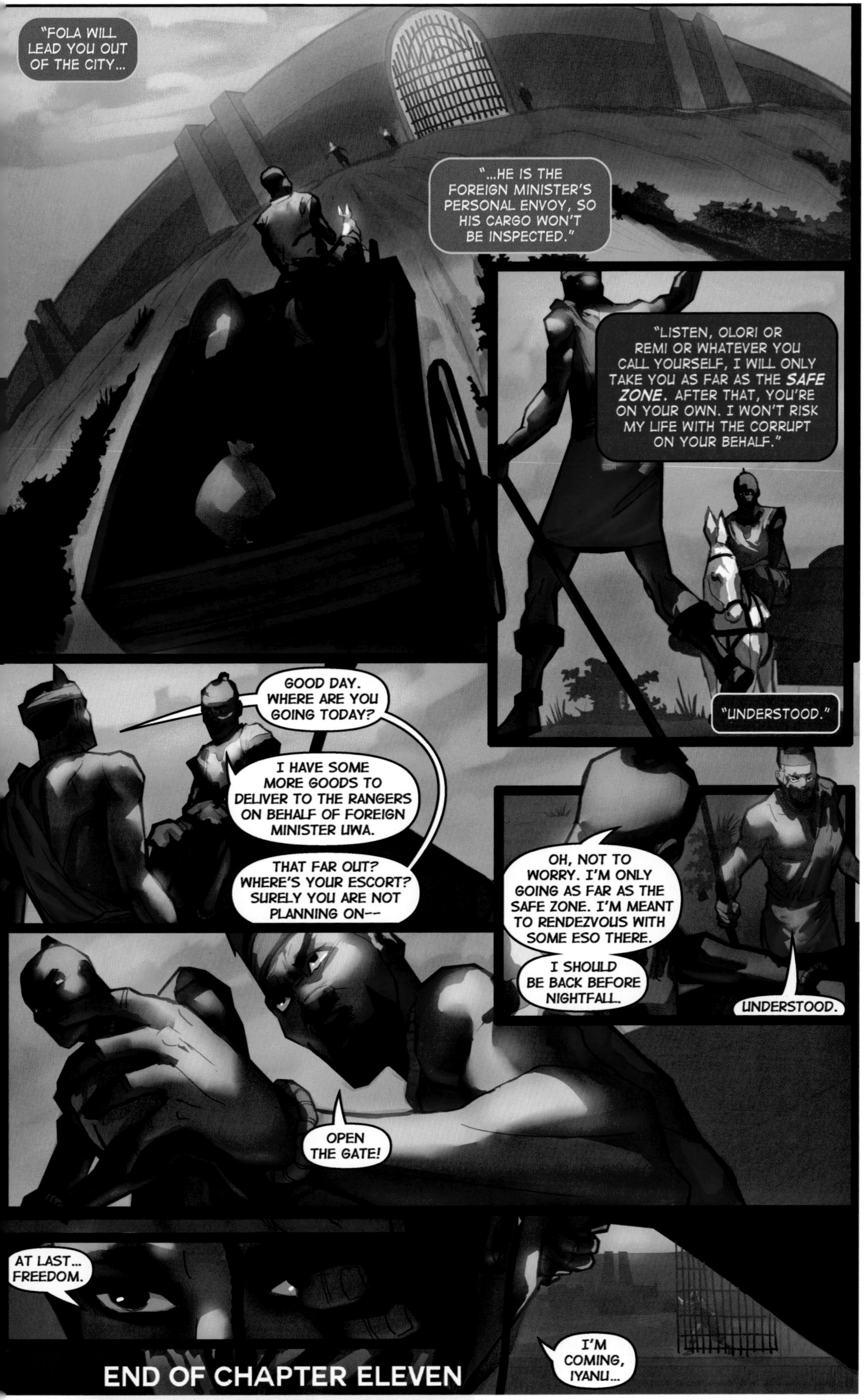
"FOLA WILL LEAD YOU OUT OF THE CITY...
"...HE IS THE FOREIGN MINISTER'S PERSONAL ENVOY, SO HIS CARGO WON'T BE INSPECTED."
"LISTEN, OLORI OR REMI OR WHATEVER YOU CALL YOURSELF, I WILL ONLY TAKE YOU AS FAR AS THE SAFE ZONE. AFTER THAT, YOU'RE ON YOUR OWN. I WON'T RISK MY LIFE WITH THE CORRUPT ON YOUR BEHALF."
"UNDERSTOOD."
GOOD DAY. WHERE ARE YOU GOING TODAY?
I HAVE SOME MORE GOODS TO DELIVER TO THE RANGERS ON BEHALF OF FOREIGN MINISTER UWA.
THAT FAR OUT? WHERE'S YOUR ESCORT? SURELY YOU ARE NOT PLANNING ON--
OH, NOT TO WORRY. I'M ONLY GOING AS FAR AS THE SAFE ZONE. I'M MEANT TO RENDEZVOUS WITH SOME ESO THERE.
I SHOULD BE BACK BEFORE NIGHTFALL.
UNDERSTOOD.
OPEN THE GATE!
AT LAST... FREEDOM.
I'M COMING, IYANU...
END OF CHAPTER ELEVEN

CHAPTER TWELVE

Divine Power

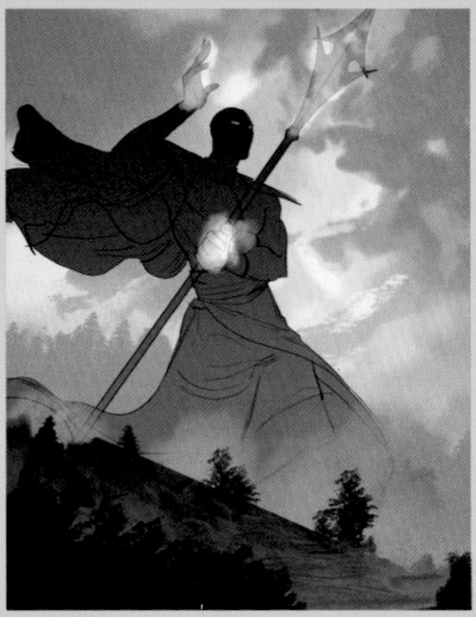

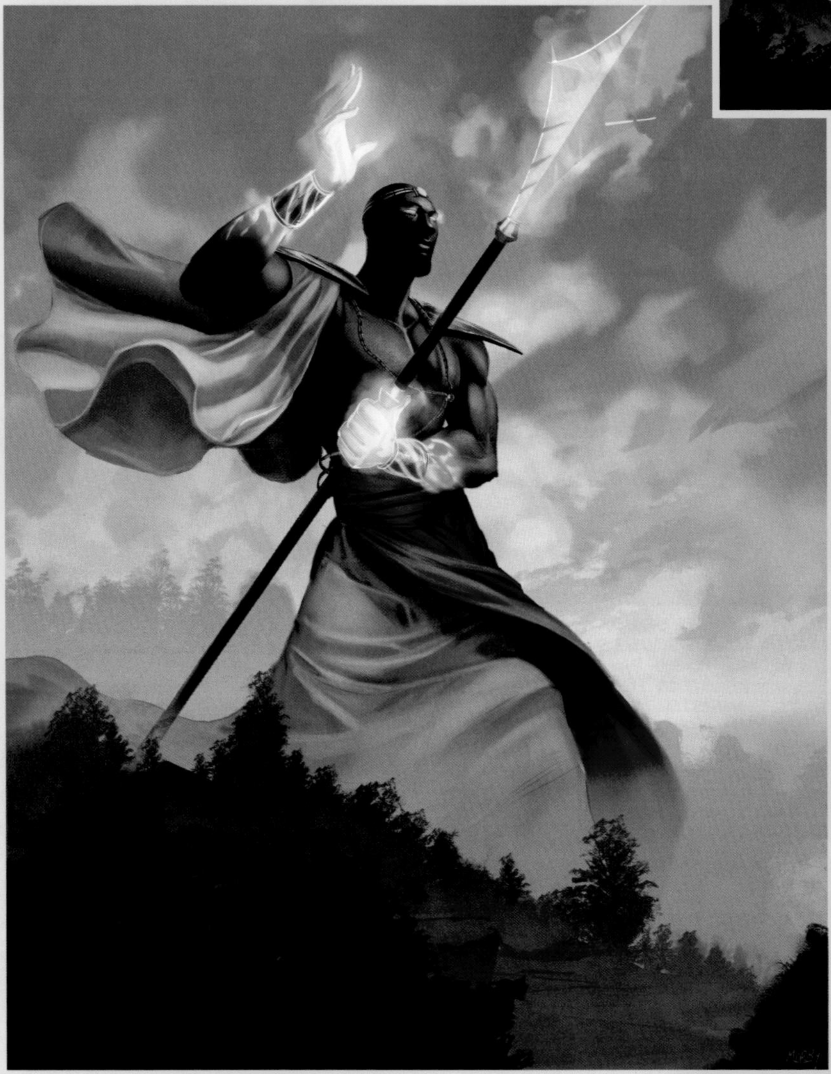

DIVINE POWER

Extraordinary and otherworldly powers that manifest themselves in infinite forms. These powers are only found in Divine Ones.

ACQUIRED DIVINE POWER

A form of Divine Power that can be passed down to mortals from Divine Ones. Nowhere as strong or powerful as Innate Divine Power.

INNATE DIVINE POWER

True Divine Power that Divine Ones are born with.

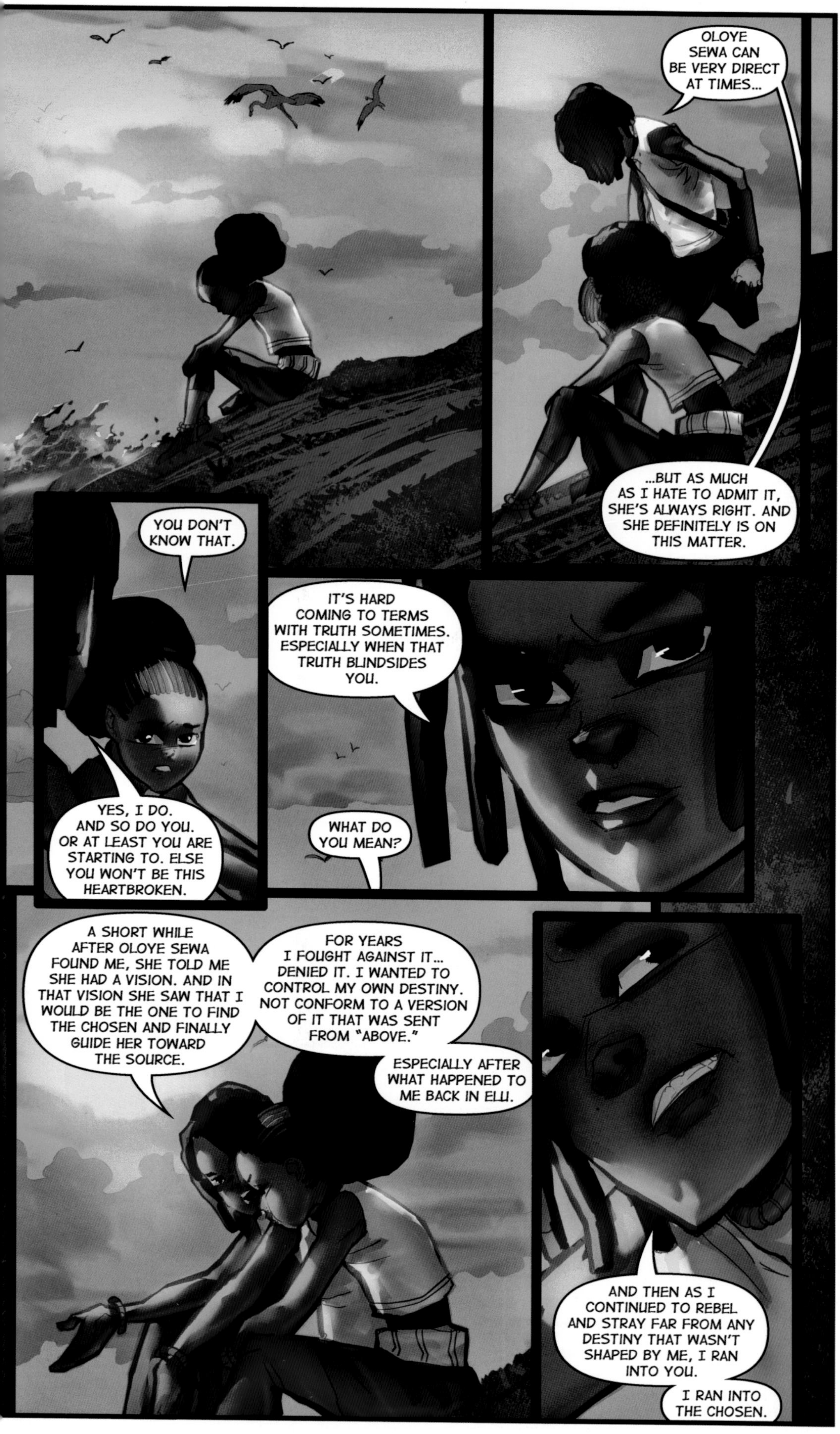
OLOYE SEWA CAN BE VERY DIRECT AT TIMES...
...BUT AS MUCH AS I HATE TO ADMIT IT, SHE'S ALWAYS RIGHT. AND SHE DEFINITELY IS ON THIS MATTER.
YOU DON'T KNOW THAT.
YES, I DO. AND SO DO YOU. OR AT LEAST YOU ARE STARTING TO. ELSE YOU WON'T BE THIS HEARTBROKEN.
IT'S HARD COMING TO TERMS WITH TRUTH SOMETIMES. ESPECIALLY WHEN THAT TRUTH BLINDSIDES YOU.
WHAT DO YOU MEAN?
A SHORT WHILE AFTER OLOYE SEWA FOUND ME, SHE TOLD ME SHE HAD A VISION. AND IN THAT VISION SHE SAW THAT I WOULD BE THE ONE TO FIND THE CHOSEN AND FINALLY GUIDE HER TOWARD THE SOURCE.
FOR YEARS I FOUGHT AGAINST IT... DENIED IT. I WANTED TO CONTROL MY OWN DESTINY. NOT CONFORM TO A VERSION OF IT THAT WAS SENT FROM "ABOVE."
ESPECIALLY AFTER WHAT HAPPENED TO ME BACK IN ELU.
AND THEN AS I CONTINUED TO REBEL AND STRAY FAR FROM ANY DESTINY THAT WASN'T SHAPED BY ME, I RAN INTO YOU.
I RAN INTO THE CHOSEN.

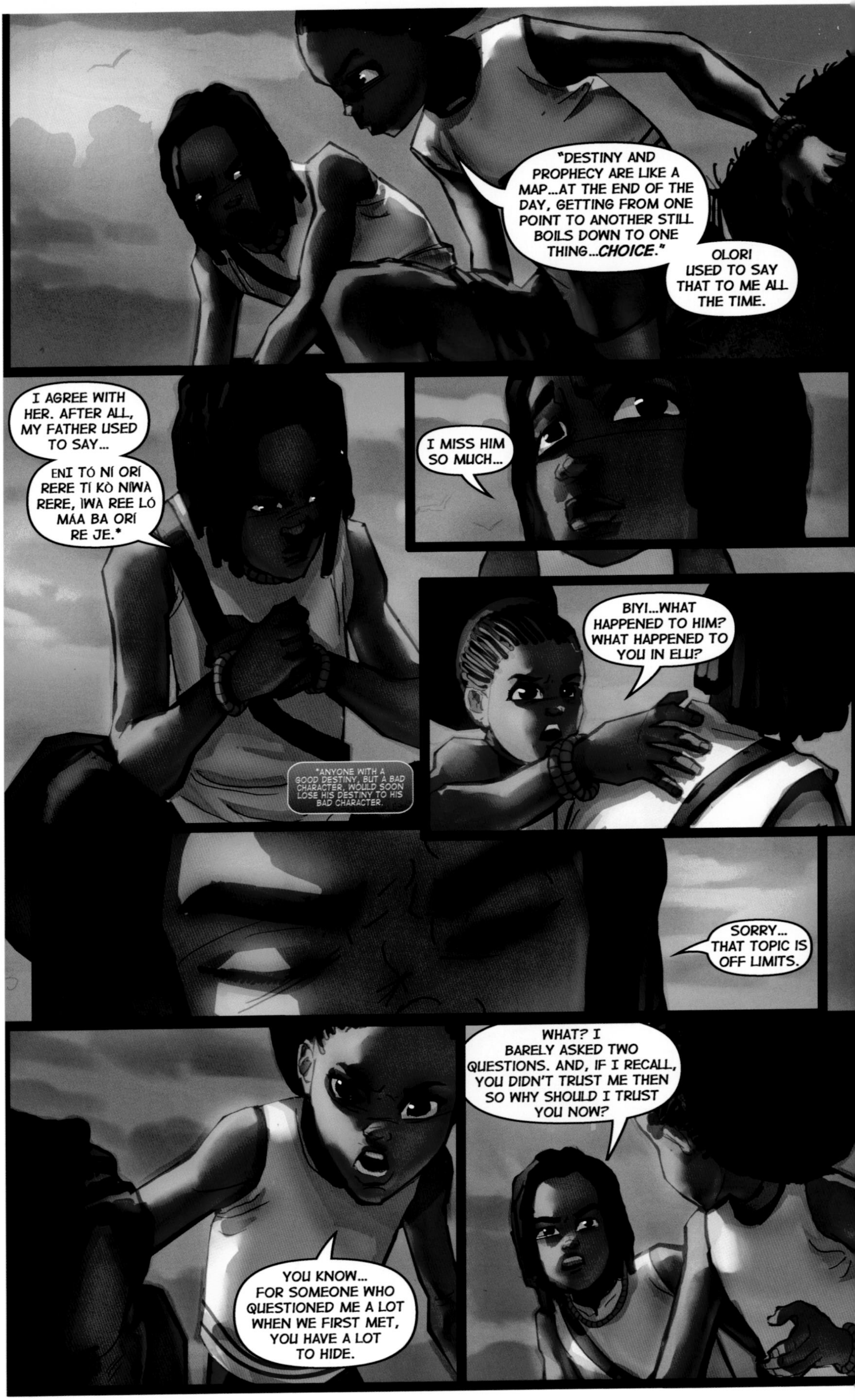
"DESTINY AND PROPHECY ARE LIKE A MAP...AT THE END OF THE DAY, GETTING FROM ONE POINT TO ANOTHER STILL BOILS DOWN TO ONE THING...*CHOICE*."
OLORI USED TO SAY THAT TO ME ALL THE TIME.
I AGREE WITH HER. AFTER ALL, MY FATHER USED TO SAY...
ENI TÓ NÍ ORÍ RERE TÍ KÒ NÍWÀ RERE, ÌWÀ REE LÓ MÁA BA ORÍ RE JE.*
*ANYONE WITH A GOOD DESTINY, BUT A BAD CHARACTER, WOULD SOON LOSE HIS DESTINY TO HIS BAD CHARACTER.
I MISS HIM SO MUCH...
BIYI...WHAT HAPPENED TO HIM? WHAT HAPPENED TO YOU IN ELU?
SORRY... THAT TOPIC IS OFF LIMITS.
YOU KNOW... FOR SOMEONE WHO QUESTIONED ME A LOT WHEN WE FIRST MET, YOU HAVE A LOT TO HIDE.
WHAT? I BARELY ASKED TWO QUESTIONS. AND, IF I RECALL, YOU DIDN'T TRUST ME THEN SO WHY SHOULD I TRUST YOU NOW?

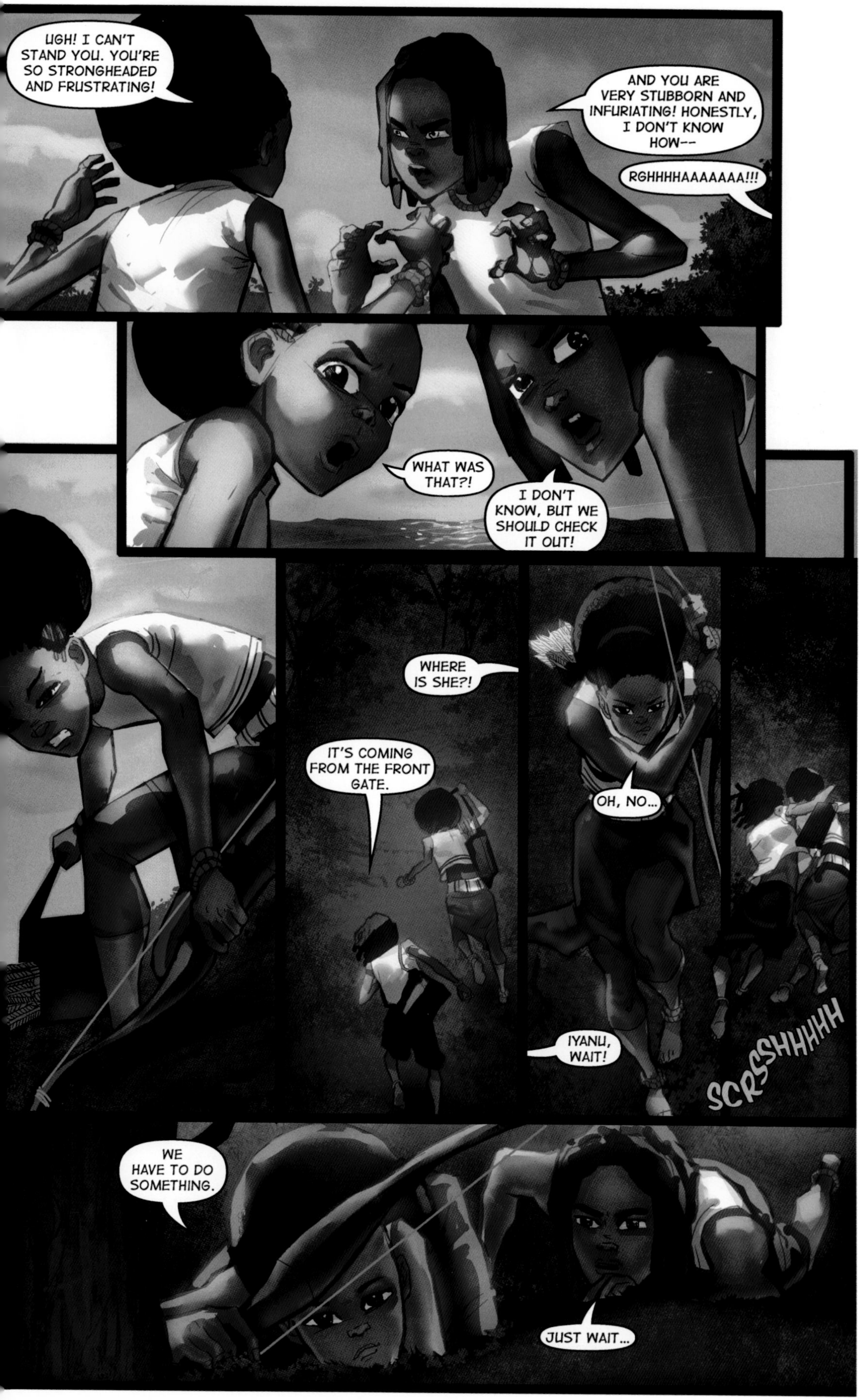
UGH! I CAN'T STAND YOU. YOU'RE SO STRONGHEADED AND FRUSTRATING!
AND YOU ARE VERY STUBBORN AND INFURIATING! HONESTLY, I DON'T KNOW HOW--
RGHHHHAAAAAAA!!!
WHAT WAS THAT?!
I DON'T KNOW, BUT WE SHOULD CHECK IT OUT!
WHERE IS SHE?!
IT'S COMING FROM THE FRONT GATE.
OH, NO...
IYANU, WAIT!
SCRSSHHHHH
WE HAVE TO DO SOMETHING.
JUST WAIT...

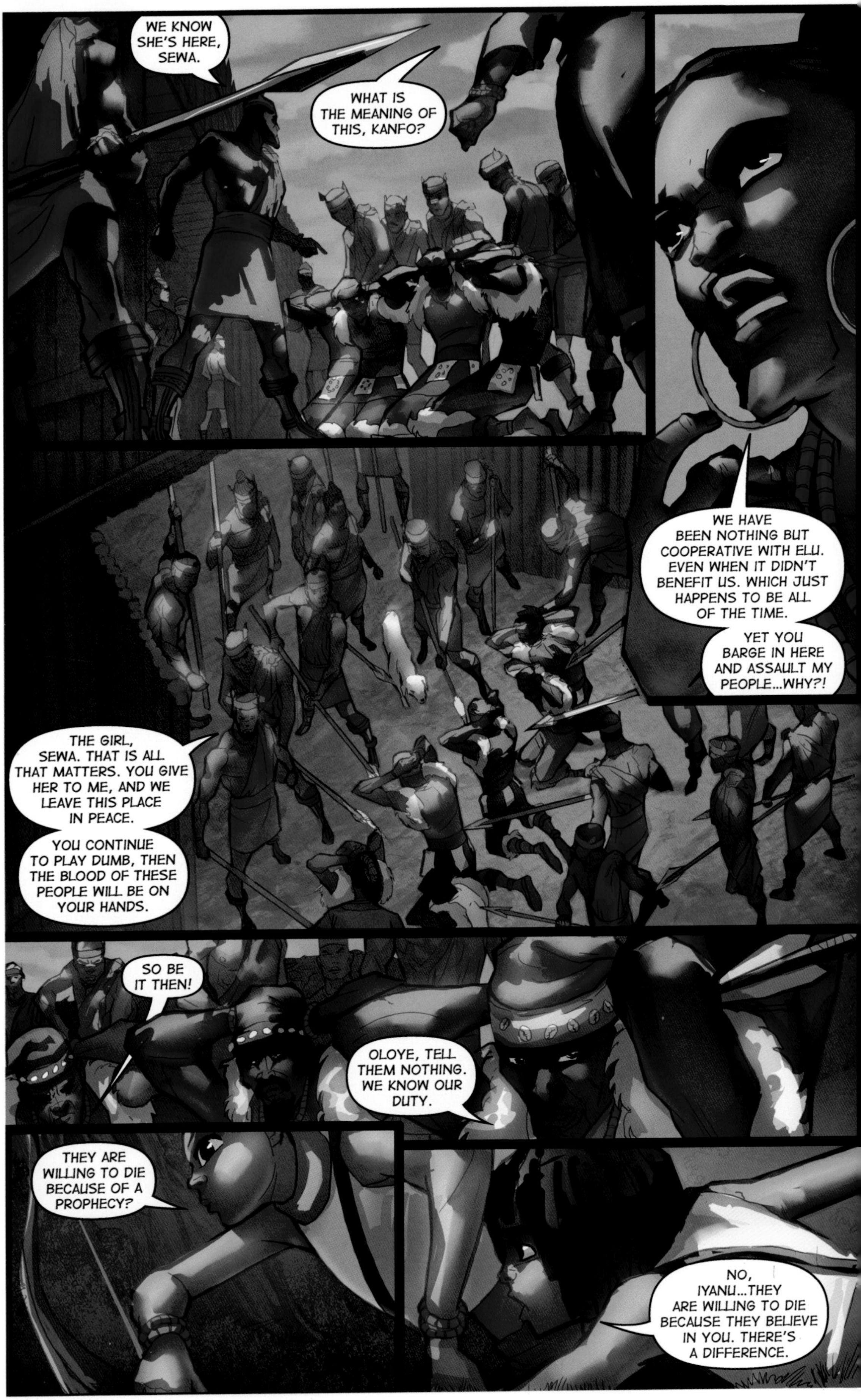
WE KNOW SHE'S HERE, SEWA.
WHAT IS THE MEANING OF THIS, KANFO?
WE HAVE BEEN NOTHING BUT COOPERATIVE WITH ELU. EVEN WHEN IT DIDN'T BENEFIT US. WHICH JUST HAPPENS TO BE ALL OF THE TIME.
YET YOU BARGE IN HERE AND ASSAULT MY PEOPLE...WHY?!
THE GIRL, SEWA. THAT IS ALL THAT MATTERS. YOU GIVE HER TO ME, AND WE LEAVE THIS PLACE IN PEACE.
YOU CONTINUE TO PLAY DUMB, THEN THE BLOOD OF THESE PEOPLE WILL BE ON YOUR HANDS.
SO BE IT THEN!
OLOYE, TELL THEM NOTHING. WE KNOW OUR DUTY.
THEY ARE WILLING TO DIE BECAUSE OF A PROPHECY?
NO, IYANU...THEY ARE WILLING TO DIE BECAUSE THEY BELIEVE IN YOU. THERE'S A DIFFERENCE.

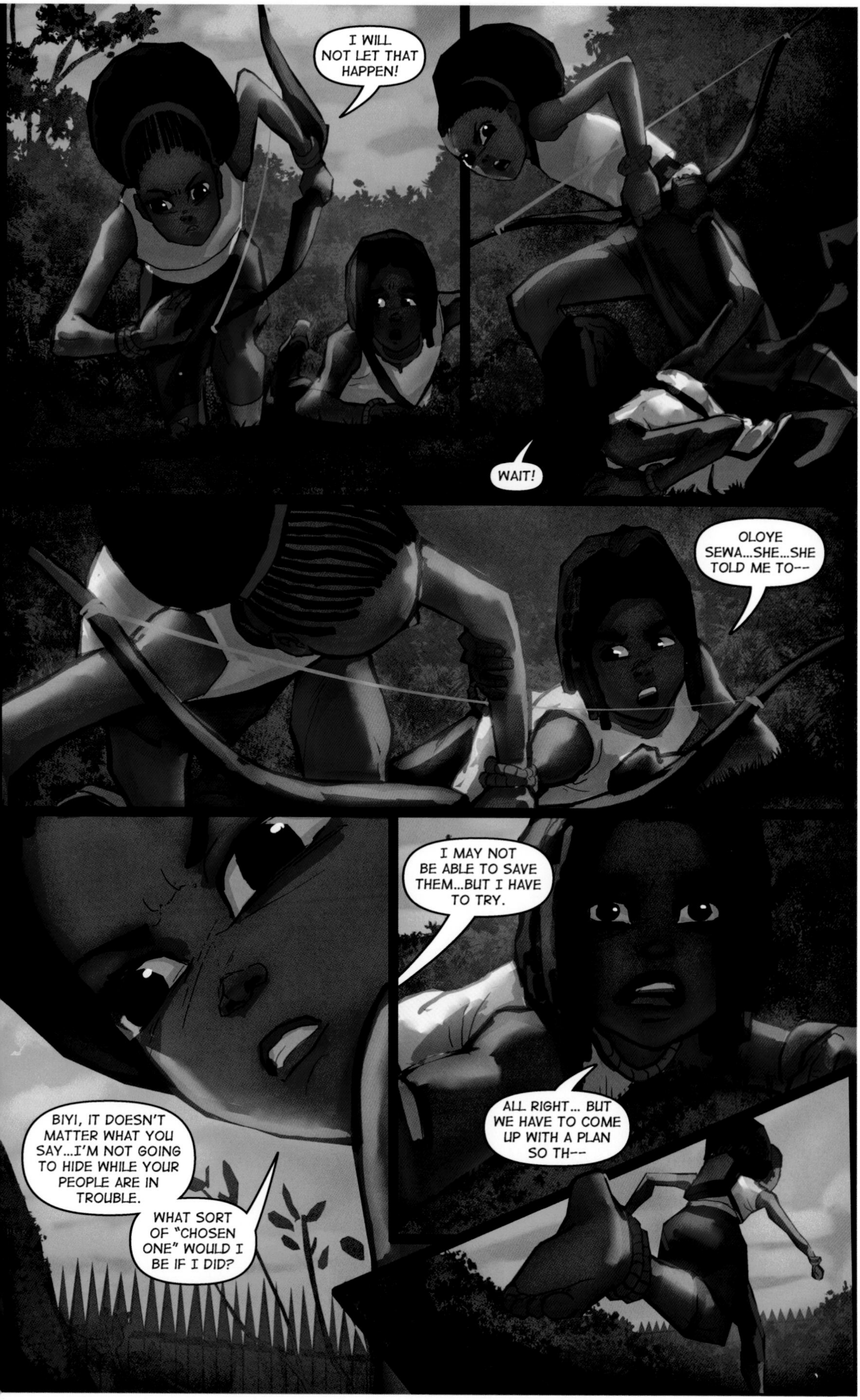
I WILL NOT LET THAT HAPPEN!
WAIT!
OLOYE SEWA...SHE...SHE TOLD ME TO--
I MAY NOT BE ABLE TO SAVE THEM...BUT I HAVE TO TRY.
BIYI, IT DOESN'T MATTER WHAT YOU SAY...I'M NOT GOING TO HIDE WHILE YOUR PEOPLE ARE IN TROUBLE.
WHAT SORT OF "CHOSEN ONE" WOULD I BE IF I DID?
ALL RIGHT... BUT WE HAVE TO COME UP WITH A PLAN SO TH--

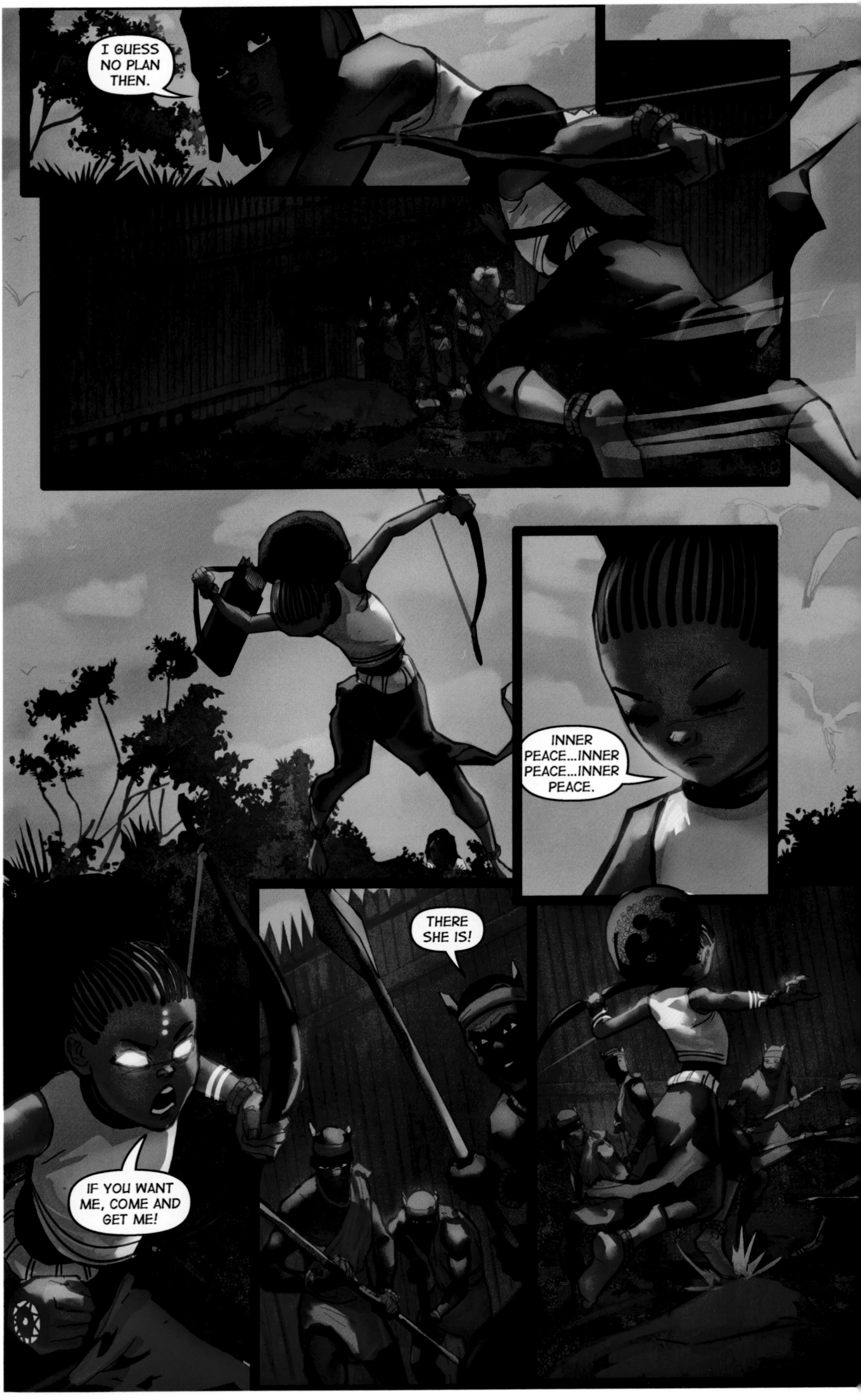
I GUESS NO PLAN THEN.
INNER PEACE...INNER PEACE...INNER PEACE.
IF YOU WANT ME, COME AND GET ME!
THERE SHE IS!

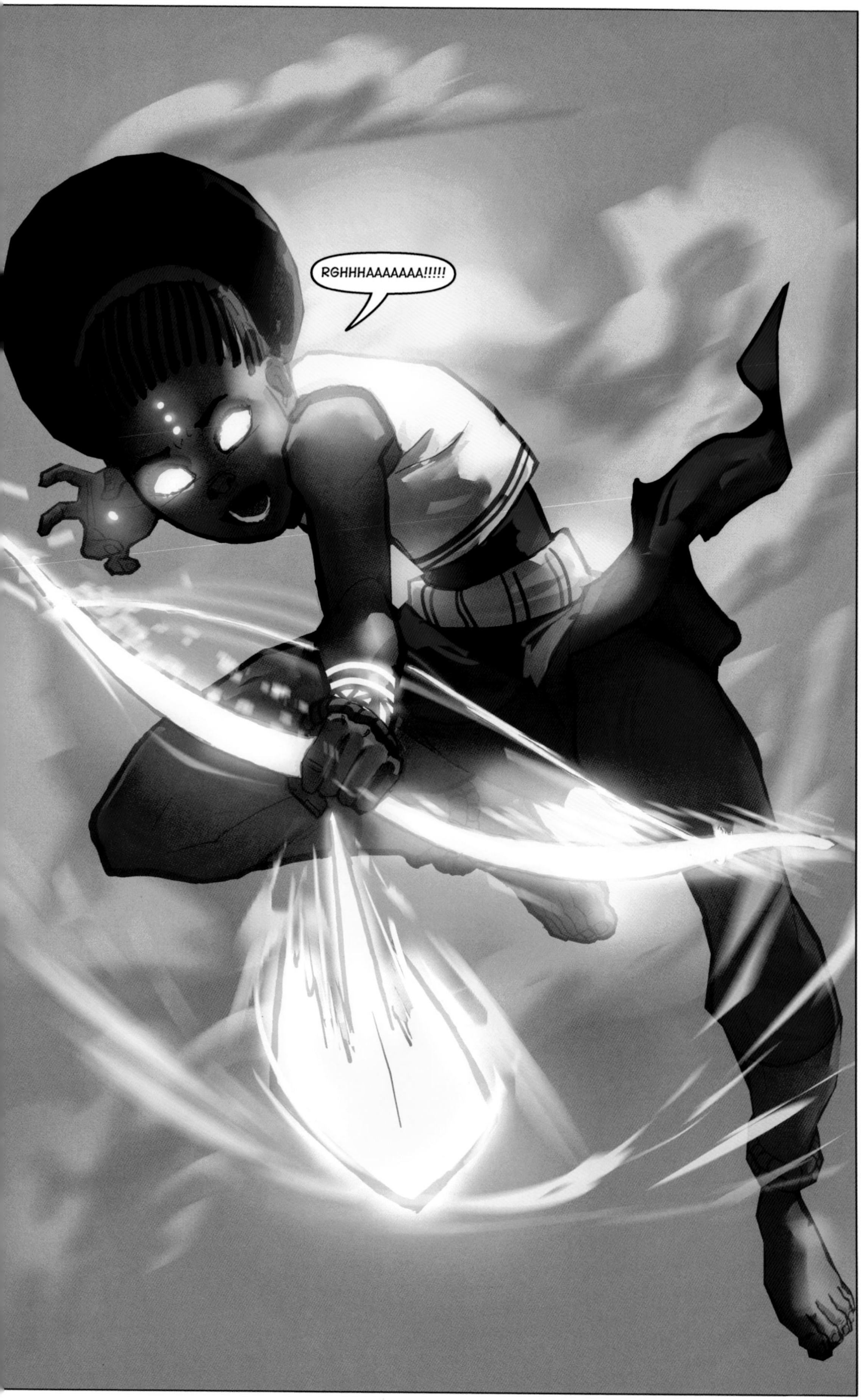
RGHHHAAAAAAA!!!!!

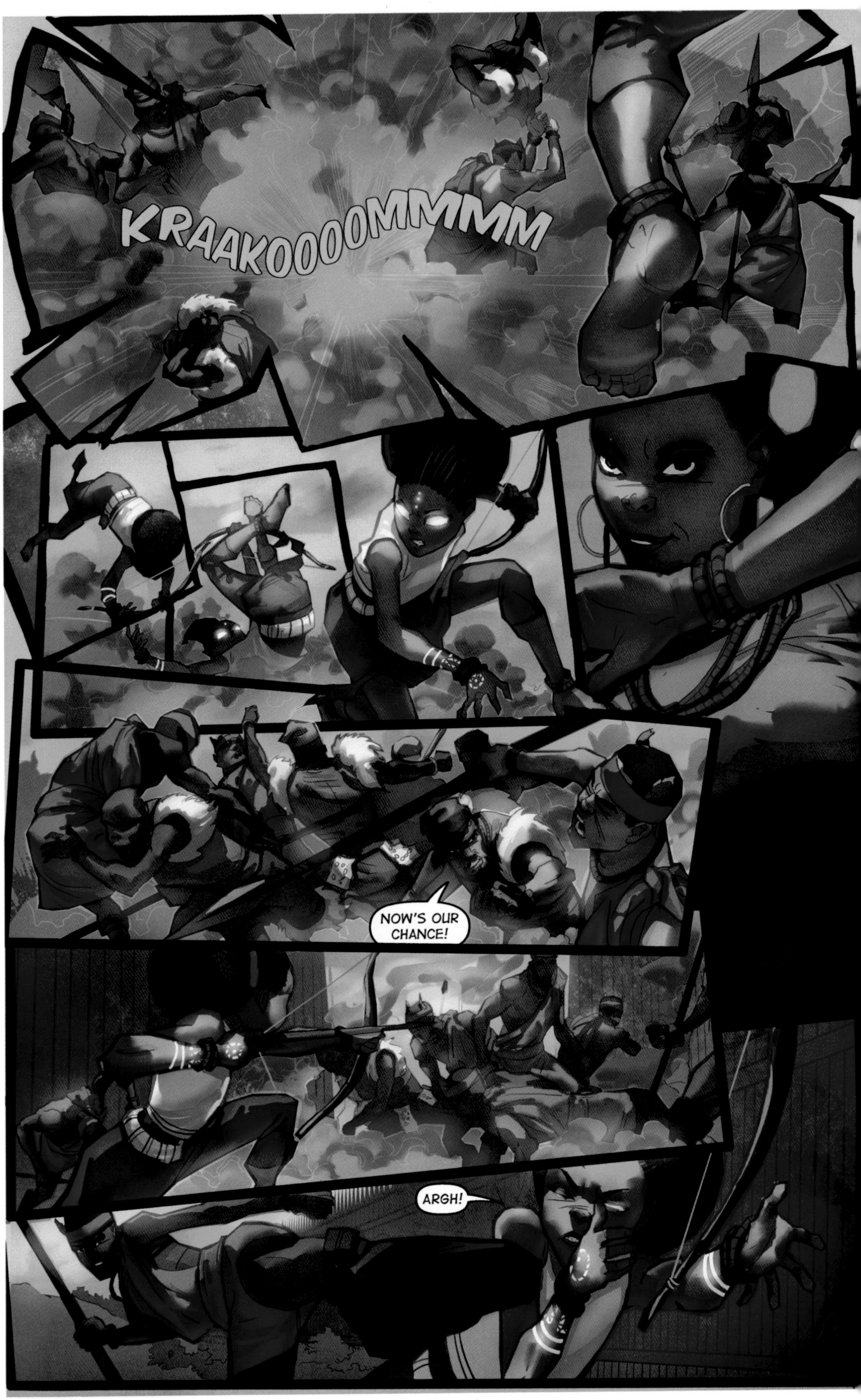
KRAAKOOOOMMMMM
NOW'S OUR CHANCE!
ARGH!

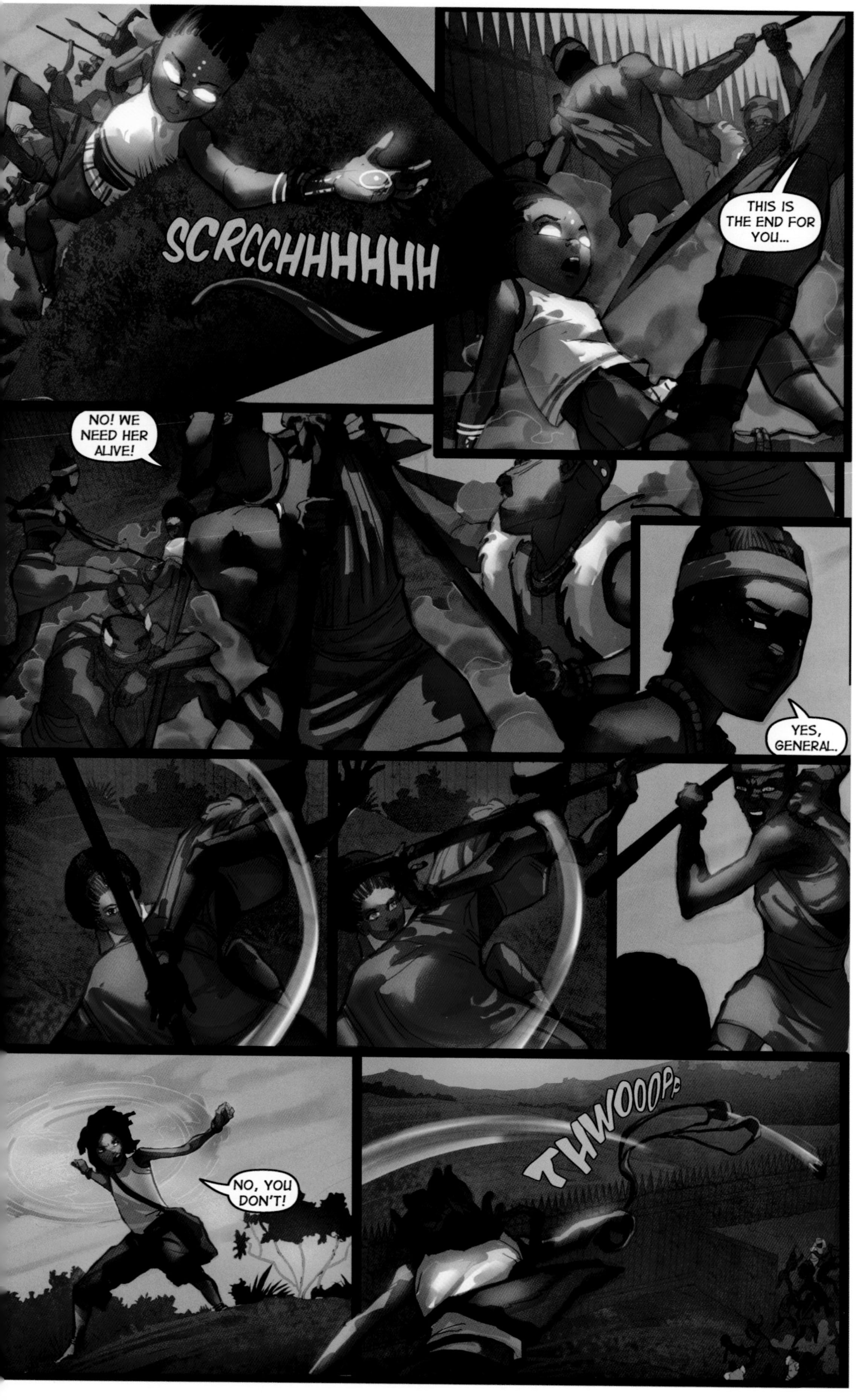
SCRCCHHHHHH
THIS IS THE END FOR YOU...
NO! WE NEED HER ALIVE!
YES, GENERAL.
NO, YOU DON'T!
THWOOOP

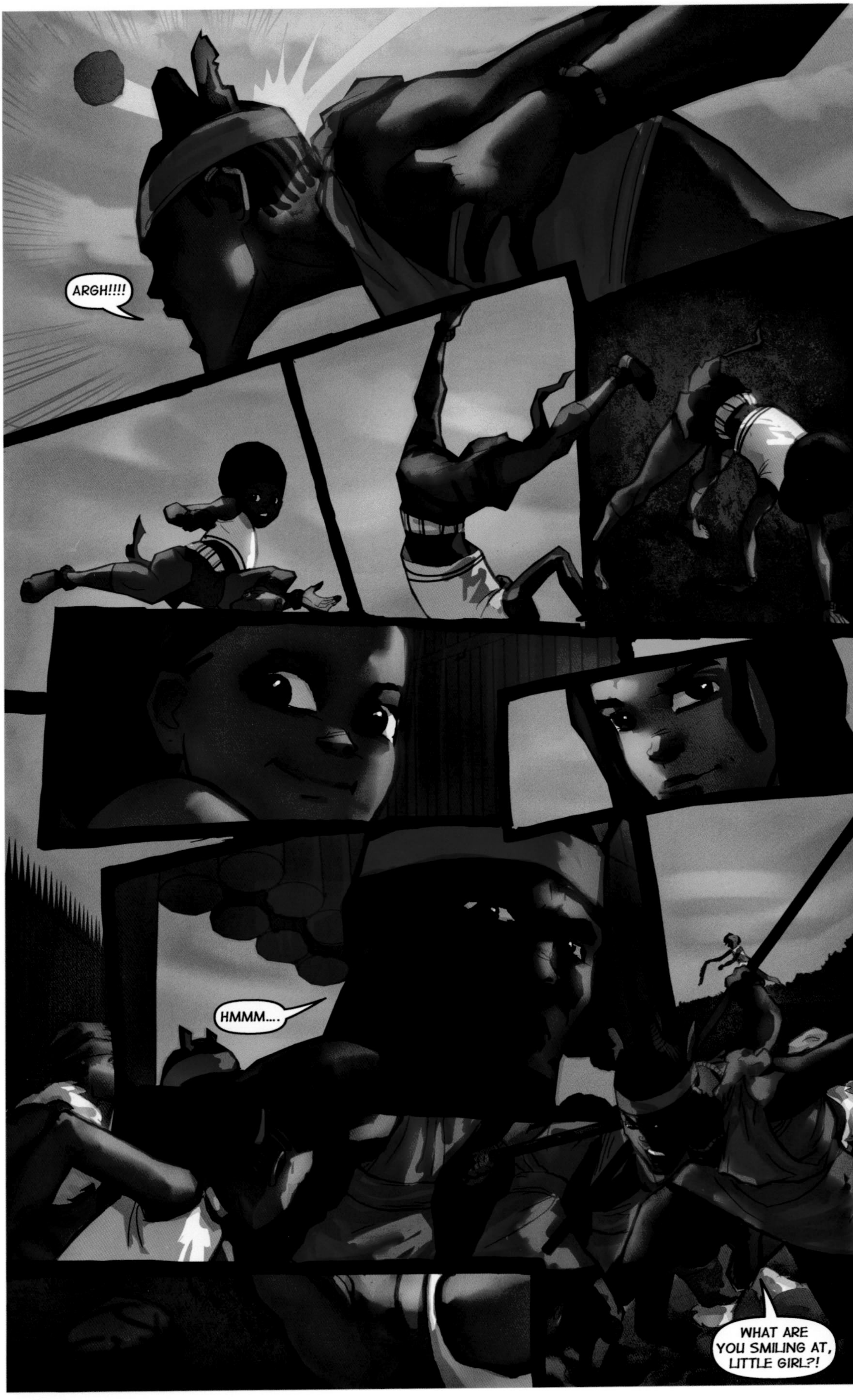
ARGH!!!!
HMMM....
WHAT ARE YOU SMILING AT, LITTLE GIRL?!

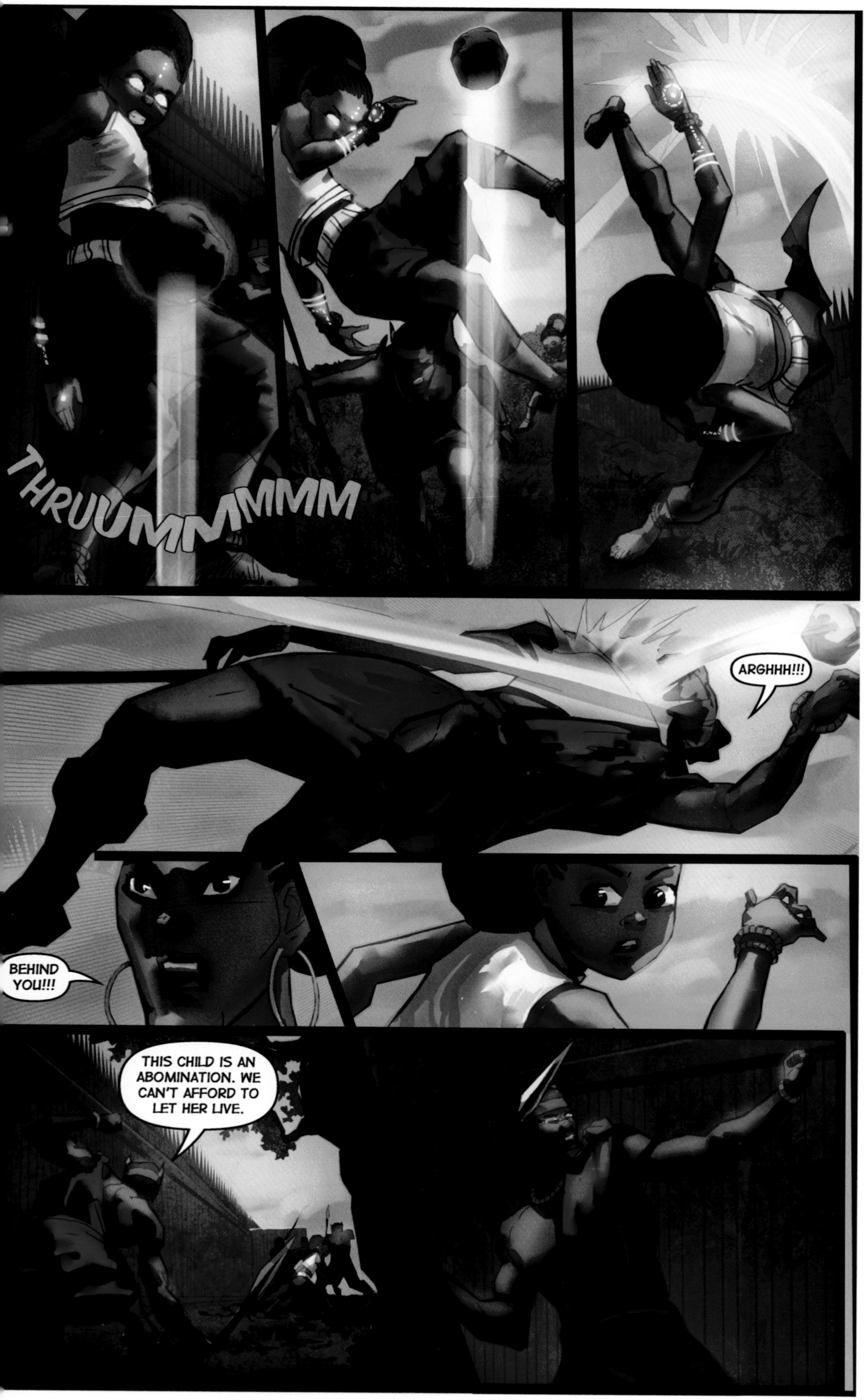
THRUUMMMMM
ARGHHH!!!
BEHIND YOU!!!
THIS CHILD IS AN ABOMINATION. WE CAN'T AFFORD TO LET HER LIVE.

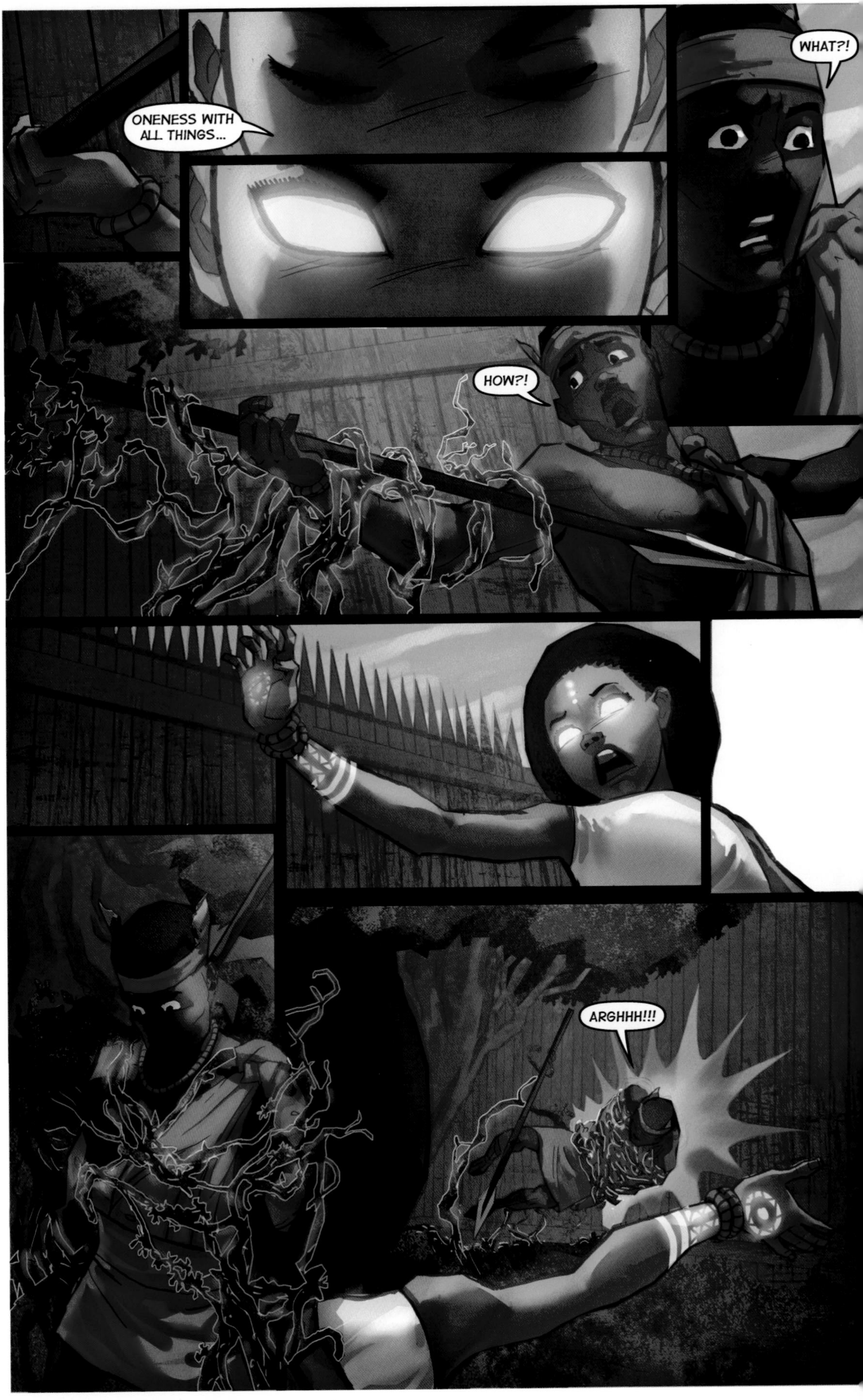
ONENESS WITH ALL THINGS...
WHAT?!
HOW?!
ARGHHH!!!

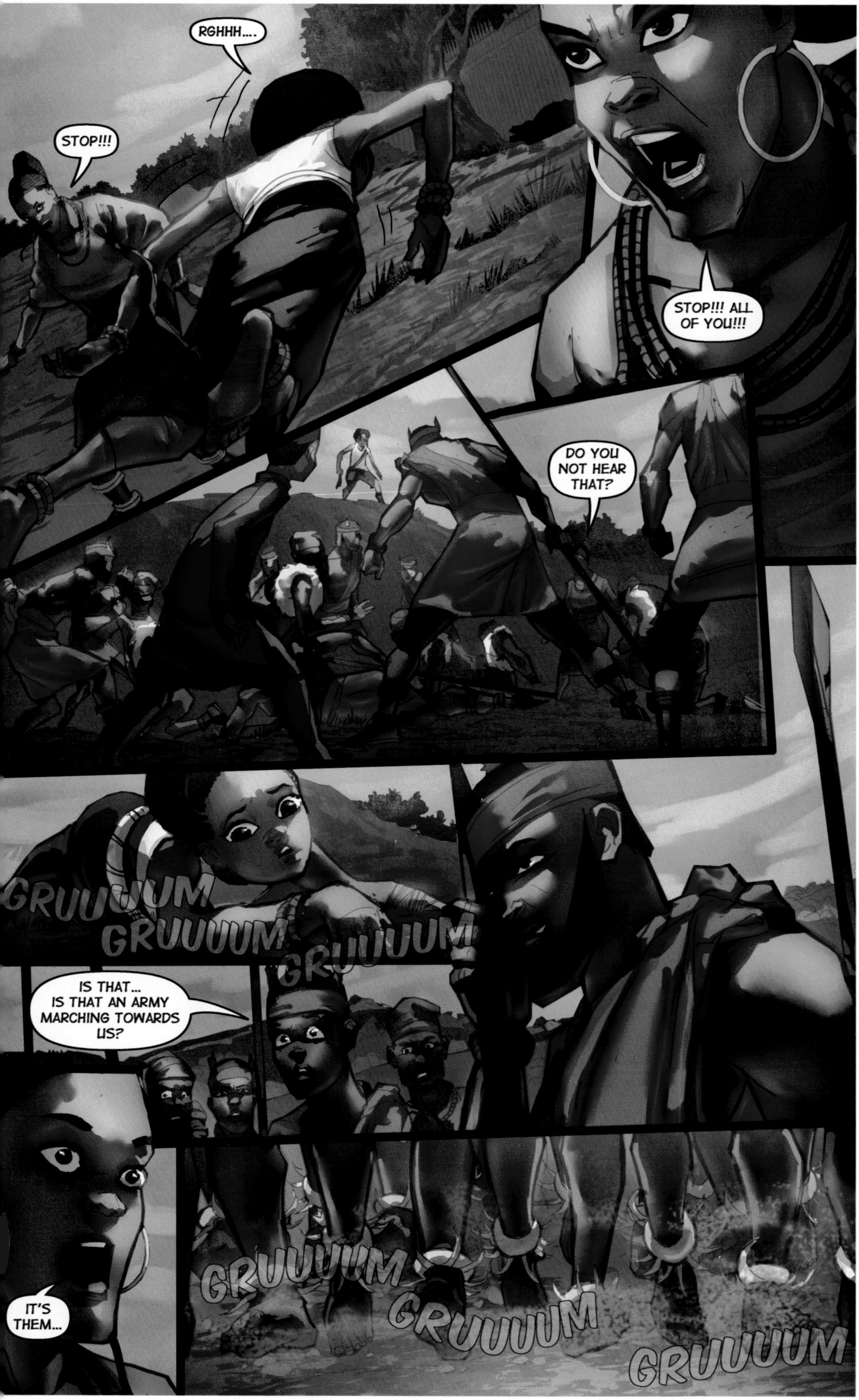
STOP!!!
RGHHH....
STOP!!! ALL OF YOU!!!
DO YOU NOT HEAR THAT?
GRUUUUM
GRUUUUM
GRUUUUM
GRUUUUM
IS THAT... IS THAT AN ARMY MARCHING TOWARDS US?
IT'S THEM...
GRUUUUM
GRUUUUM
GRUUUUM

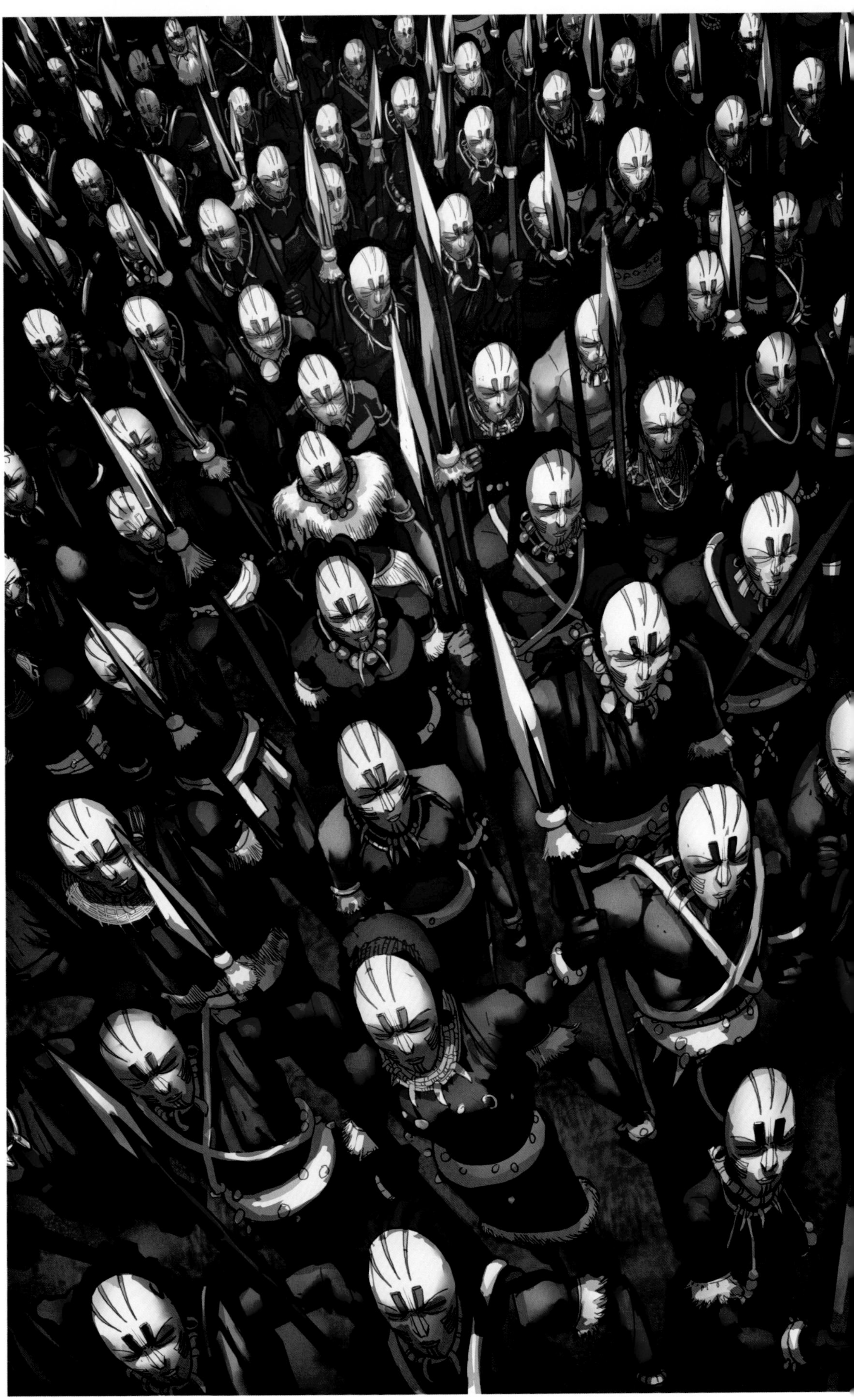

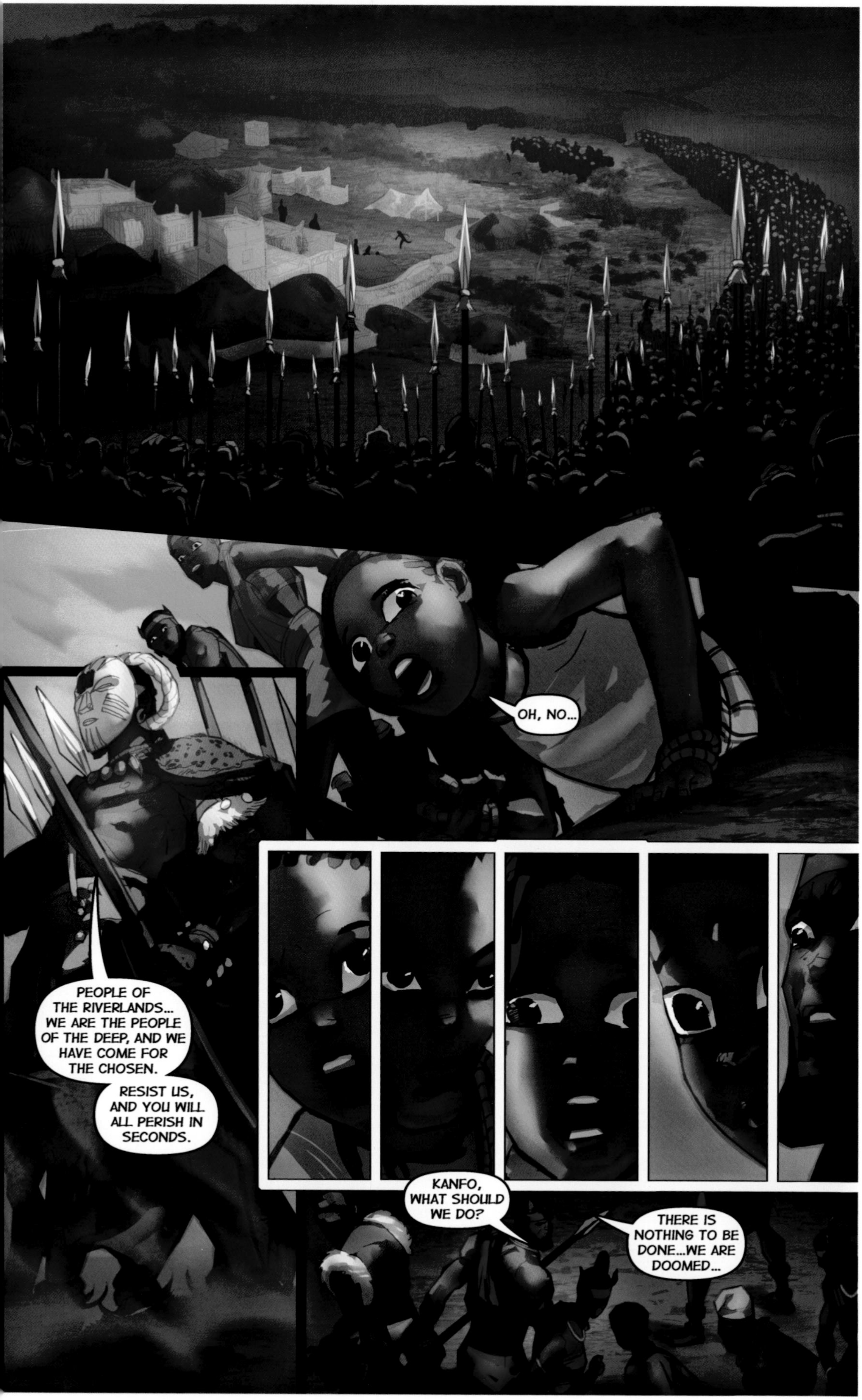
OH, NO...
PEOPLE OF THE RIVERLANDS... WE ARE THE PEOPLE OF THE DEEP, AND WE HAVE COME FOR THE CHOSEN.
RESIST US, AND YOU WILL ALL PERISH IN SECONDS.
KANFO, WHAT SHOULD WE DO?
THERE IS NOTHING TO BE DONE...WE ARE DOOMED...

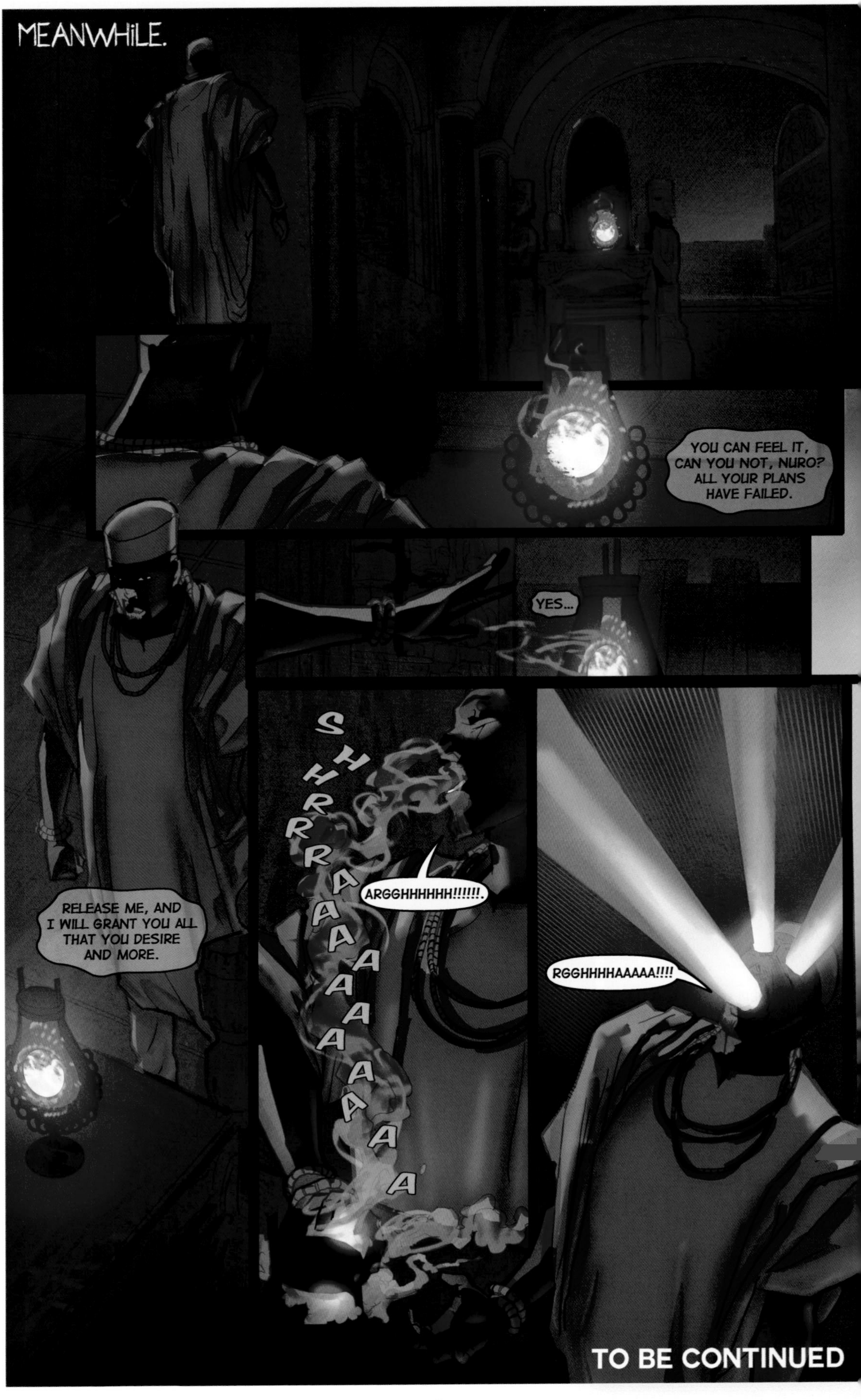
MEANWHILE.
YOU CAN FEEL IT, CAN YOU NOT, NURO? ALL YOUR PLANS HAVE FAILED.
YES...
RELEASE ME, AND I WILL GRANT YOU ALL THAT YOU DESIRE AND MORE.
SHHRRRAAAAAAAAAAAA
ARGGHHHHHH!!!!!!.
RGGHHHHAAAAA!!!!
TO BE CONTINUED

The Chosen • Art by Toyin "Morby" Ajetunmobi

Creator's Corner with Roye Okupe

HEY, GUYS! ROYE HERE! I hope you've enjoyed *Iyanu: Child of Wonder* Volume 2. Just like with Volume 1, I thought it'd be a cool idea if I added, as a bonus, some more backstory to peel back the layers of this beautiful, massive world and geek out with you a bit about it. For the next few pages, I'll be giving some behind-the-scenes backstory about key characters, locations, and events pertaining to the world of Iyanu in chronological order. We'll pick up from where we stopped in the Iyanu Volume 1 "Creator's Corner" section . . . **400 ADW**.

Once again, I've used the conclusion of the main event, the Divine Wars, as an anchor point to measure time. So **BDW** stands for "Before the Divine Wars," while **ADW** stands for "After the Divine Wars."

Art by Chima Kalu

The Vengeance of Prince Debo
(400 - 475 ADW)

ONCE THEY MADE IT to the **Deep**, Prince Debo and his followers managed to settle within the dense forest. Although life was not anything close to what it was within the walls of Elu, **The People of the Deep**, as they were now known, made what they could of the life they had. But losing almost half of your family, relatives, and friends is a devastating tragedy that would break anyone. And that is exactly what tragedy did to Prince Debo. For all that was on his mind from the moment he and his people arrived in the Deep was revenge and the reclamation of Elu. A notion he was sure to pass down to all his people and most especially his descendants.

The Death of Prince Debo
(475 ADW)

UNFORTUNATELY, PRINCE DEBO would not live to see the inside of the walls of Elu again or his revenge enacted. He would die of natural causes in 475 ADW, at the age of 100. He was survived by four children, ten grandchildren, and seventeen great-grandchildren. All of whom were at his side when he uttered his final words, "reclaim our land . . . Avenge the dead."

The Children of The Deep (485 - 525 ADW)

THE PEOPLE OF THE DEEP are very hard and violent people. The saying "Take before it can be taken from you" has been passed down from generation to generation as a motto for all who are born and live in the Deep.

With over a hundred years spent outside the walls of Elu finding their footing and ten years after the passing of Prince Debo, in 485 ADW, the People of the Deep begin to plot their return to and reclamation of Elu. But the approach they choose will be an indirect one.

In 485 ADW, **Prince Dele (short for Bamidele)**, grandson of Prince Debo and current ruler of the Deep, devises an infiltration plan. To do this, he would need two of his brightest young warriors.

From birth, the children of the Deep are trained (sometimes against their will) to be ruthless warriors and vicious marauders. And it just happened that the two of their brightest young warriors, **Oye** and **Remi**, were Prince Dele's nephew and niece, respectively.

Oye and Remi were both great-grandchildren of Prince Debo. Ever since their father, who was a single parent, passed away, Prince Dele cared for both of them—meaning there was no one he trusted more with his mission to destabilize Elu from within. Meanwhile, back

People of the Deep • Art by Godwin Akpan

in Elu, it had been over a hundred years since the exile of Prince Debo, and since then, many more people had been thrown out the walls of Elu. Haunted by the guilt of the horrible decisions of his ancestors, Oba Adeniyi, the then-current king of Elu, began a pilot program to bring orphaned children from outside the walls back into Elu. It was the first program of its kind, and one many within the walls frowned upon.

Back in the Deep, Prince Dele saw this as an opportunity to use his nephew and niece to finally complete the mission of his grandfather. Oye, a teenager, would infiltrate the political system (the Council) while Remi, his little sister, would infiltrate the spiritual (the Agoni). Oye bought in immediately to the mission. But Remi, still grieving the loss of her father, struggled with the idea of leaving the only home she ever knew.

Eventually, the two would get to Elu and be accepted as orphans into society. For forty years, both of them would rise through their individual ranks until Oye, who was now known as **Nuro**, became Chancellor of the Elu Mesi (the Council) and Remi, who was now known as **Olori**, became the last Agoni!

The Agoni Rebellion
(520 ADW)

THROUGHOUT THEIR ASCENT within the walls, Nuro (formerly Oye) and Olori (formerly Remi) intentionally kept communication between themselves to a minimum. Conversely, the brother and sister pair maintained ongoing communications with their comrades in the Deep via a network of spies both within the Walls of Elu and many of the exiled settlements.

However, as they both got a taste of more power during their respective rise, communication with the Deep eventually slowed, coming to a complete halt when Nuro became Chancellor of the Elu Mesi—the de facto #2 in Elu. But as the saying goes, absolute power corrupts absolutely. And no man's life properly exemplified this phrase as much as Nuro's, who once he became Chancellor, ceased all communication with the Deep. Olori, on the other hand, stopped communicating with her former people for a much more noble reason. Having finally found a home and family again with the Agoni, she no longer saw the appeal in betraying the people she had now come to love. It would seem that both their uncle's (Prince Dele) and great-grandfather's (Prince Debo) plot to reclaim Elu had failed. At least for the time being.

As soon as Nuro became Chancellor, he quickly began to plot how to consolidate his power. His next target,

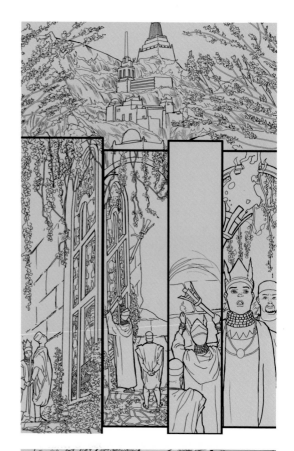

Art by Chima Kalu

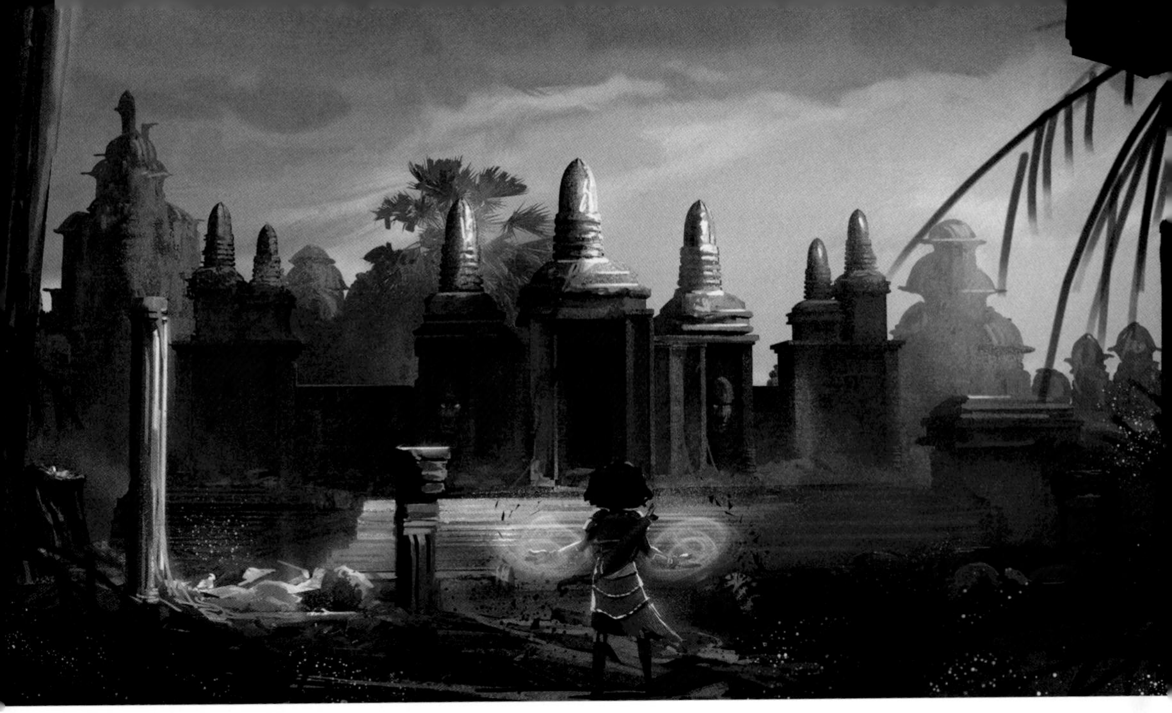

Concept art by Godwin Akpan

the Agoni, who for centuries had held secrets that were vital to the well-being of Elu. The most important being the concoction (Abo Dust) that purified the corrupt. The Agoni holding such secrets didn't bode well for Nuro's plans to become all-powerful. So, by manipulating the members of the Elu Mesi (the Council), Nuro would turn them and the majority of the masses against the Agoni. Soon after, the current King, Oba Adeniyi, would have no option but to send the Eso to detain the leaders of the Agoni. But they resisted and thus began the Agoni rebellion.

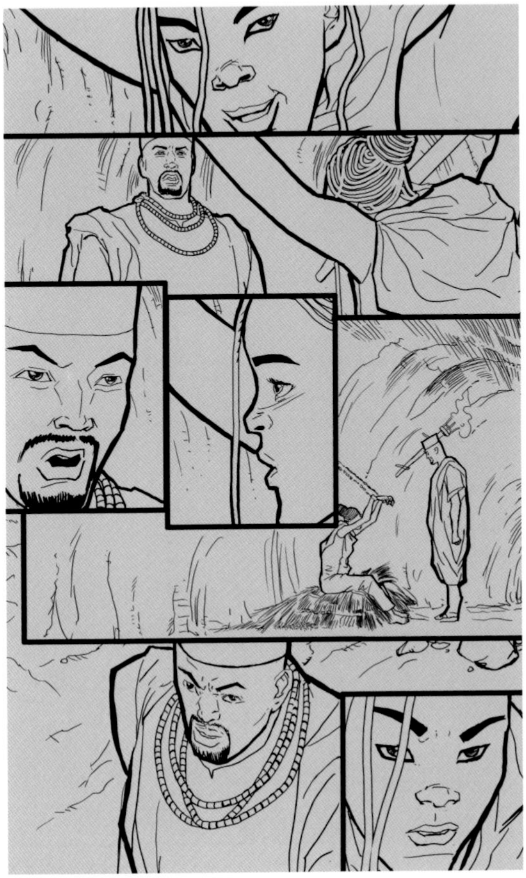

Art by Chima Kalu

After a skirmish outside the Forbidden Temple, all of the Agoni were wiped out in a matter of hours, leaving Olori as the last of the Agoni. This unfortunate genocide would further distance brother from sister as Olori now mourned the loss of yet another family at the hands of her brother Nuro. In exchange for her life, Olori, who refused to give up the secrets of the Agoni, would keep on purifying the Corrupt. She would also vacate the Land of the Forgotten, a place that had been home to the Agoni for over five hundred years, and be banished to the forest region north of the Outer Walls to live out the rest of her days. Thus allowing Nuro full access to the Forbidden Temple to begin extracting the knowledge the Agoni had kept secret for centuries.

Conclusion

Now that you're all caught up with both the history of Yorubaland and the history of the People of the Deep, I can't wait for you to see what's in store for *Iyanu: Child of Wonder* Volume 3. Stay tuned!

–ROYE OKUPE, FEBRUARY 2022

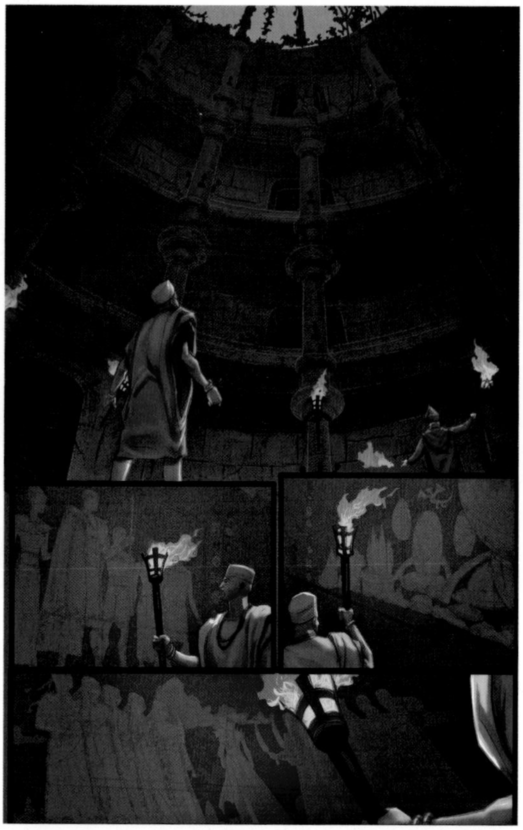
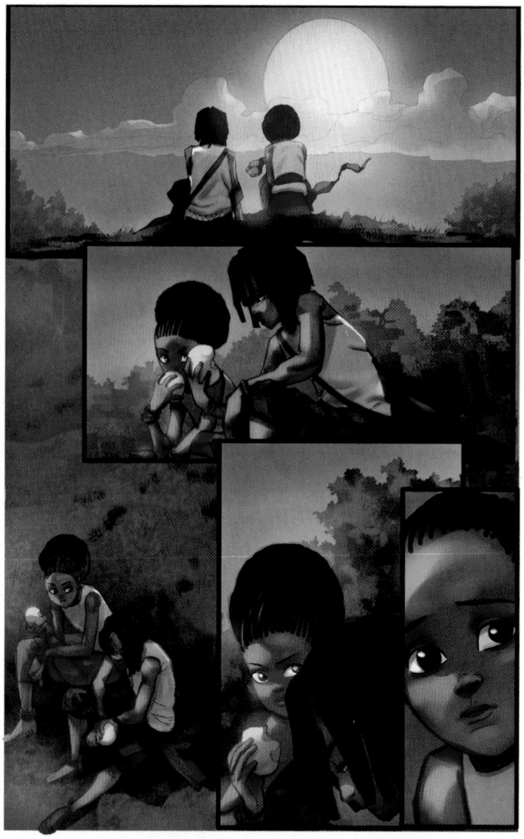
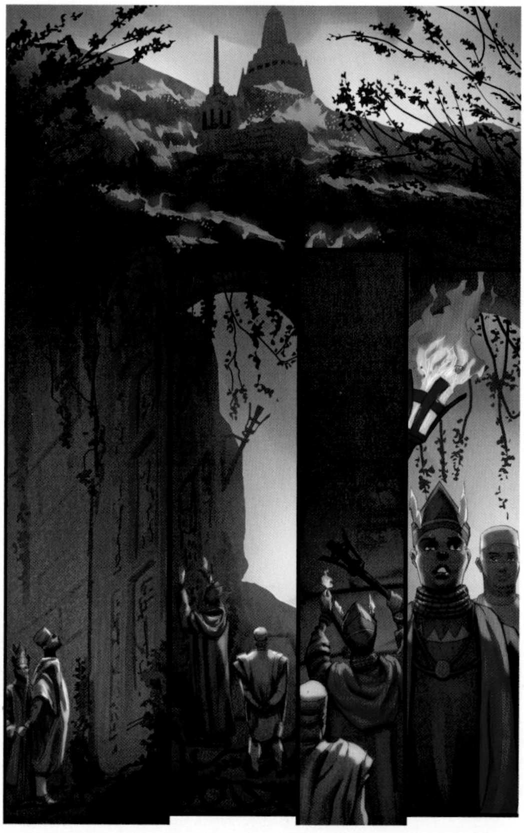
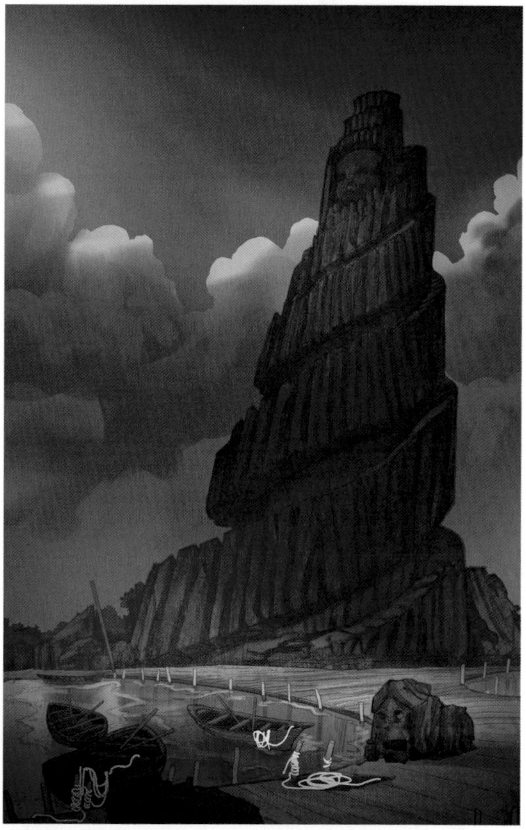

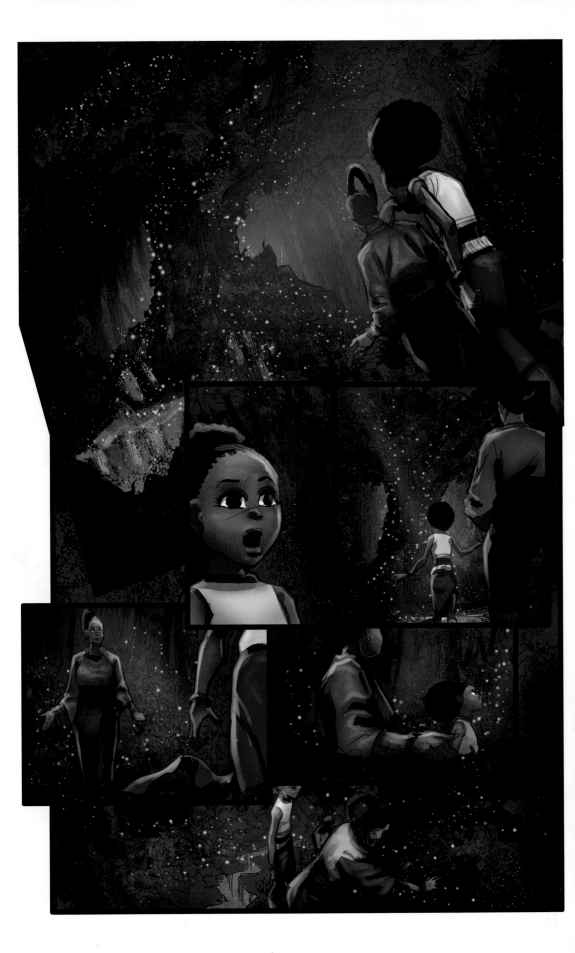

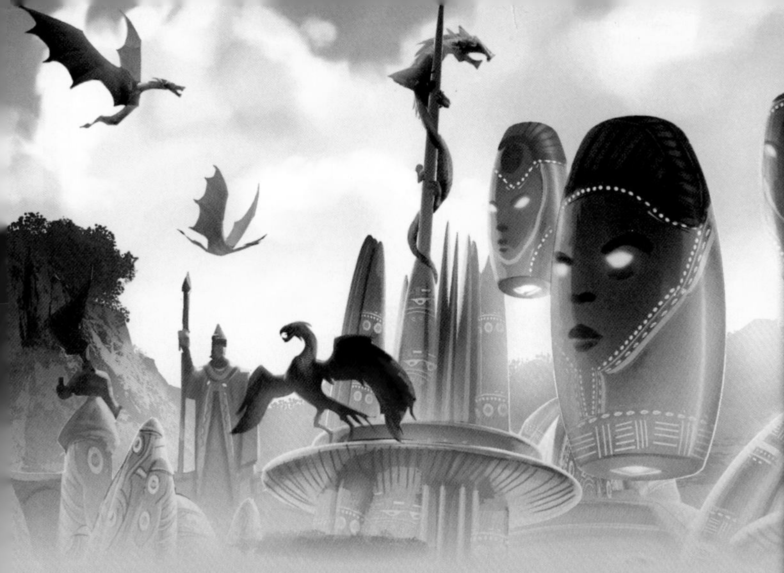

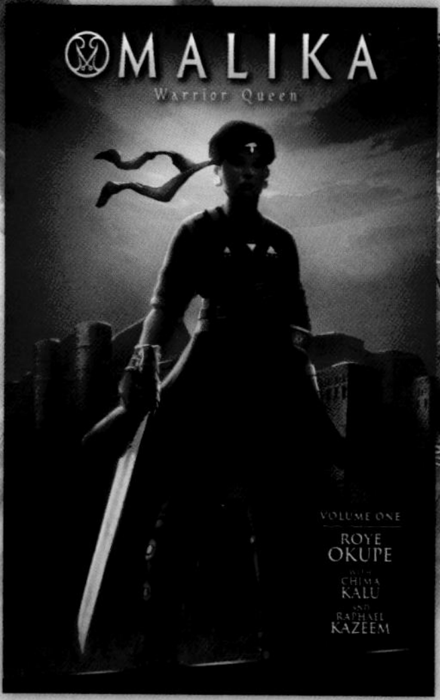
MALIKA
Warrior Queen
VOLUME ONE
ROYE OKUPE
CHIMA KALU
RAPHAEL KAZEEM

Dark Horse Books and YouNeek Studios are proud to present a shared universe of fantasy and superhero stories inspired by African history, culture, and mythology—created by the best Nigerian comics talent!

Malika: Warrior Queen Volume 1

(pronounced: "Ma-Lie-Kah")

Written by Roye Okupe.
Illustrated by Chima Kalu.
Colors by Raphael Kazeem.
Letters by Spoof Animation.

Begins the tale of the exploits of queen and military commander Malika, who struggles to keep the peace in her ever-expanding empire, Azzaz.

Sept. 2021 Trade Paperback 336 pages
$24.99 US $33.99 CA • 9781506723082

Malika: Warrior Queen Volume 2

Written by Roye Okupe.
Illustrated by Sunkanmi Akinboye.
Colors by Etubi Onucheyo and Toyin Ajetunmobi.
Letters by Spoof Animation.

Dec. 2021 Trade Paperback 280 Pages
$24.99 US $33.99 CA • 9781506723075

Iyanu: Child of Wonder Volume 1

(pronounced: "Ee-Yah-Nu")

Written by Roye Okupe.
Illustrated by Godwin Akpan.
Letters by Spoof Animation.

A teenage orphan with no recollection of her past discovers that she has abilities that rival the ancient deities told of in folklore. These abilities are the key to bringing back an "age of wonders," to save a world on the brink of destruction!

Sept. 2021 Trade Paperback 112 Pages
$19.99 US $25.99 CA • 9781506723044

WindMaker Volume 1

Written by Roye Okupe.
Illustrated by Sunkanmi Akinboye and Toyin Ajetunmobi.
Letters by Spoof Animation.

The West African nation of Atala is thrust into an era of unrest and dysfunction after their beloved president turns vicious dictator.

April 2022 Trade Paperback 144 Pages
$19.99 US $25.99 CA • 9781506723112

E.X.O.: The Legend of Wale Williams Volume 1

Written by Roye Okupe.
Illustrated by Sunkanmi Akinboye.
Colors by Raphael Kazeem.
Letters by Spoof Animation.

The oldest son of a world-renowned scientist, Wale Williams—aka tech-savvy superhero EXO—tries to save Lagoon City from a deadly group of extremists. But before this "pending" superhero can do any good for his city, there is one person he must save first—himself!

Oct. 2021 Trade Paperback 280 Pages
$24.99 US $33.99 CA • 9781506723020

E.X.O.: The Legend of Wale Williams Volume 2

Written by Roye Okupe.
Illustrated by Sunkanmi Akinboye.
Colors by Etubi Onucheyo and Tarella Pablo.
Letters by Spoof Animation.

Feb. 2022 Trade Paperback 280 Pages
$24.99 US $33.99 CA • 9781506723037

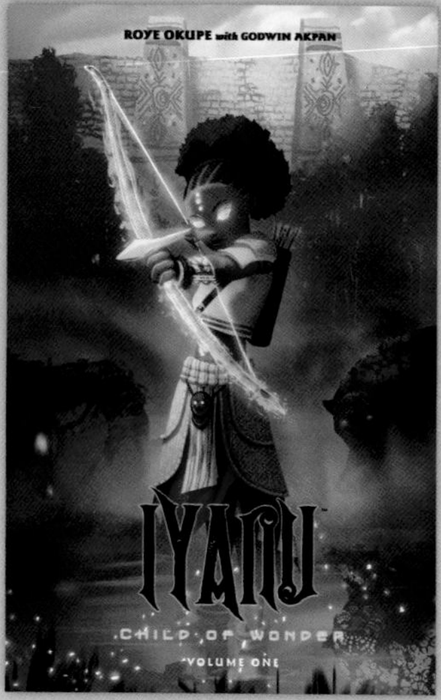
ROYE OKUPE with GODWIN AKPAN
IYANU
CHILD OF WONDER
VOLUME ONE

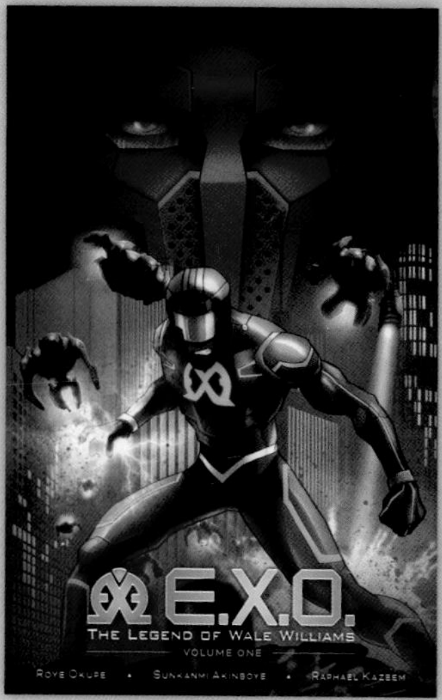
E.X.O.
THE LEGEND OF WALE WILLIAMS
VOLUME ONE
ROYE OKUPE • SUNKANMI AKINBOYE • RAPHAEL KAZEEM

DarkHorse.com

Press Inquiries:
pr@darkhorse.com

Sales Inquiries:
tradesales@darkhorse.com